Contents

Law and Film

Edited by

Stefan Machura
and
Peter Robson

BLACKWELL
Publishers

Copyright © Blackwell Publishers Ltd

ISBN 0-631-22816-0

First published 2001

Published simultaneously as Vol. 28 No. 1 of
Journal of Law and Society ISSN 0263-323X

Blackwell Publishers
108 Cowley Road, Oxford OX4 1JF, UK
and
350 Main Street, Malden, MA 02148, USA.

British Library Cataloguing in Publication Data applied for

Library of Congress Cataloguing-in-Publication Data applied for

Typeset by MHL Typesetting Limited, Coventry
Printed and bound in Great Britain by J W Arrowsmiths, Bristol, UK.

JOURNAL OF LAW AND SOCIETY
VOLUME 28, NUMBER 1, MARCH 2001
ISSN: 0263-323X, pp. 1–8

Law and Film: Introduction

STEFAN MACHURA* AND PETER ROBSON**

What we have brought together in this collection is a selection of contemporary scholarship in Law and Film in a range of jurisdictions. Law and Film has been a focus of the Law and Society Association at its Annual Meetings through the 1990s and has attracted scholars from different backgrounds. We include four pieces from Germany, three from Britain, and four from the United States of America. Inevitably the concentration within most of the essays is, however, on the dominant cultural products of Hollywood. The paucity of material other than American in the area of law films is itself an issue which is addressed in a number of the essays presented here. We have provided a selected chronological bibliography of writing on law and film at the end of this introduction. This bibliography indicates how recent has been scholarly work on law and film and the recent genesis of this scholarship has helped shape the varied nature and style of the works presented here.

Not surprisingly there is no consensus about what to look at in law and film nor in what form these studies are best conducted. There is then a variety of approaches to the issue of how film looks at law. Some of the writers in this volume have based their analysis on a wide range of films, whilst others have provided a close reading of the work of either a particular era, film-maker or writer. The interests and paradigms the writers adopt include social theory, literary theory, and film studies. Further, a number of films recur within the essays and are the subject of analysis from these distinctive perspectives. We welcome this diversity which is inevitable in a field of scholarship that seeks to cross traditional boundaries.

There are a number of strands of inquiry which have emerged in this collection. Three principal areas can be identified. The collection looks at the nature of the films produced portraying law and lawyers. The essays look at the significance and impact of these law films on the public perception of law and the legal process and the influence on the practice of law itself.

* Law Faculty, Ruhr-Universitat Bochum, Gebäude GC 8/135, D-44780 Bochum, Germany
** The Law School, University of Strathclyde, 173 Cathedral Street, Glasgow G4 0RQ, Scotland

1

Finally there is an assessment of how and why the various themes in writing on the topic of law and film have developed. First, it is important for readers to gain an appreciation of how the law film has developed. Nicole Rafter provides a brief guide to the different kinds of films which have emerged in this area. In 'American Criminal Trial Films', she provides an overview of their development from 1930 to 2000. She identifies and describes three different phases of film-making and locates them in their cultural context. Steve Greenfield takes up this theme in his contribution 'Hero or Villain? Cinematic Lawyers and the Delivery of Justice'. He suggests that there have been different emphases over the years and that the unethical lawyer has always existed alongside the Atticus Finch figure. The dominant theme in law films has, however, been how the lawyer pursues justice. The contrast over the years between the lawyer of the 1960s and the 1990s is a notion which Gerald Thain examines in 'Cape Fear – Two Versions and Two Visions Separated by Thirty Years'.

Michael Böhnke, in 'Myth and Law in the Films of John Ford', takes the opportunity to explore the whole question of the nature and legitimacy of law. He looks at the way Ford portrays law in some of his work as being imposed on society and in other work he stresses how it emerges from social interaction and represents community values. In the rather different context of inter-war Germany, Peter Drexler, in 'The German Courtroom Film During the Nazi Period', points out how very different kinds of films were used in this period to bolster a myth about law. He describes a conscious manipulation of law in film to reinforce a notion of community which justified Nazi policies of 'ethnic and social cleansing'.

Mathias Kuzina, in 'The Social Issue Courtroom Drama as an Expression of American Popular Culture', looks at how law films relate to the tradition of social issues film-making. In 'Patterns of Courtroom Justice', Jessica Silbey then addresses the critique of David Black in *Law in Film: Resonance and Representation* that lawyers have failed to make any contribution to the discipline of film studies. She goes beyond the dominant concerns of lawyers with film, which Meyer and Osborn have noted, to look at the narrative and aesthetic conventions which the Hollywood law films share. In her paper she notes the techniques film-makers have used to emphasize aspects of law and to involve the viewer in the story.

Looking to the questions of significance and impact, Stefan Machura and Stefan Ulbrich examine the dominance of Hollywood law films in contemporary German popular culture and explore reasons for this phenomenon. In 'Law in Film: Globalizing the Hollywood Courtroom Drama', they also draw on Niklas Luhmann's systems theory to provide an explanation for the fascination of the film industry with the legal process. Phil Meyer looks at the role of cinema in the way in which law is practiced in contemporary United States courts in 'Why a Jury Trial is More Like a Movie Than a Novel'. He also notes the flattening effect of adaptation on their journey from the printed page to the screen. Peter Robson, in 'Adapting the Modern Law Novel:

2

Filming John Grisham', takes up this theme of the relationship between fiction and film. He examines how the blockbusting book success of John Grisham has been transformed into film. He suggests that the adaptation process has produced a type of film which, perhaps surprisingly, beyond the surface, emphasizes Grisham's concerns with the inequality of legal services and the parasitic nature of the legal profession in the American system.

It is worth noting the context in which the examination of law films operates. Not only does it operate in the professional sphere as Meyer notes but it is an expanding area with higher education. In his essay 'Borders and Boundaries: Locating The Law in Film', Guy Osborn outlines the development of Law and Film as a sub-discipline within law schools in Britain and the whole question of what counts as the subject matter of such inquiries. He notes that there are a range of educational reasons for film and law as a subject on the law school curriculum.

From our experience teaching, presenting at symposia, and attending conferences in the area of law, society, and popular culture, we feel that this collection provides a fair representation of the concerns and interests of scholars working in this field. As can be seen from the bibliography, the full range of interests is, however, even wider than what can be presented in a single collection. We are confident that work in this area will build on these foundations and that Law and Film will continue to provide a worthwhile and increasing input to legal education, theory, and even film studies.

SELECTED WRITINGS ON LAW AND FILM – A CHRONOLOGY
1986–1999

1986

A. Chase, 'Towards a Legal Theory of Popular Culture' (1986) *Wisconsin Law Rev.* 527–69.
A. Chase, 'Lawyers and Popular Culture: A Review of Mass Media Portrayals of American Attorneys' [1986] 2 *Am. Bar Foundation Research J.* 297.

1987

T.J. Harris, *Courtroom's Finest Hour in American Cinema* (1987).
S. Macaulay, 'Images of Law in Everyday Life: The Lessons of School, Entertainment and Spectator Sports' (1987) 21 *Law and Society Rev.* 185–218.
R.C. Post, 'On the Popular Image of the Lawyer: Reflections in a Dark Glass' (1987) 75 *California Law Rev.* 379–89.
S.D. Stark, 'Perry Mason meets Sonny Crocket: The History of Lawyers and the Police as Television Heroes' (1987) 42 *University of Miami Law Rev.* 229–83.

1989

L. Friedman, 'Law, Lawyers and Popular Culture' (1989) 98 *Yale Law J.* 1579–1606.

3

S. Gillers, 'Taking L.A. Law More Seriously' (1989) 98 *Yale Law J.* 1607–23.
R.E. Rosen, 'Ethical Soap: *L.A. Law* and the Privileging of Character' (1989) 43 *University of Miami Law Rev.* 1229–61.
C. Rosenberg, 'An L.A. Lawyer Replies' (1989) 98 *Yale Law J.* 1625–9.

1990
A. Sokolsky, 'The Case of the Juridical Junkie: Perry Mason and the Dilemma of Confession' (1990) 2 *Yale J. of Law & the Humanities* 189–99.

1991
N. Rosenberg, 'Young Mr. Lincoln: The Lawyer as Super-Hero' (1991) 15 *Legal Studies Forum* 215–31.

1992
O. Castendyk, '*Recht und Rechtskultur. Das Recht im Fernsehen als "Popular Legal Culture" – ein vielversprechender Ansatz aus den USA?*' (1992) 25 *Zeitschrift für Rechtspolitik* 63–7.
P.N. Meyer, 'Law Students Go to the Movies' (1992) 24 *Connecticut Law Rev.* 893–913.

1993
D.L. Gunn (ed.), *The Lawyer and Popular Culture* (1993).
S. Greenfield and G. Osborn, 'Lawyers in Film: Where Myth Meets Reality' (1993) 43 *New Law J.* 1791–2.
P.N. Meyer, 'Visual Literacy and the Legal Culture: Reading Film as Text in the Law School Setting' (1993) 17 *Legal Studies Forum* 73–93.
R. Sheffield, 'On Film: A Social History of Women Lawyers in Popular Culture 1930 to 1990' (1993) 14 *Loyola of Los Angeles Entertainment Law J.* 73–114.

1994
E. Kennedy, 'The Gorgeous Lesbian in L.A. Law: The Present Absence?' in *The Good, the Bad and the Gorgeous: Popular Culture's Romance with the Lesbian*, eds. D. Hamer and B. Budge (1994).
C.L. Miller, '"What a Waste, Beautiful, Sexy Gal, Hell of a Lawyer": Film and the Female Attorney' (1994) 4 *Columbia J. of Gender & Law* 203.
K.J Neuhaus, 'Jura Goes Hollywood' part 1 (1994) 2 *JUSTUF* 36–42; part 2 (1995) 1 *JUSTUF* 34–40.
N. Rosenberg, 'Hollywood on Trials: Courts and Films 1930–1960' (1994) 12 *Law and History Rev.* 341–67.
M.P. Schraf and L.D. Robert, 'The Interstellar Relations of the Federation: International Law and "*Star Trek:The Next Generation*"' (1994) 25 *University of Toledo Law Rev.* 577–665.
R. Sherwin, 'Law Frames: Historical Truth and Narrative Necessity in a Criminal Case' (1994) 47 *Stanford Law Rev.* 39–83.

4

1995

L.E. Graham and G. Maschio, 'A False Public Sentiment: Narrative and Visual Images of Women Lawyers in Film' (1995/96) 84 *Ky. Law. J.* 1027–73.

S. Greenfield and G. Osborn, 'Law's Imagery: The Representation of Lawyers in Film', Socio-Legal Studies Association Conference, Leeds 1995.

S. Greenfield and G. Osborn, 'Where Cultures Collide: the Characterisation of Law and Lawyers in Film' (1995) 23 *International J. of the Sociology of Law* 107–30.

S. Greenfield and G. Osborn, 'The Living Law: Popular Film as Legal Text' (1995) 29 *The Law Teacher* 33–42.

C. Shapiro, 'Women Lawyers in Celluloid: Why Hollywood Skirts the Truth' (1995) 25 *University of Toledo Law Rev.* 955.

1996

M. Asimow, 'When Lawyers Were Heroes' (1996) 30 *University of San Francisco Law Rev.* 1131.

R. Berets, 'Changing Images of Justice in American Films' (1996) 20 *Legal Studies Forum* 473–80.

P. Bergman, 'Pranks For The Memory' (1996) 30 *University of San Francisco Law Rev.* 1235.

P. Bergman and M. Asimow, *Reel Justice – The Courtroom Goes to the Movies* (1996).

C.P. Blum, 'Images of Lawyering and Political Activism in *In the Name of the Father*' (1996) 30 *University of San Francisco Law Rev.* 1065

J. Denvir, *Legal Reelism – Movies as Legal Texts* (1996).

J. Grant, 'Lawyers As Superheroes: *The Firm, The Client* and *The Pelican Brief*' (1996) 30 *University of San Francisco Law Rev.* 1111.

S. Greenfield and G. Osborn, 'Pulped Fiction? Cinematic Parables of (In)Justice' (1996) 30 *University of San Francisco Law Rev.* 1181.

R.M. Harding, 'Celluloid Death: Cinematic Deceptions of Capital Punishment' (1996) 30 *University of San Francisco Law Rev.* 1167.

J.L. Harrison and S. Wilson, 'Advocacy in Literature: Storytelling, Judicial Opinions and *The Rainmaker*' (1996) 26 *University of Memphis Law Rev.* 1285–302.

P. Joseph and S. Carton, 'The Law of the Federation: Images of Law, Lawyers and the Legal System in "*Star Trek: The Next Generation*"' (1996) 24 *University of Toledo Law Rev.* 43–85

C. Lucia, 'Women on Trial: The Female Lawyer in the Hollywood Courtroom' in *Feminism, Media and the Law*, eds. M. Fineman and M. McCluskey (1997) 146–67.

I. Lurvey and S.E. Eiseman, 'Divorce Goes To The Movies' (1996) 30 *University of San Francisco Law Rev.* 1209.

N. Minow, '"An Idea Is A Greater Monument Than A Cathedral": Deciding How We Know What We Know In *Inherit The Wind*' (1996) 30 *University of San Francisco Law Rev.* 1225.

5

L.J. Moran, 'Heroes and Brothers in Love: The Male Homosexual as Lawyer in Popular Culture' (1998) 18 *Studies in Law, Politics and Society* 3–27.

C. Musser, 'Film Truth, Documentary, and the Law: Justice at the Margins' (1996) 30 *University of San Francisco Law Rev.* 963.

F.M. Nevins, '*Man In The Middle*: Unsung Classic Of The Warren Court' (1996) 30 *University of San Francisco Law Rev.* 1097.

B. Nichols, 'The Unseen Jury' (1996) 30 *University of San Francisco Law Rev.* 1055.

J.J. Osborn Jr., 'Atticus Finch-The End Of Honor: A Discussion Of *To Kill A Mockingbird*' (1996) 30 *University of San Francisco Law Rev.* 1139.

D.R. Papke, 'Peace Between The Sexes: Law And Gender In *Kramer vs. Kramer*' (1996) 30 *University of San Francisco Law Rev.* 1199.

P. Robson, 'Law and Lawyers in Film – Globalising Atticus Finch' (Law and Society Association 1996).

N. Rosenburg, 'Professor Lightcap Goes To Washington: Rereading *Talk Of The Town*' (1996) 30 *University of San Francisco Law Rev.* 1083.

C. Ryan, 'Lawyers As Lovers: *Gold Diggers Of 1993* Or "I'd Rather You Sue Me Than Marry Me"' (1996) 30 *University of San Francisco Law Rev.* 1123.

J. Seaton, 'Review of Bergman and Asimow's *Reel Justice*' (1996) 20 *Legal Studies Forum* 145–52.

S. Shale, 'The Conflicts of Law and the Character of Men: Writing *Reversal of Fortune* and *Judgment at Nuremberg*' (1996) 30 *University of San Francisco Law Rev.* 991.

C. Shapiro, 'Do Or Die: Does *Dead Man Walking* Run?' (1996) 30 *University of San Francisco Law Rev.* 1143.

R.K. Sherwin, 'Cape Fear: Law's Inversion and Cathartic Justice' (1996) 30 *University of San Francisco Law Rev.* 1023.

R. Strickland, 'The Cinematic Lawyer: The Magic Mirror and the Silver Screen' (1997) 22 *Oklahoma City University Law Rev.* 13.

G.F. Uelmen, 'The Trial As A Circus: *Inherit The Wind*' (1996) 30 *University of San Francisco Law Rev.* 1221.

R.L. Waring, '*Z*' (1996) 30 *University of San Francisco Law Rev.* 1077.

1997

J.P. Brooks, 'Will Boys Just Be Boyz 'N the Hood? African-American Directors Portray a Crumbling Justice System in Urban America' (1997) 22 *Oklahoma City University Law Rev.* 1.

A. Chase, 'Subterranean Government, Underground Film'(1997) 22 *Oklahoma City University Law Rev.* 167

J.M. Burkoff, 'If God Wanted Lawyers to Fly, She Would Have Given Them Wings: Life, Lust and Legal Ethics in *Body Heat*' (1997) 22 *Oklahoma City University Law Rev.* 187.

R. Coyne, 'Images of Lawyers and the Three Stooges' (1997) 22 *Oklahoma City University Law Rev.* 247.

C.A. Corcos, 'Presuming Innocence: Alan Pakula and Scott Turow Take On The

6

Great American Legal Fiction' (1997) 22 *Oklahoma City University Law Rev.* 129.

S.N. Gatson, '"It's About Law": Accessible Sources for Law and Society' (Law and Society Association, 1997).

P. Robson, 'Between Detachment and Violence: The Private Eye and the Rule of Law in the Movies' (Law and Society Association, 1997).

C.M. Selinger, 'Dramatizing on Film the Uneasy Role of the American Criminal Defense Lawyer: True Believer' (1997) 22 *Oklahoma City University Law Rev.* 223.

1998

S. Machura, '*Rechtsfilme und Rechtsalltag*' (1998) 10 *Richter ohne Robe* 39–42.

S. Machura and S. Ulbrich, *Recht im Film* (1998).

F.M. Nevins, 'Through TV's Golden Age on Horseback: Legal Themes in Western Series 1949–1975' (Law and Society Association, 1998).

P. Robson, 'The Judge in Film' (Law and Society Association Annual Meeting, 1998).

B. Scholdan, 'The Virtuous Lawyer: The Construction of Citizenship in Legal Melodrama' (Law and Society Association Annual Meeting, 1998).

1999

D.A. Black, *Law in Film: Resonance and Representation* (1999).

S.F. Fulero, E. Greene, V. Hans, M.T. Nietzel, M.A. Small, and L.S. Wrightsman, 'Undergraduate Education in Legal Psychology' 23 (1999) *Law and Human Behavior* 137–53.

2000

M. Asimow, 'Divorce in the Movies: From the Hays Code to *Kramer v* Kramer' (2000) 24 *Legal Studies Forum* 221–67.

M. Asimow, 'Bad Lawyers in the Movies' (2000) 24 *Nova Law Rev.* 533–91.

N. Rafter, *Shots in the Mirror* (2000).

WEBARTICLES

Trial Run: Hollywood Goes to Court (http://www.amctv.com/ontheair/realtoreel/archives/trial.html)

Articles from *Picturing Justice* website (http://www.usfca.edu/pj/articles/ plus citation noted).

M. Asimov, 'Return of the Heroic lawyers ... and the Heroic Client: *The Winslow Boy* and *The Castle*' (January 2000 winslow_boy.html).

J. Denvir, '*Chinatown*' (March 1998 chinatown.html).

J. Denvir, '*The Last Wave*' (May 1998 LastWave.html).

J. Denvir, '*The Law of Rules*' (November 1999 ruleoflaws.html).

J. Grant, '*The Rainmaker*' (December 1997 Rainmaker2.html).

C. Jackson, 'Judging *Judging Amy*' (December 1999 amy.html).

C. Jackson, 'Mamet's *The Winslow Boy*: Traps and Loopholes' (winslow_jackson.html).

J.C. Suggs, 'Adams Ribs: Get 'em While They're Hot', *Picturing Justice* (March 1998 AdamsRib.html).

R.A. Waring, 'Civil Action – Another Government Bailout?' (February 1999 Civil_Action-Waring.html).

R. Waring, '*Not for Ourselves Alone* and *Salt of the Earth*: The Interplay of Gender and Race' (December 1999 gender.html).

R.L. Waring, 'The Winemaker' (November 1997 Rainmaker.html).

R.L. Waring, *The Devil's Advocate* (November 1997 devilsad.html).

R.A. Waring, *The Sweet Hereafter* (May 1998 sweethearafter.html)[sic]

JOURNAL OF LAW AND SOCIETY
VOLUME 28, NUMBER 1, MARCH 2001
ISSN: 0263-323X, pp. 9–24

American Criminal Trial Films: An Overview of Their Development, 1930–2000

NICOLE RAFTER*

The history of American trial films – and I am speaking of trial films in general at the moment, not of the sub-division of criminal trial films - has been shaped both by changes in public attitudes toward law and lawyers and by shifts in viewer tastes. These same factors have necessitated changes in the way we define 'American trial films'. In earlier years one could recognize a trial film with relative ease: it was a drama in which a heroic lawyer or lawyer surrogate solved the film's dilemmas in the course of a civil or criminal trial, usually a trial held within a courtroom. Contemporary movies, in contrast, are more interested in action than in debate and oratory, and they are more cynical about the effectiveness of legal processes. Thus they tend to embed a short trial scene in a longer adventure story, and they seldom depict lawyers as heroes on the grand scale or courts as places where fundamental social and moral issues are settled. In sum, the trial film genre is undergoing major change, if not dissolution.[1]

The purpose of this paper is to establish the general lines of development of an important sub-group within the trial film genre: American criminal trial films. The research forms part of a larger project on crime in American movies and the impact of crime movies on United States society.[2] The paper's secondary purpose is to formulate generalizations about the characteristics of United States films that include criminal trials in the hope that these generalizations may contribute to understanding of the broader, generic category 'trial film'. In the following historical overview, I use terms such as 'criminal trial films' and 'criminal court films' even though in a few cases, such as *The Ox-Bow Incident* (1943), the trial takes place outside a

---

* *Law, Policy and Society Program, Northeastern University, Boston, MA 02115, United States of America*
I wish to thank Charles Alexander Hahn for assistance with this analysis.

1 For remarks on definitions of genre and the issue of on-screen duration, see D.A. Black, *Law in Film* (1999) ch. 3.
2 N. Rafter, *Shots in the Mirror: Crime Films and Society* (2000).

9

conventional courtroom. In a few other cases, such as *Call Northside 777* (1948), the film emphasizes legal processes designed to correct the mistaken results of an earlier criminal trial. To keep the study manageable in size, I have limited coverage to Hollywood movies.[3] I also exclude silent movies, comedies, sci-fis, Westerns, and war films with criminal trials, although I do cover *The Ox-Bow Incident,* which has Western elements, and films on military criminal trials during peacetime, such as *Judgment at Nuremberg* (1961) and *A Few Good Men* (1992).[4] I begin by making some generalizations about the characteristics of criminal court dramas over time, after which I discuss the evolution of films of this type, identifying three developmental stages. I conclude with observations about both the limitations of criminal trial films and their ideological significance.

CHARACTERISTICS OF MOVIES WITH CRIMINAL TRIALS

Criminal trial films set up a tension between two sorts of law: immutable natural law or justice on the one hand and fallible man-made law on the other. They let us know what justice would consist of in the current case and then use that ideal as a template for what should happen.[5] At the same time they show us how, in the current case, man-made law fails (or is about to fail) to reach the goal of true justice, and they proceed to play with the discrepancy between the actual and ideal.

Criminal trial films usually include an *injustice figure*, the person responsible for creating or maintaining the gap between justice and man-made law. Most criminal trial films also include a *justice figure*, a hero who tries to move man-made law ever closer to the ideal until it matches the justice template. In most criminal trial movies produced before 1980, the film's resolution occurs when man-made law becomes identical to the underlying pattern. The justice figure is usually (but not always) a lawyer; and in a few criminal court dramas, the position of justice figure is held by several characters at once. In *Marked Woman* (1937), for example, a 'clipjoint hostess' (Bette Davis) and the district attorney (Humphrey Bogart)

---

3 This means skipping Fritz Lang's *M* (1931), made in Germany and perhaps the greatest of all trial films. My concentration on criminal court films also means that I will not cover such well-known civil trial films as *The Verdict* (1982), in which lawyer Paul Newman is rehabilitated, and *Music Box* (1989), in which lawyer Jessica Lang discovers a former Nazi in her own family.

4 However, I omit *The Caine Mutiny* (1954), which is set during World War II.

5 Robert C. Post makes a similar point when his distinguishes between two images of law in popular culture. Post writes that 'the concept of "law" itself has assumed a double meaning. Law is on the one hand the positive enactments of the state. law in this sense is technical, ambiguous, and complex. It can almost always be circumvented ... (L)awyers stand accused of breaking a different kind of law, the law which is associated with justice and with our values as a community' (R.C. Post, 'On the Popular Image of the Lawyer' (1987) 75 *California Law Rev.* 383).

10

work together to convict an organized crime boss who has been taking over New York City's nightclubs. On rare occasions, movies with significant criminal court scenes have no justice figure at all. *A Place in the Sun* (1951), *The Postman Always Rings Twice* (1946), and *The Wrong Man* (1956) lack justice figures, and, significantly, they also have no villains, absences that flow from their bleak views of the world as a place where people either create their own tragedies or are struck down randomly by fate.[6]

In criminal trial movies made before 1980, the closing of the gap between law and justice usually occurs in the trial scene, where the triumph of the good lawyer over the nasty one signals resolution of the film's basic dilemma. However, many of these films include other or additional signs of resolution and success. Some conclude with a return to the setting of the first scene, a demonstration that the original equilibrium has been restored.[7] Films in which injustice has driven happy couples apart often end with a scene of reunion. In Alfred Hitchcock's *The Paradine Case* (1947), for instance, the lawyer (Gregory Peck) and his wife reunite after an estrangement caused by his all-too-impassioned defence of a beautiful woman.

Yet another device that criminal court films use to resolve their plots is to show, at the end, that good personal relationships parallel good legal relationships, with everyone recognizing and happily accepting the rule of a wise father/judge. These movies are full of confusions over authority and legitimacy, disorders that manifest themselves in both law-breaking and the dissolution of previously strong relationships. Many conclude with a good father or father-figure (who may also be a judge) settling the case and restoring order. Varying this pattern, *To Kill a Mockingbird* (1962) contrasts a lack of resolution in the legal arena, in which Atticus Finch loses his case, with resolutions in the sub-plot, in which the tension between Boo Radley and the Finch children dissolves and Atticus, the perfect father, shields Boo from a murder prosecution.

Nearly all criminal trial films sound the same theme: the difficulty of achieving justice. While they take up and explore a wide range of secondary issues, their overriding point is that as a goal, justice is elusive, demanding, and often more ambiguous than it first appears. Criminal trial films sound this theme in various ways, some through stories of false convictions (*Call Northside 777* (1948); *I Want to Live!* (1958); *In the Name of the Father* (1993); *The Ox-Bow Incident* (1943); *True Believer* (1989)) or mistaken acquittals (*Jagged Edge* (1985); *The Juror* (1996); *Trial by Jury* (1994)).

---

6 The second version of *The Postman Always Rings Twice* (1981) becomes flaccid partly because it lacks the legal framework of the first. Scriptwriter David Mamet retains some courtroom material from the first version; but without the opening scene in which the main character, Frank, is delivered into the movie by the D.A., and without the last scene in which the D.A. leads Frank off to execution, the other material becomes incoherent.

7 *Jagged Edge* (1985) wittily inverts this pattern, returning at the end to another scene of the masked killer stalking a woman in bed.

11

Some stress the difficulty of identifying the true culprit (*Presumed Innocent* (1990); *Primal Fear* (1996); *Reversal of Fortune* (1990)), while others emphasize systematic faults in the criminal justice process (*And Justice for All* (1979); *The Lady from Shanghai* (1948); *The Star Chamber* (1983)). Criminal trial movies also put forth various opinions about the complexities of justice, with some condemning courts for delays and others praising them for patient deliberations, some despising lawyers and others glorifying them. Many show justice officials triumphing after a long struggle with injustice; others openly mock trial procedures. Few, however, fail to stress that justice is an exacting goal, reached only through arduous quests and multiple sacrifices.

THE EVOLUTION OF CRIMINAL TRIAL MOVIES

Hollywood began producing criminal trial films with soundtracks in the early 1930s and continues producing them in large quantity today. Lines of development are neither steady nor clear-cut, but it is possible to discern three phases in the evolution of these films: an experimental period that began in the 1930s and bore fruit in the 1940s and 1950s with law *noirs*; a brief heroic period that began in the mid-1950s and petered out in the early 1960s; and a period of depletion, 1970 till the end of the century and beyond, during which trial movies tried but often failed to meet the challenges posed by a new set of cinematic and political circumstances.

1. *1930s to the mid-1950s: experimentation and the law* noirs

The 1930s were a time of experimentation, a decade during which directors of the new soundtracked movies searched for ways to depict legal struggles that would be both persuasive and entertaining. The start of the decade saw the release of *Manhattan Melodrama* (1934), a movie that pits a good lawyer against a criminal by following Myrna Loy as she tries first to reform her gangster boyfriend, Blackie (Clark Gable), and then becomes the wife of a crusading district attorney, Jim (William Powell). Although the two men have been best friends since childhood, Jim prosecutes Blackie and eventually, having become the state's governor, denies commutation of Blackie's death sentence. At this point *Manhattan Melodrama* runs into a problem inherent in its design. The experiment was to dramatize the struggle for justice in two contrasting but equal characters; the problem is that Blackie is too engaging a villain for viewers to approve of his execution. Moreover, although Jim is supposedly the good guy, his lack of generosity toward his old friend undercuts what was meant to be a triumph of justice.

The end of the decade saw the release of *Young Mr. Lincoln* (1939), the most heroic of all heroic-lawyer movies. Law itself is dignified by Lincoln's attraction to it, and the film reveres the future President as not only a superb

12

lawyer but also a perfect American. Featuring Henry Fonda as a lanky Lincoln look-alike, the film anticipates *To Kill a Mockingbird* with a scene in which the attorney blocks the door to the jail where his defendants are incarcerated, thus holding an angry crowd at bay. The trial becomes the movie's most dramatic moment as Lincoln adroitly unmasks the true killer. But *Young Mr. Lincoln*'s hero needs more loathsome opponents. The experiment here was to embody justice in a single character and then follow that character's struggles. But in this film, justice is less a struggle than a foregone conclusion.

Director Fritz Lang explored yet another approach to the courtroom film in *Fury* (1936), a proto-*noir* that locates the struggle for justice in a wronged character. The most bitter criminal trial film in Hollywood history,[8] *Fury* stars Spencer Tracy as Joe Wilson, a young man who is mistakenly arrested and imprisoned on kidnapping charges. A lynch mob gathers outside his jail and sets it on fire – the first instance of fury. With his fiancée Catherine looking on, Joe appears at his cell's window, seemingly in flames; and presumably his body is destroyed in the subsequent explosion. Joe lives, however, and plots revenge against the would-be lynchers, who are brought to trial *en masse* for his murder. Keeping even Catherine in the dark about his survival, Joe plans to sit back and allow all the defendants to be convicted and executed – the second instance of fury – and he relents only because he cannot bear the thought of life without Catherine. At the most dramatic moment, Joe interrupts the trial and reveals himself. Sparing the defendants brings him no joy, however; Joe remains deeply resentful, and the criminal justice system stands condemned for a second failure to achieve justice. If *Fury* leaves a sour aftertaste, it is because injustice goes unpunished and the justice figure, Joe, in fact fights solely for himself.[9]

After this decade of experimentation, the criminal court film hit its stride in the 1940s with the cycle of cynical and stylistically expressionistic films that movie scholar Norman Rosenberg has deftly named 'law *noirs*.' Law *noirs*, Rosenberg writes, present a 'baleful view of lawyers' and 'portray people, some entirely innocent and others not-so-innocent, trapped in a

---

8 *Fury*'s bitterness, critics speculate, may have derived from the personal background of director Fritz Lang, who had recently fled Nazi Germany for the United States. For example, Lotte Eisner suggests that there may be 'a parallel between the gradual and menacing growth of hatred in [*Fury*'s] crowd lusting for a lynching, and the Hitler terror' (quoted in A. Chase, 'Lawyers and Popular Culture: A Review of Mass Media Portrayals of American Attorneys' [1986] 2 *Am. Bar Foundation Research J.* 297, fn. 44).

9 Less successful is a criminal trial film released the next year (1937), *The Life of Emile Zola*. Starring Paul Muni as the French author on trial for slandering army officials whom he accused of framing Alfred Dreyfus, the Jew sent to Devil's Island for a crime he did not commit, this film is impressive for its courtroom setting, but the lengthy speeches become stilted and preachy. At the end, to escape his jail sentence, Zola flees to England, where he waits till the scandal runs its course, Dreyfus is freed, and he himself is exonerated.

13

highly fallible legal system.'[10] Unlike more traditional Hollywood fare, law *noirs* 'raise doubts about the ability of the trial process to achieve satisfactory closure.'[11] The cycle begins with *The Letter* (1940), which sets a story of mistaken acquittal in colonialist Malaysia, and with *Stranger on the Third Floor* (also 1940), a tale of false conviction in which justice is again achieved only outside the court system. Those movies were followed by *The Postman Always Rings Twice*, with its double-crossing prosecutor and despicable defence attorney, and by *They Won't Believe Me* (1947), *Call Northside 777*, and *The Lady From Shanghai* (1948). *Knock on Any Door* (1949) features Humphrey Bogart as a defence attorney who, having grown up in slums, can match the bad guy punch for punch. The cycle extends into the 1950s with a late law *noir*, Hitchcock's *The Wrong Man* (1957), the story of a family ruined by a mistaken arrest.[12]

The Ox-Box Incident, although released in 1943, is less closely related to the law *noirs* than to the experimental courtroom films of the 1930s and the heroic court dramas of the 1950s and 1960s. It focuses on neither a justice figure nor an injustice figure but rather on witnesses to a struggle over legal authority. Two outsiders (one of them Henry Fonda) are passing through an isolated Western town when they become witnesses to mob violence. Local ranchers capture three other travellers, quickly 'try' them for a recent murder, and hang them from a tree limb. These travellers have hardly been 'finished' with bullets before the sheriff gallops up to announce that the man whom they thought had been murdered is not dead after all. Depressed and repentant, the lynchers troop into the local bar and listen while Fonda reads a last-minute letter from one of the condemned men to his wife. 'Law is a lot more than words you put in a book,' the letter explains. 'It's everything people ever have found out about justice and what's right and wrong. It's the very conscience of humanity.' These ringing words anticipate the adulation of law in trial films of the next period.

From the 1930s into the 1950s, criminal trial dramas attracted outstanding directors including John Ford (*Young Mr Lincoln*), Alfred Hitchcock (*The Wrong Man, The Paradine Case*), Fritz Lang (*Fury* and *Beyond a Reasonable Doubt* (1956)), Nicholas Ray (*Knock on Any Door*), Orson Welles (*The Lady from Shanghai*), William Wellman (*The Ox-Bow Incident*), and William Wyler (*The Letter*). Intriguing visually, many of these films use the extreme camera angles and striking black-and-white patterns for which *noirs* in general are admired. Law *noirs* make justice

10 N. Rosenberg, 'Law Noir,' in *Legal Reelism: Movies as Legal Texts*, ed. J. Denvir (1996) 282.
11 N. Rosenberg, 'Hollywood on Trials: Courts and Films, 1930–1960' (1994) 12 *Law and History Rev.* 345.
12 Hitchcock's earlier criminal court film, *The Paradine Case*, does not fit the law *noir* category due to its lack of sense of corruption and its upper-class setting and characters. *The Paradine Case* is in fact as much a mystery as a criminal courtroom film.

14

figures engaging by turning them into outsiders of one sort or another: the journalist who gets a mistaken conviction overturned in *Call Northside 777*, the Malaysian widow who stabs the exonerated killer in *The Letter*, the tough-guy attorney in *Knock on Any Door*. In addition, law *noirs* give these justice figures worthy opponents, goliaths of injustice that sometimes turn out to be the criminal justice system itself. Thus viewers can have it both ways, identifying with outsiders to the justice system who, in the end, become saviours of law and order.

2. Mid-1950s through the 1960s: the heroic tradition

Criminal trial dramas became more overtly laudatory of the law with the 1957 release of *Twelve Angry Men*, first in a series of films that conclude that justice can be achieved through the courts. *Witness for the Prosecution* (1957), *Anatomy of a Murder* (1959), *Inherit the Wind* (1960), *Judgment at Nuremberg*, and *To Kill a Mockingbird* went on to portray lawyers as men who labour heroically within the system to ensure that man-made law coincides with the justice ideal. Rooted in *Young Mr. Lincoln* and *The Ox-Bow Incident*, these movies became the classics of trial movies, representatives of what many consider to have been the genre's Golden Age.

In their generally uncritical perspective on the judicial system, these classics are products of their times, reflections of a society that was wealthier, more secure, and less chaotic than the America of the Depression and World War II years. Like the best-selling novels on which a number of them are based, the courtroom classics present criminal trials in mythic terms, as battles of good against evil; their courts are hallowed halls, places where the truth, after a titanic contest, emerges victorious. Turning lawyers into cultural heroes, the classic courtroom movies present them as professional wizards and guardians of the country's sacred traditions.

The classic courtroom films are also traditional cinematically. They use standard devices such as close-ups of nervous witnesses and dramatic outbursts by onlookers, punctuated by the hammer of a judge's gavel. Compared to law *noirs*, their photography is straightforward and somewhat static. While they are cinematically skilful, their camera work is less dramatic than that of law *noirs* and less radical – one might almost say more respectful.

Twelve Angry Men, in which the action is confined entirely to the claustrophobic room in which a murder-trial jury is deliberating its verdict, at first seems like an attack on criminal law, for few jurors take the process seriously. One wants to hurry to a guilty verdict so he can go to a baseball game; another concludes that the defendant is probably guilty because he is a foreigner. *Twelve Angry Men,* however, actually mounts a powerful argument for the jury system, demonstrating that a lone but courageous individual can assure justice. The system may not be perfect, the film tells us, but it works well in the end, and it is a microcosm of the democratic process in which the search for consensus eventually leads to wise decisions.

Reverence for the law again runs strong in *Witness for the Prosecution*, starring Charles Laughton as an ageing, ailing barrister who, defying his nurse, decides to defend an accused murderer. Director Billy Wilder's courtroom is a large, grand place, full of tradition and great men. Bewigged and fiendishly clever, Laughton wins a 'not guilty' verdict from the jury, only to discover that the defendant did in fact commit the murder. 'Vole, you have made a mockery of English law,' the barrister admonishes, charging his client with a sin that is clearly much worse than murder. When Vole is stabbed by his common-law wife (Marlene Dietrich), whom he has also double-crossed, Laughton vows to defend *her*, and *Witness for the Prosecution* ends with him charging off to the next contest, revitalized by the thrill of striving for justice.

Judgment at Nuremburg places a judge in the hero's role. Portraying an actual post-World War II trial of men who themselves served as judges during the Nazi regime, it concentrates, uniquely, on what one character describes as 'crimes committed in the name of the law'. The key issue is whether judges are fundamentally responsible to man-made law or natural law. Is it true, as one defence attorney argues, that 'A judge does not make the laws; he carries out the laws of his country', or must judges answer to a higher kind of law, justice itself? The film responds to this question primarily through the character of the presiding justice, Judge Dan Haywood (Spencer Tracy), depicting him as a modest, tolerant man who wants to understand how the wisest judges in Germany could have participated in the Nazi regime. Haywood goes out of his way to be fair.

Judge Haywood's counterpart is the chief figure on trial (Burt Lancaster), a jurist famous for having 'dedicated his life to justice – to the concept of justice'. Although at first this German judge refuses to participate in the trial, he comes to accept his responsibility for the failures of the Nazi regime, admitting that he and the other defendants knew that the people they sentenced were sent to concentration camps. In effect, this injustice figure condemns himself for choosing man-made over natural law. In *Judgment at Nuremberg* as in *Twelve Angry Men* and *Witness for the Prosecution*, a solitary figure's moral courage carries the day. Judge Haywood convicts the defendants and, despite international pressure for leniency, sentences them to life imprisonment. He bases his decision on belief in a moral law that transcends man-made laws and must be followed by all human beings. The very first time a Nazi judge condemned an innocent man, Haywood declares, he transgressed this moral law.

Inherit the Wind re-enacts the 'monkey trial' case of 1925 in which fundamentalist William Jennings Bryan squared off against liberal Clarence Darrow to argue that religious beliefs should dictate how science is taught in the schools. Spencer Tracy plays Drummond, the Darrow character who defends a local teacher facing criminal charges for discussing evolution in the classroom. The prosecuting attorney (Frederick March) is a demagogic religious conservative, and the trial takes place in Hillsboro, 'the buckle on the Bible belt'. With small-town bigotry and self-righteousness permeating

16

the courtroom along with the fetid southern heat, the teacher's chances for a fair trial seem nil. Drummond's arguments on behalf of freedom of thought chip away at Hillsboro's prejudices, however, and the teacher, though convicted, is merely given a nominal fine. Tracy's monumental performance as Drummond, slaying the dragon of Biblical literalism, makes this one of the most satisfying of all trial films.

Anatomy of a Murder, concerning an Army lieutenant accused of killing a man who allegedly raped his wife, is less dramatic in presentation, at least from today's perspective. At the time of release, audiences may have found it racy, for it was one of the first movies to deal explicitly with rape and extra-marital affairs, and lawyer James Stewart, breaking with all previous standards of decorum, presents a pair of torn panties in evidence. Nonetheless, Stewart's portrait of a homespun attorney, simple yet crafty, reinforces the archetype of the heroic, all-American lawyer. This Lincolnesque figure triumphs through honesty, brilliance, and perseverence, a victory only slightly diminished by the surprise ending. Similarly, Atticus Finch, the lawyer-hero of *To Kill a Mockingbird*, triumphs through character, even though he loses his case in court.

While not themselves classics, other criminal trial films of the period contributed to the heroic tradition. In *The Young Philadelphians* (1959), Paul Newman plays the tax lawyer as all-around guy: friend first to construction workers, then wealthy old ladies and heading for complete class sell-out but redeemed when he risks his career defending a friend falsely accused of murder. *Compulsion* (1959), retelling the famous 1924 murder case of Leopold and Loeb, features a holy trinity of lawyers – the judge, prosecutor, and defence attorney – who labour mightily to achieve justice for the ungrateful young killers. Particularly through the impassioned rhetoric of the defence attorney (Orson Welles), *Compulsion* portrays law as impartial, majestic, even godlike – quite the opposite of the self-indulgent murderers.

A few films of the period hung back from the stampede to glorify criminal law and lawyers. *A Place in the Sun* presents an enigma, a man who did indeed plan to kill his pregnant fiancée but is unsure about his responsibility for the boating accident in which she drowned. Thus the menacing and vengeful prosecutor (Raymond Burr) somewhat misses the mark in demanding the death penalty, and as the young man (Montgomery Clift) walks to his execution, we wonder whether this is justice or legalistic brutality. *I Want to Live!* goes even further, showing that criminal justice officials framed an innocent woman (Susan Hayward) and knowingly sent her to the gas chamber. Based on the actual case of Barbara Graham, executed at San Quentin in the 1950s, this film is narrated by a journalist who repents of his sensationalist reporting of the case and decides to expose the miscarriage of justice.[13] However, few other mid-century films bucked the trend toward adulation of the law.

13 In an unusual combination, the journalist's character thus functions as both an injustice and a justice figure.

17

3. From the 1970s to 2000: depletion of the criminal trial film

As if pausing for rest after their heroic exertions, criminal trial films made few appearances between 1962 (*To Kill a Mockingbird*) and 1979 (*And Justice for All*).[14] During the hiatus, massive changes occurred in the movie industry, the judicial system, and the country's attitudes toward authority. Cinematically, films became more reliant on action and violence. Colour film became the rule, forcing photographers to learn how to work in what was in some respects a new medium. Criminal law underwent a civil rights revolution with new requirements for *Miranda* warnings, appointed counsel, and (in serious cases) automatic appeals. Vietnam and Watergate made veneration for the law seem sentimental, while the entry of women and people of colour into law schools exposed the biases behind images of the ideal lawyer as a white male. Justice and injustice had to be reconceptualized.

Situated at the nexus of these aesthetic, legal, and social changes, criminal court dramas released after the 1962–1979 hiatus had trouble finding their footing. *And Justice for All*, for instance, is an awkward, uncertain film Starring Al Pacino as a rebellious young defence lawyer, the film spends much of its energy criticizing the adversary system for being more concerned with wins and losses than with truth. Vignettes in which justice miscarries show that the guilty may go free and the innocent be incarcerated. *And Justice for All* succeeds mainly in its gritty portrayal of state courts as, not dignified halls of justice, but corridors crowded with deal-making cynics. *The Onion Field* (1979) and *The Star Chamber* (1985) are similarly jaded in their view of justice and equally uneven cinematically, but in these movies, the legal material is less central, edged out by psychopaths and action sequences. In such post-hiatus criminal court films, we see less a continuation of earlier traditions than stumbling efforts to develop new forms and formulae. Film-makers were in fact redesigning the criminal trial movie, struggling to create new justice and injustice figures and to find fresh ways to depict gaps between natural and man-made law.[15]

A series of woman-lawyer movies revived criminal trial films in the mid-1980s. The series began, spectacularly, with *Jagged Edge* (1985), the tale of a corporate lawyer who reluctantly agrees to defend a man accused of the gruesome knife murder of his heiress-wife. Glenn Close plays the lawyer, Teddy Barnes, who has an affair with her client, Jack Forrester (Jeff Bridges), before discovering that he actually is the killer. Masked and clad in

---

14 One exception was Orson Welles's *The Trial* (1963), a film that closely follows Franz Kafka's hallucinatory novel; however, it bears little resemblance to any other criminal courtroom movie and in any case is far from standard Hollywood fare. Another exception was *Madame X* (1966), a Lana Turner vehicle that may be the worst trial film ever made.

15 Also see R. Berets, 'Changing Images of Justice in American Films' (1996) 20 *Legal Studies Forum* 473–80.

18

black, Jack comes after Teddy as she lies in bed – a repeat of the wife's death scene. This time, however, the intended victim is prepared.

Jagged Edge set off a debate over whether Teddy Barnes and the woman lawyers of subsequent trial films represent successful professionals or failed females, women who violate their true nature by straying from the kitchen. Carolyn Lisa Miller argues that *Jagged Edge* in fact transforms Teddy Barnes 'from powerful attorney to powerless woman, resituating her in her "proper" role'.[16] The film pivots on 'the power of men to violently reshape or destroy female identity', Miller continues, noting that we never learn Teddy's full 'female' name or why she has a man's nickname.[17] From the start, *Jagged Edge* protects the killer by concealing his identity. Moreover, 'by assuming his point-of-view in the [wife-murder] scene, [it] adopts his identity as its own'.[18] The movie shows Teddy breaking her professional code of ethics by becoming involved with Jack; and in court, when his relationship with another woman is revealed, it depicts her as a stereotypical hysterical woman.

Blinded by love, the lonely professional woman is unable to see through Jack's camouflage until she stumbles upon conclusive evidence of his guilt. Miller points out that the discovery scene occurs while the heroine is changing the sheets in Jack's bedroom suite:

> Why is this attorney functioning as a maid in her client's mansion, and why upon discovering this inculpatory evidence does she fail to call the police? In a single move, she is robbed of her public power and placed within the domestic sphere, where she remains[19]

– till the film's end.

Two of the next three woman-attorney films share *Jagged Edge*'s assumptions about the incompatibility of the statuses of 'attorney' and 'woman'. *Suspect* (1987), starring Cher as Riley, a hard-working attorney, implies that Riley is destroying her femininity through over-exertion. Angst-ridden and dateless, she revives only when she has an affair with a juror in a case she is defending. Thus committing an ethical violation that could lead to disbarment, Riley places her need for a man before her career, and implicitly before justice. With a similar lack of professionalism, in *Physical Evidence* (1989) defence lawyer Theresa Russell falls in love with her client (Burt Reynolds).[20] Only in *The Accused* (1988), the Jodie Foster film that probes the guilt of bystanders in the infamous 'Big Dan' rape case, does a 1980s

---

16 C.L. Miller, '"What a Waste, Beautiful, Sexy Gal, Hell of a Lawyer" Film and the Female Attorney' (1994) 4 *Columbia J. of Gender and Law* 212.
17 id., p. 212, fn. 32.
18 id., p. 213.
19 id., p. 215, fn. 39.
20 *Nuts* (1987), centred around a female character who is not an attorney but a high-priced call-girl accused of murder, avoids gender-stereotyping of lawyers but introduces another negative female stereotype, that of the hysteric – the 'nut' of the title.

courtroom drama present a woman criminal lawyer (Kelly McGillis) who is a true justice figure, strong, competent, and capable of concentrating on her work even with men around.[21]

Courtroom dramas proliferated in the 1990s, but as the numbers went up, their quality fell. While criminal trial scenes continued to be used to create suspense and bring finality to the resolution, seldom did an entire movie build toward a trial scene.[22] Instead, these scenes were now enmeshed in a fabric of other, more animated sequences. They had become episodes in thrillers. Reflecting actual criminal trials (such as those involving O.J. Simpson and the assailants of Rodney King) in which justice seemed to many to have gone astray, courtroom films of the nineties mistrusted the criminal justice system's ability to accomplish its mission. Many began with the assumption that the system was broken beyond repair.

Presumed Innocent features Harrison Ford as Rusty Sabich, a criminal lawyer indicted for killing a female colleague with whom he had had an affair. The plot line conceals Sabich's guilt or innocence until the climax. Although he is ultimately exonerated, the judicial system is portrayed as a hollow shell of its former nobility. The trappings remain – the ornate courtrooms, the legal formalities – but beneath the veneer, something is rotting. The bad smell emanates in part from the judge, who pushes for Sabich's acquittal in order to conceal his own earlier malfeasance in another trial.

The judicial system blunders again in *Primal Fear* (1996), where Richard Gere defends a choirboy who murdered a priest. When the audience learns that the accused was molested by the priest and suffers from multiple personality disorder, it roots for the outcome Gere ultimately secures – not guilty by reason of insanity. However, Gere learns in the final scene that the choirboy (Edward Norton) faked his psychosis and is in fact a sadistic killer. At this point, there is nothing Gere can do. He, and the entire system, have been duped. So, in a sense, have viewers, for we have been kept in the dark by the film, much as Gere was kept ignorant by his client.

Criminal trial films of the nineties showed little sustained interest in the social issues that engrossed earlier courtroom dramas. They feigned interest in equality by using multiethnic and multiracial casts (the Hispanic defence attorney (Raul Julia) in *Presumed Innocent*, a female African-American judge in *Body of Evidence* (1992)), but they said little about ethnic or racial injustice. While they included female attorneys in their courtrooms, they

---

21 For another analysis of female attorney movies, see F.Y. Bailey, J.M. Pollock, and S. Schroder, 'The Best Defense: Images of Female Attorneys in Popular Films' in *Popular Culture, Crime, and Justice*, eds. F. Bailey and D. Hale (1998) ch. 12, 180–95.
22 An exception is *A Few Good Men*, a film that takes place mainly in the courtroom and has little or no 'action'. Successful at the box office, *A Few Good Men* won over audiences through dialogue and exposition – a rare feat in the nineties.

seem gripped less by gender issues than by a desire to show libidinous lawyers undressing. The gap between human law and true justice had become a plot gimmick.

Woman-lawyer films remained popular in the 1990s, with attorney Barbara Hershey sleeping with her pornographer client in *Defenseless* (1991) and attorney Susan Sarandon finding an outlet for her thwarted maternalism in *The Client* (1994). *A Few Good Men* (1992) features Demi Moore as a marine attorney defending two young marines charged with murder. The film, however, concentrates on another lawyer, played by Tom Cruise, whose character develops from lazy slacker to champion of justice. The movie's title is perhaps more accurate than the film-makers intended, for although Demi Moore's character outranks Tom Cruise's, her role in court is limited to passing him papers so he can argue the case.

In Sidney Lumet's *Guilty as Sin* (1993), another brilliant blond attorney (Rebecca DeMornay) defends another creep (Don Johnson) against another charge of wife-killing. In this case, however, the lawyer does not succumb sexually, and when she realizes that she is dealing with a serial woman-killer, she tries to frame him. He instantly sees through her ruse, however, and as soon as the jury returns the not-guilty verdict, he comes after her. In the ensuing struggle, both fall from a balcony, he to his death, she to multiple fractures and the wry observation, as an ambulance drives her away, that this is a tough way to get rid of a client. 'She has not won a legal case, however', a critic observes, 'since client-killing is not in the Model Code of Professional Responsibility'; and once again the female attorney has functioned 'as the erotic object for the audience as well as for the characters in the film'.[23]

There are, of course, exceptions to both the generally poor quality of nineties criminal trial films and their tendency to portray women lawyers as flying pigs, creatures that were not meant to be. *In the Name of the Father*, director Jim Sheridan's account of a 1970s frame-up of Irish men and women by the British government, opens with a dazzling spectacle of Irish commoners battling British police, and although it alternates trial scenes with action sequences, it keeps track of its themes. That the defence lawyer is a woman (Emma Thompson) is incidental here, and her sexuality is no more at issue than is Atticus Finch's in *To Kill a Mockingbird*.

The disappointing quality of most recent criminal court films stems from not their negativity about the law but their mindless reliance on shopworn conventions and depleted traditions. In fact, they do not say much at all. Lacking anger or other signs of conviction, they seem to be written by computers programmed to reproduce formulae. Their usual theme – the impossibility of achieving justice – cannot be persuasively conveyed through camera tricks, manipulative scripts, and recycled plots. The criminal trial film is unlikely to be revitalized in the foreseeable future. Rather, it is likely

23 Miller, op. cit., n. 16, pp. 227, 224.

to be replaced by films like *Do the Right Thing* (1989) and *Thelma and Louise* (1991) that pose questions about justice and responsibility outwith courtroom settings.

LIMITATIONS AND IDEOLOGICAL SIGNIFICANCE

While criminal trial films of the 1980s and 1990s criticize the justice system, none renounces the feel-good devices of Hollywood to present an oppositional view in which injustice not only prevails but causes profound social harm. To be sure, *individuals* are hurt in *The Star Chamber*, *Jagged Edge*, *The Accused*, and so on, but we know most of them will recover. Teddy Barnes will return to corporate law, right-wing judges will learn to live with defendants' rights, and rape bystanders will realize they should assist victims. Moreover, injustice figures are usually punished in these movies, and their evil does not survive them to infect society. There is simply no courtroom equivalent of *Bad Lieutenant* (1992), Abel Ferrara's police film in which injustice rages out of control, consuming innocents in its path and reducing the very idea of justice to ashes.

This lack of tragic vision in late twentieth-century criminal trial films can be illustrated with *The Rainmaker* (1997), a film about an idealistic young lawyer who wins his first case to the tune of $50 million, in the process exposing the criminality of the insurance company that refused to cover medical costs for a young man dying of leukemia. The hero, Rudy Baylor (Matt Damon) also helps old ladies and battered wives, and he is legally ambidextrous, equally capable in criminal and civil law. To be sure, *The Rainmaker* does provide a host of shysters and crooked attorneys to counterbalance Rudy's perfection. It blocks Rudy from collecting the $50 million in punitive damages from the insurance company, and at the end he renounces the practice of law because he cares 'how I do it'. 'Every lawyer', Rudy concludes with a wisdom far in advance of his experience, 'at least once in every case, feels himself crossing a line he doesn't really need to cross; it just happens, and if you cross it enough times it disappears forever, and then you're just another lawyer joke, just another shark in the dirty water'. Thus *The Rainmaker* enables us to venerate the law, in the character of its hero, even while exposing the law's weaknesses. Such uplifting material shields us from injustice rather than exposing us to it.

The absence of criminal trial films with a tragic or even deeply critical message reveals something fundamental about the nature of these dramas. *Bad Lieutenant* and other anti-feel-good cop films of the late twentieth-century (*Chinatown* (1974), *Normal Life* (1996), *Q & A* (1990), *Romeo is Bleeding* (1993), *To Live and Die in L.A.* (1985)) grew out of the bleakness of detective *noirs*, with their morally ambiguous private investigators and acceptance of crime as a normal condition. Although criminal court films, too, went through a *noir* phase, law *noirs* did not reject Hollywood conventions as completely as did detective *noirs*, nor did they argue that justice is beyond reach. For example, *Call Northside 777*, while hardly a joyful film, has a hero, the crusading journalist, who gets the falsely convicted men out of prison. Similarly, while *Stranger on the Third Floor* demonstrates the unreliability of eyewitness testimony, it concludes with the capture of the real villain.[24] *Knock on Any Door* has a hero – a strong one in Humphrey Bogart as Nick Romano's tough but understanding defence attorney. *Fury* might have led the way toward a darker tradition had Fritz Lang's studio not forced him to tack on a happy ending in which the reunited couple embraces in front of the judge.[25] Due to this ending, however, even *Fury* suggests that criminal trials can resolve social and personal problems. Thus law *noirs* failed to create a base on which present-day critical criminal court movies might have been built.

Another reason for criminal court films' lack of an alternative, more tragic vision of legal justice lies with the genre itself. Trial scenes are rigid in their requirements, permitting little in the way of plot innovation. In terms of character, too, they tend to inflexibility. By definition, most of their justice figures must be lawyers; and given the limited role of judges in United States trials, most of those lawyers must be defence attorneys or prosecutors.[26] In addition, trial scenes are limited cinematically; the ways to film a legal dispute are finite in number. Due to this overall rigidity, film-makers have been unable to use the genre to evolve more diverse, complex, or sorrowful views of criminal court injustice.

24 The only exception to the rule that law *noirs* retained Hollywood's happy-ending conventions seem to be *They Won't Believe Me* (1947), in which the innocent defendant, despairing of a fair trial, kills himself just before the jury returns with a not-guilty verdict. But this is only a partial exception (after all, the jury does recognize the defendant's innocence), and in any case *They Won't Believe Me* had little if any influence on other movies.

25 In an interview, Fritz Lang said that:

> I *hated* the kiss, because I think it wasn't necessary. A man [Spencer Tracy's character, Joe Wilson] gives a speech that ... is very well written and extremely well delivered, and then suddenly, for no reason whatsoever – in front of the judge and the audience and God knows who – they turn around and kiss each other ... It's such a coy ending now.

> Lang as quoted in P. Bogdanovich, *Fritz Lang in America* (1967) 26–8 (emphasis in original).

26 In an unpublished paper on Hollywood courtroom dramas, Machura and Ulbrich argue that the relative weakness of the judge in American trials strengthens conflicts between prosecution and defence and pushes the trial itself into the center of the stage (S. Machura and S. Ulbrich, 'Law in the Movies: Image of Legal Reality or Self-Reference of Film?', paper presented at Annual Meeting of the Law & Society Association, June 4–7, 1998, Aspen, Colorado). Thus the relative weakness of the judge in actual trials is one reason for the international popularity of American trial films.

23

As a group, criminal trial films make no dominant type of ideological declaration. According to one, justice can be achieved; according to the next, it is out of reach. Individually, these films do send powerful ideological messages. The characters in *Twelve Angry Men*, for example, have been carefully designed to drive home a message about pluralism and consensus,[27] and, as indicated, the woman-lawyer films of the eighties and nineties can be seen as part of the backlash against feminism. Over time, however, criminal court films have staked out a wide range of ideological positions.

Criminal court films' ideological significance ultimately lies less in what they say than in the images they use to say it – in their mythologies about what happens during criminal trials. The reality of criminal justice processes is of course very different from movie depictions; in the United States, 85 per cent of all criminal cases are plea-bargained, for instance, and the 15 per cent that do go to trial are as likely to have trials with judges sitting alone as jury trials.[28] Few people, however, are aware of these realities; most of us derive our fundamental assumptions about the workings of criminal law from the media. Representations of law furnish raw material for public debates about justice; in our haste to discuss the issues, we may not notice that there is something odd about the materials, especially if we lack actual courtroom experiences to compare them with.[29]

The influence of movies' representations of criminal law is now international in scope. Due to the worldwide dominance of American films, viewers in countries with very different legal traditions think their trials follow the United States movie pattern. Stefan Machura and Stefan Ulbrich report that in interviews, German defendants expressed surprise at the physical arrangement of their courtrooms, which did not look like the courtrooms they were used to seeing in American television shows. Machura and Ulbrich describe another study in which German children and adults, when asked what they knew about courts, said that they got most of their information from movies, especially American crime films.[30] If ideology is the myths people live by, then the images of trial films constitute a rich and globally powerful source of ideology about the nature of criminal justice processes.

27 P. Biskind, *Seeing is Believing* (1983): 10–20.
28 For a film-by-film analysis of differences between film trials and actual trials, see P. Bergman and M. Asimow, *Reel Justice* (1996).
29 For a critique of this and related developments, see R.K. Sherwin, *When Law Goes Pop*. (2000).
30 Machura and Ulbrich, op. cit., n. 26.

JOURNAL OF LAW AND SOCIETY
VOLUME 28, NUMBER 1, MARCH 2001
ISSN: 0263-323X, pp. 25–39

Hero or Villain? Cinematic Lawyers and the Delivery of Justice

STEVE GREENFIELD*

This essay is concerned with two specific issues that have as their backdrop the heroic central figure, the trial lawyer. First it considers the role of screen lawyers in seeking to maintain public (in this sense the public is the community within the film) support for the due process of law. The issue is the link between the lawyer and the initiation of the formal legal process. Essentially it is the extent to which the lawyer defends the institution of law. The second part of the piece considers when screen lawyers are permitted to go outside the formal process of law to ensure that the right result is achieved. It examines instances of where lawyers have been prepared to go 'beyond law' to achieve justice. Such acts raise a number of questions concerning how such behaviour affects perception of the legitimacy of the law, professional ethics, and the relationship between law and justice

INTRODUCTION

Within the area of film and the law there are a number of distinct approaches that have been adopted by different academics. There is clearly a growing interest in films that are concerned with the portrayal of law and lawyers and this is reflected in a wide variety of works. Some analysis of legal film is rooted in a desire to understand the nature of the broader relationship between law and popular culture and this has emerged as the study of popular culture itself has itself moved further forward into the mainstream.[1]

* School of Law, University of Westminster, 4 Little Titchfield Street, London W1P 7FW, England
Many thanks to Guy Osborn for his learned thoughts and comments on the original drafts of this piece.

1 See, for example, A. Chase, 'Towards A Legal Theory of Popular Culture' (1986) *Wisconsin Law Rev.* 527–69; G. Newman, 'Popular Culture and Criminal Justice: A Preliminary Analysis' (1990) 18 *J. of Crim. Justice* 261–74; S. Macaulay, 'Popular Legal Culture: An Introduction' (1989) *Yale Law J.* 1545; D. Papke, 'Law in American Culture: An Overview' (1992) 15 *J. of Am. Culture* 3.

Other studies have concentrated on individual films,[2] true events converted to film,[3] the representation of women or ethnic minorities,[4] legal institutions,[5] or the relationship between the portrayal of the profession and real life lawyering.[6] There have also been some admirable attempts to construct legal filmographies which is a fundamental though difficult task.[7] A key, as yet largely unresolved dimension, to the study of cinematic portrayals of law and lawyers has been the causal link between what the public sees (the cultural representation) and the effect of such representation. One of the apparent contradictions is between a historically generally positive screen image of lawyers and a general lay dislike for the activities of the profession, most crudely indicated by the range of (anti-) lawyer jokes. The contemporary view, that lawyers are now getting a bad press or rather a bad review, finds some favour within the professional associations.[8] Bander however argues that this is far from a new phenomenon:

> The American Bar Association (ABA), in a recent issue of its journal, bemoaned that lawyer-bashing has become the current fad. I have news for the ABA; lawyer bashing has been with us for thousands of years.[9]

Gordon argues that a more complex and almost schizophrenic relationship between the American public and lawyers has long existed.[10] The American dimension is an important consideration as the vast majority of the films are American in content which is a reflection of the construction of the international film industry.[11]

2 See the (1996) 30(4) issue of the *University of San Francisco Law Rev.* that was devoted to film and law and contains a section on analysis of individual films including, amongst others, *Kramer vs. Kramer, To Kill a Mockingbird, Inherit the Wind, Dead Man Walking, In the Name of the Father*.
3 See, for example, S. Greenfield and G. Osborn, 'Pulped Fiction? Cinematic Parables of (In)Justice' in id., p. 1181.
4 See, for example, R. Sheffield, 'On Film: A Social History of Women Lawyers in Popular Culture 1930–1990' (1993) 14 *Loyola of Los Angeles Entertainment Law J.* 73.
5 See, for example, G. Hambley, 'The Image of the Jury in Popular Culture' (1992) 12 *Legal Reference Services Q.* 171.
6 See, for example, R. Strickland, 'The Cinematic Lawyer: The Magic Mirror and the Silver Screen' (1997) 22 *Oklahoma City University Law Rev.* 13.
7 See P. Mastrangelo, 'Lawyers and the Law: A Filmography' (1983) 3 *Legal References Q.* 31.
8 T. Weidlich, 'Will "The Firm" Further Hurt Bar's Image' *National Law J.*, 28 June 1993(a); T. Weidlich, 'A Cynical Age Sees Few Heroes In Its Lawyers' *National Law J.*, 29 November 1993(b).
9 D. Gunn, *The Lawyer and Popular Culture* (1993).
10 J. Gordon, 'The Popular Image of the American Lawyer: Some Thoughts on its Eighteenth and Nineteenth Century Intellectual Bases' (1989) 46 *Washington and Lee Law Rev.* 763.
11 There are some notable English films such as *Brothers in Law* (Roy Boulting, 1957) and *Witness for the Prosecution* (Billy Wilder, 1957). This latter film is American-made but has the English legal system as its content.

26

Americans have always had ambivalent feelings about lawyers. Almost every generation has expressed its distaste for this profession which lives by subtlety and conflict, but each generation has put its most important public and private affairs into the hands of persons trained to the law. This fact is true whether one looks to positions of private or public power. Nowhere has the bar been so heavily criticized and in no other place have its members had such honors and powers bestowed upon them.

The Hollywood treatment of lawyers often seems to only reflect the positive side of this relationship with a seemingly marked reluctance to catalogue lawyers as unfaithful to the principles of justice. However there is some evidence of a more critical portrayal of lawyers at different times within cinematic history; it may be the prevailing genre that determines the nature of the character:

> The world of film *noir* or the dark cinema is inhabited with as disreputable a bunch of lawyers as ever flickered across the silver screen. Some of these attorneys are scheming and corrupt, like Calhern in *The Asphalt Jungle*, others are the weak pawns of powerful, devastating femmes fatales like Barbara Stanwyck, who dominates Kirk Douglas in his very first film, *The Strange Love of Martha Ives.*[12]

With respect to contemporary legal films, there is a developing line of argument that we are now seeing a new type of lawyer compared to the great heroic lawyer of whatever era:

> wisdom has rotted into calculation, justice into dealmaking. The lawyer today is forced to face all manner of complex problems confusing his moral authority: matters economic, racial, sexual, political. The magic circle is broken.[13]

Specifically this concerns a comparison between more modern portrayals and that of the great screen lawyer heroes from the mid 1950s through the 1960s. This is an era Rafter describes as 'the heroic tradition' in which lawyers are portrayed 'as men who labour heroically within the system to ensure that man-made law coincides with the justice ideal.'[14] Whether there are examples of unsavoury screen lawyers at different times does not disguise the long line of films that develop the notion of the lawyer as a superhero.

The great hero-lawyer, whether of this period or before or after, has often been confronted with a significant moral question. Contentious ethical issues, surrounding the practice of law, have long been used as part of the

---

12 R. Strickland, 'The Cinematic Lawyer: The Magic Mirror and the Silver Screen' (1997) 22 *Oklahoma City University Law Rev.* 19.
13 T. Appelo, 'Atticus Doesn't Live Here Anymore' (1992) 8 *California Lawyer* 174–7, at 177.
14 N. Rafter, *Shots in the Mirror: Crime Films and Society* (2000) 102. The other periods she identifies are: The 1930s to the Mid-1950s; Experimentation and the Law *Noirs* ... From the 1970s to the Present; Depletion of the Genre.

character construction of cinematic lawyers. The handling of difficult moral and ethical dilemmas are often marks of the 'great' law film and the 'great' film lawyer. This is not confined to any particular period, for example, a more recent film, *Philadelphia*,[15] confronted issues of homophobia and AIDS and employment. The perception of the lawyer as an American hero figure certainly persists as far back as the seminal *Young Mr Lincoln*[16] in 1939. There are a number of idyllic portrayals of the lawyer as virtuous, almost godlike in demeanour and ability, with a willingness to tackle issues such as racism and discrimination. Clark, however, argues that the modern portrayal:

> ... portrays the humanity of the lawyer in a more honest light. The conflict of values paints a more ambivalent picture of the modern lawyer but ultimately the heroic aspect wins out, not only in the external battle of good versus evil, but also in an internal moral confrontation.[17]

These early portrayals are echoed in some of the more modern comparisons though the contemporary examples may exhibit more complex characteristics. This latter point does to some extent depend upon the depth of analysis of the characters concerned. It is a mistake to consider that the early portrayals were of pure heroes without flaws. For example, Lincoln (in *Young Mr. Lincoln*) is shown resorting to threats of physical violence on more than one occasion and, furthermore, he is not beyond cheating, albeit only at a tug-of-war or influencing the fall of the stick that is to determine his career choice. Today's misdemeanours are far more serious: unfaithfulness, cheating, lying, as well as a whole host of breaches of professional practice rules. Modern cinema requires more detailed and fast-moving works and this is reflected in the characters and the flaws they have; cheating at a tug-of-war is simply not bad enough. Frank Galvin in *The Verdict* is a modern-day example of the heroic lawyer who delivers justice, yet he is imbued with personal deficiencies such as his heavy drinking. It is possible to see that certain characteristics of the cinematic lawyer have remained fairly constant, and that some features are central to the portrayal of lawyers and the legal process.[18]

This argument about the development of common characteristics and whether the hero-lawyer still exists is an interesting and important debate and will develop as work in the area increases and more examples are unearthed. One of the problems with assessing the way in which lawyers are portrayed is determining the 'type' of film in question and the role of the lawyer within the film. In one sense the whole issue of genre is vital though in many ways seeking to define law films may, in itself, be problematic. If,

---

15 Jonathan Demme, 1993.
16 John Ford, 1939.
17 G. Clark, 'The Lawyer as Hero?' in Gunn, op. cit., n. 9.
18 S. Greenfield and G. Osborn, 'Where cultures collide: the characterisation of law and lawyers in film' (1995) 23 *International J. of the Sociology of Law* 107–30.

by definition (whichever we choose), the film does not qualify as a law film, can we subsume the characteristics into our general analysis? Put simply, is a dishonest character who happens to be a lawyer, but not acting as a lawyer, of any significance? But to find lawyers we have to find law films and this creates more problems than it solves. Unless we adopt an incredibly restrictive approach and ring-fence courtroom drama (whatever that may be) as legal films, then, in a sense, many films which on the surface are not about law are within the field.[19]

PRESERVING THE RULE OF LAW

The representation of an unpopular defendant is often a key moral issue that the cinematic lawyer must embrace in order to distinguish him from other, more mortal lawyers. In part, this contributes to the heroic dimension, neatly depicted by Chase as:

> ... a protector who stands with his or her client against the world no matter what the odds; indeed, no matter what the attorney's personal political views or estimate of the client's 'guilt' or 'innocence', a matter left to judge and jury.[20]

Unafraid of thinking the unthinkable, or representing the unrepresentable, moral issues have been raised as hurdles for the cinematic lawyer to cross. The resolution of such dilemmas enables the lawyer to claim and maintain the high moral ground and develop as an individual. Representing the unpopular puts the lawyer outside and above the local community, especially given that the crime at stake is almost inevitably murder. There are two elements here, which often cross over, first the right to representation and secondly the sanctity of the rule of law. This latter point is concerned with the relationship between lawyers and the legal process. The due process of law is legitimized and raised to an important level, supported by the lawyers.

A prime example of representing the unpopular is to be found within the revered *To Kill A Mockingbird*.[21] The film contains perhaps the most oft cited example of the ultimate hero-lawyer, Gregory Peck's portrayal of Atticus Finch.[22] Carver (a lawyer) makes a personal point about the strength

---

19 Chase reinforces this point: 'Just as legal education has been too preoccupied with materials produced by courts, our study might also fall into a trap by narrowing its focus exclusively to popular culture materials which concern courtrooms and trials.' Chase, op. cit., n. 1, p. 527.
20 A. Chase, 'Lawyers and Popular Culture' (1986) *Am. Bar Foundation* 282.
21 Robert Mulligan, 1962.
22 Appelo, op. cit., n. 13, argues that Finch's authority extends beyond the courtroom into the problems of society but is buttressed by the force of law:

> ... Atticus Finch had the moral authority of a world-historical figure. Mockingbird is about the real issues of race, violence and justice that were making Americans

29

of the portrayal when she notes that 'Atticus made me believe in lawyer-heroes.'[23] She further explains that it is not just the 'larger moral issue of Tom's arrest and trial' which demonstrates his occupation of the moral high ground but also the aspects of his mundane life:

> He found time, somehow, for tender talks with his children. On walks home from his office, he paused at the fence of his grumpy lady neighbor, to say 'good day' and praise her garden. He was intolerant of prejudice and unkindness at every level.[24]

This stresses not his greater morality but his ordinariness and, as with Lincoln, his relationship with the common folk. Atticus Finch may have an influential position within the community but he is prepared to stand aside from local society by representing Tom Robinson. He agrees without undue hesitation to defend Robinson despite the hostility that he knows this will cause. Furthermore, Finch is physically prepared to defend his client from a prospective lynch mob and is aided and abetted by his children. In a similar move to Lincoln's, his daughter picks out an individual in the crowd and disarms the collective will. The unpopular defendant and the resolute defence of the legal process contribute to make Finch the heroic man and lawyer that he must be.

This feature of the celebrated position of the lawyer within the community can also be seen in *Young Mr Lincoln*. This is an interesting and important film for a number of reasons, not least the status of the main character and the director. Consequently it has been subject to detailed analysis within the context of work in the area of film and the law.[25] One crucial scene involves two brothers, one of whom it is alleged have murdered a local figure, Scrub White. When a crowd are informed of White's murder they attempt to storm the jail, where the two boys have been taken, and lynch the pair. Lincoln meanwhile informs the mother that he is her (and her sons) lawyer and proceeds to the jailhouse to deal with the crowd. Lincoln quietens the stone-throwing crowd and, after threatening physical violence, attempts to reason with them, adopting both a high moral tone and a practical rationale (his own

fear for the structural integrity of the state circa 1962. As Finch, Peck is crowned with the white fedora of truth and walks with a stately asymmetry, the result of an actual back injury but put to immortal use. His gait emphasises his gravity, the essence of the law. it doesn't come agross as a limp; it makes him seem to be striding straight from Mount Olympus. Arguably the most physically beautiful male product in Hollywood, Peck makes an ever better symbol of incorruptibility than Burr. His coiffure is as resonant as the wig of a British judge: His forelock only falls out of place and onto his forehead at significant moments, such as when he must take off his reading glasses to shoot a rabid dog, or when he's assaulted by the film's white-trash villain, or when he finds that character murdered.

23 C. Carver, 'Lawyers as Heroes' (1988) 13/14 *Los Angeles Lawyer* 13.
24 id.
25 See, for example, N. Rosenberg, 'Young Mr Lincoln: The Lawyer as Super-Hero' (1991) XV *Legal Studies Forum* 215.

greenness and inability) for a trial to proceed:

Lincoln:	All joking aside lets look at this matter from my side. Why you all know I'm just a fresh lawyer trying to get ahead but some of you boys act like you want to do me out of my first clients.
	(*laughter from the crowd*)
	I'm not saying that you fellas are not right maybe these boys do deserve to hang. But with me handling their case don't look like you'll have much to worry about on that score.
	(*laughter from the crowd*)
	All I'm asking is to have it done with some legal pomp and show.
	(*crowd mutters*)
Man with rope:	We've gone to a heap of trouble not to have at least one hanging
Lincoln:	Sure you have Mac and if these boys had more than one life I'd say go ahead, maybe a little hanging mightn't do 'em any harm, but the sort of hanging you boys 'ed give em would be so ... so ... permanent.
	(*crowd laughs*)
	Trouble is when men start taking the law into their own hands they's just as apt in all the confusion and fun to hang somebody who's not a murderer as somebody who is. And the next thing you know they're hanging one another just for fun. Until it gets to a place when a man can't pass a tree or look at a rope without feeling uneasy. We seem to lose our heads in times like this. We do things together that we might be ashamed to do by ourselves.

Lincoln singles out an individual in the crowd who he describes as a good and decent bible-reading man, quotes a piece of scripture with regard to mercy, and effectively shames the crowd into abandoning their protest. Ford's Lincoln figure is, in some ways, a contradiction; a man who decries the use of force without allowing the law to run its course whilst on the other hand prepared to use brute force to his own ends. This latter point is illustrated by his threat to knock two protagonists' heads together to solve a dispute. What is apparent throughout the film is the crucial importance of the figure of Lincoln and the contribution of this film towards a mythical, almost divine, status. Lincoln is obviously, given his political position, a funda-mental subject for film; interestingly it was Fonda, rather than Ford, who was recorded as having reservations about playing the character.[26]

26 T. Gallagher, *John Ford: The Man and his Films* (1986) 164:

> When Ford discussed Lincoln there was such an extraordinary sense of intimacy in his tone that somehow it was no longer a director speaking of a great President, but a man talking about a friend ... But he cajoled Henry Fonda into being Lincoln 'You think you'd be playing the goddam great emancipator, huh? He's a goddam fucking jake-legged lawyer in Springfield, for Christ's sake!'

Gallagher argues that the myth of Lincoln contributes to both the physical characteristics of the portrayal but also controls the character's freedom. The myth subsumes the man:

> It requires the viewer's active participation to detect Lincoln's ignobility, silliness, awkwardness, arrogance and fear. Comedic frontier roughness exonerates Lincoln for cheating at tug-of-war, or for ruthlessness towards two farmer plaintiffs or towards Jack Cass; and we admire his foxiness rather than his obnoxious guile in the way he dupes everyone during the trial.[27]

This is a vital point. Gallagher demonstrates that Ford's Lincoln is in many ways not a superhero, rather, a product of myth and history. If you dissect the character there are many flaws and inconsistencies.[28] However, by the end of the film, his status within the community is enhanced and he is seen as a powerful and influential character. There are differences between the blemishes in the character of Lincoln and those in Lincoln the lawyer. Many of the features in *Young Mr Lincoln* and the characteristics of Lincoln the lawyer, are replicated in later films.

The adoption of high moral values and defence of the legal system need not be confined to legal representatives. In the classic Sidney Lumet film, *Twelve Angry Men*,[29] the clear moral question is the depth of the legal process required to convict and execute a young man accused of the murder of his father. The jury is shown to be prepared to convict the young man without any serious debate apart from the objections of one juror, and they vote 11–1 in favour of guilty. This dissenting juror, played by Henry Fonda, insists that the case be discussed before such an important decision is made.

Fonda:	I just want to talk
Second Juror:	What is there to talk about? Eleven men in here think he's guilty, no one had to think about it twice except you.
Third Juror:	I want to ask you something, do you believe his story?
Fonda:	I don't know whether I believe it or not. Maybe I don't.
Second Juror:	So how come you vote not guilty?
Fonda:	Well there were eleven votes for guilty it's not easy to raise my hand and send a boy off to die without talking about it first
Second Juror:	Well now who says it's easy?
Fonda:	No-one.

---

27 id., p. 165.
28 Interestingly Gallagher argues that this is reflected in his relationship with the law:

> Although supposedly a man of the people and peace, Lincoln receives Law from God, uses it with violence, and represses most human instincts in himself and others. When not outrightly ridiculous, Lincoln is a mediocrity, a mere agent of truth; rather than a human, he is an unchanging, glacial monster, a sort of Nosferatu.

id., p. 171.
29 Sidney Lumet, 1957.

Second Juror:	What just because I voted fast? I honestly think the guy's guilty, you couldn't change my mind if you ... talked for a hundred years.
Fonda:	I am not trying to change your mind it's just that we're talking about someone's life here, we can't decide it in five minutes, supposing we're wrong?

Fonda plays the role of both sceptic juror and the boy's 'defence counsel' in opening debates about the key points of the evidence. What the film does is support the notion that the legal process requires the intervention of good men to make sure that it runs according to liberal values:

> At a sociological level, clearly Lumet's film reflects strong concern with the constituent parts of a living democracy, as the wiser and more emotionally stable jurors must responsibly lead those men with less self awareness and self knowledge than they, if democracy is to have any chance to work fairly and justly. Though the film contains little doctrinaire preaching on the subject of democracy, the audience is led to respond favourably to those jurors – Fonda, Joseph Sweeney, George Voskovec – for whom reason and the liberal vision of the world and of humankind are paramount.[30]

This links together the idea of the hero (lawyer) and the importance of the legal process. The public may not appreciate the vital role of law to democracy and it needs the lawyer to demonstrate that the law must be allowed to function. Fonda, as a juror in *Twelve Angry Men*, is given this task of guiding the other jurors towards what is 'right'. Often though this is the role to be played by the defence lawyer who is given a superior moral capacity to make such important judgements. This reflects a more general theme of the lawyer being portrayed as ethically superior to those around him. Being able to see beyond the immediate problem to see a broader picture sets our hero aside both inside and outside of the community.

What these films demonstrate is absolute integrity when dealing with a major moral problem. The defence of the rule of law and the right to a fair trial may well find theoretical supporters, but here are Fonda (twice) and Peck showing that there may be consequences, such as vilification, for standing up for this right. This element of the character may also provide an attractive dimension to those playing the part: 'actors relish the role of the lawyer, it can offer them depth and breadth and the opportunity to play the heroic saviour'.[31] This is an important point and may, partly at least, explain why lawyers have been treated so favourably by scriptwriters. Within a method of film production that relies on a star system the central figure, played by the star, may need to contain prescribed features. As Goldman wryly notes:

30 F. Cunningham, *Sidney Lumet: Film and Literary Vision* (1991) 111.
31 Greenfield and Osborn, op. cit., n. 18, p. 112.

33

here is one of the basic lessons a screenwriter must learn and live with. Stars will not play weak and they will not play blemished, and you had better know that now.[32]

What is apparent from a fairly rudimentary analysis of legal films is that fundamental issues surrounding the application of law have played an important role in the construction of the screen lawyer. This figure has also stood in the forefront of the defence, sometimes even physical, of the importance to democracy of the rule of law. The next issue is whether that firm conviction of the law taking its course becomes subsumed within a more general desire for the hero to deliver justice by any means.

DELIVERING JUSTICE AND SIDE-STEPPING THE LEGAL PROCESS

The issue here is the role of the hero-lawyer in the delivery of justice. More fundamentally it concerns the leeway, given to the central figure, to ignore the procedures of law where he feels it necessary to reach the 'right' result. In essence this is part of the subjective core of the lawyer's function.[33] One part of this is the narrower issue of professional legal ethics and how these have been dealt with within legal films. An important point is how the cinematic lawyer is influenced by such professional ethics in his association with clients, the legal process and ultimately justice. The emphasis here is on the relationship between the lawyer, the court, and the client and whether procedural rules and ethical requirements can be ignored in order to achieve a higher ideal. This has implications for the sanctity and probity of the legal profession, the relationship between law and justice, and the fundamental question of to whom does a lawyer owe a duty.

The Verdict,[34] a further offering from Sydney Lumet, highlights some of the inconsistencies of character that lie in a more concealed fashion within both Lincoln (*Young Mr Lincoln*) and Atticus Finch (*To Kill A Mockingbird*). Here the weaknesses, of the central legal figure, are laid bare from the outset. Frank Galvin (Paul Newman) is immediately presented as a broken alcoholic who cannot find many clients or satisfy those he does.[35] He is given a last-

---

32 W. Goldman, *Adventures in the Screen Trade* (1993) 37.
33 Friedman makes the point that there may be a significant difference between how lawyers and the public view the operation of law: 'Freedom and democracy, in the minds of lawyers, in contrast with the public at large, tend to be conceived of largely in *procedural* terms. Lawyers are taught and trained to regard "due process" as the very essence of fairness and the rule of law'. L. Friedman, 'Law, Lawyers and Popular Culture' (1989) 98 *Yale Law J.* 1579–606, at 1603.
34 Sidney Lumet, 1982.
35 The film is an interesting one for analysis as at first instance it seems to run contrary to the 'heroic formula'. The starting point of the down-at-heel Galvin did cause a problem in casting:

ditch chance to redeem his legal career and, by analogy, himself.[36] The drunken ambulance-chaser is given a final offer of moral, spiritual, and legal redemption. The case itself contains a strong moral element, the paralysis of a patient by a negligent doctor and the legal problem of proof. Against a strong defence team who plant a spy (which also provides a sexual dimension) on Galvin, and with little evidence, the case seems unwinnable. Frank Galvin is offered a settlement by the defence but he rejects the offer, without ever informing his clients, that it has been made. After all a settlement would only leave him back in a professional and personal void. Galvin is then confronted by the husband of the plaintiff:

> *Plaintiff's husband:* Hey Galvin. You said you were going to call me. What do you think you are? What do you think you are?
> *(punches Galvin)*
> They tell me I could have you disbarred. I am going to have your ticket, you know what you did? I said did you know what you did?
> *(tries to punch Galvin again, third party intervenes)*
> *Frank Galvin:* OK, it's OK.
> *Plaintiff's husband:* You've ruined my life mister, me and my wife and now I'm going to ruin yours. You didn't have to go out there to see that girl we've been going for four years now. See four years, my wife has been crying herself to sleep. For what they did to her sister.
> *Frank Galvin:* I swear to you. I wouldn't. I wouldn't turn down the offer if I thought I couldn't win the case.
> *Plaintiff's husband:* What you thought. I am a working man and I'm trying to get my wife out of town. Now we hired you and I'm paying you and I gotta find out from the other side that they offered $200,000.

Redford is still interested in doing a movie about medical malpractice – but the main role, that of the lawyer, Galvin, that's the problem. He's a boozer and a womaniser and Zanuck and Brown (the producers) hear that Redford thinks the character could be bad for his image.

Goldman, op. cit., n. 32.

36 An interesting slant was placed on these issues with *Devil's Advocate* (Taylor Hackford, 1997). This takes the theme of the powerful lawyer, indeed this depiction shows law's 'unbridled power' and a much more unequivocal unflattering portrayal of law and lawyers. Here Satan is the chief partner. John Milton (Al Pacino) cites the law as being 'the ultimate backstage pass' and 'the new priesthood' and this depiction appears to run counter to the general trend of lawyer as positive force, fighting for what is 'right and good'. However, Kevin Lomax (Keanu Reeves) who begins as the unscrupulous lawyer with little truck for legal and ethical protocol (he is after all the son of Satan!) rejects his father's Faustian pact to continue the 'priesthood' and chooses redemption by killing himself. His higher moral act of self sacrifice demonstrates this innate heroic quality.

35

Once the offer is withdrawn, after his unilateral rejection, Galvin is obliged to look beyond the immediate case and fight for the 'truth'. He needs to win and win spectacularly in order to find his own personal redemption. Only by winning this case and achieving justice can he put his own past behind him. Of course he is ultimately successful and the jury foreman asks the hostile judge whether they are limited in how much they can award as they wish to exceed the amount sought. The film stresses that truth and justice are dependent not upon strict rules of legal procedure but upon human behaviour and interpretation of those rules. The rules are secondary to justice and Galvin can abuse both the rules of practice and the rules of procedure in order to achieve the truth. The film starts with him drinking spirits in a bar and unable to pick up the glass because of his shaking hand, and rejecting the advances of Charlotte Rampling. Yet, by the end of the film Galvin is drinking coffee. Galvin's career is resurrected, as is his own personal morality. Whilst ultimately spectacularly victorious, he acts outside his legal duty by not taking instructions at that point and proceeds with the case without consulting his clients.

This bending of procedural rules or those relating to client conduct is a commonplace means of revealing the independence, from both the law and the legal community, of our screen hero. For example, Lincoln, in an aggressive cross-examination, reveals the truth only after he has badgered and ridiculed the witness. He freely admits to knowing little of the law but rather knowing what's right and wrong. The process of law is second to the need to demonstrate a just result. Similarly, in *Suspect*,[37] the defence attorney Kathleen Riley (Cher) establishes an unethical relationship with one of the jurors in an attempt to find the truth for her (unpopular client). This also raises the question of the detective role of the lawyer which is again a favourite theme. If the process of law is obstructive to the delivery of justice then the lawyer is expected to physically investigate the case and gather evidence. This contributes to the construction of the omnipotent figure responsible for making up for the deficiencies of others.

The majority of these portrayals show the lawyer acting in the best (long-term) interests of the client at the expense of the formal rules. However, with respect to Galvin, it is arguable that he was acting entirely selfishly, and that any objective assessment of the case would have revealed a poor chance of success. Indeed, in his memorable summing-up, he has to appeal to the jury's sense of justice to override the deficiencies in his own case that are exacerbated by the rules of evidence. An interesting development of this notion, of abusing the rules on client conduct, is to be found within the remake of *Cape Fear*.[38] Here, though, the action taken by the lawyer is not in the interests of the client, Max Cady (Robert De Niro), whom Sam Bowden (Nick Nolte) is defending, but in the interests of the community

37 Peter Yates, 1987.
38 Martin Scorcese, 1991.

36

(this is discussed in greater depth below). These films and others demonstrate that the cinematic lawyer will often freely flaunt the procedural rules and disregard client considerations in order to achieve a subjective notion of justice.

CONCLUSION

The question is where does this analysis take us? There are a number of interrelated aspects of the portrayals that contribute to our overall impression of screen lawyers. First we have the concept of the hero-lawyer, whatever films may be brought as evidence of other attributes it is difficult to argue that in general terms even those screen lawyers who do not make hero status are treated pretty favourably. The 'greats' are often distinguished by their ability to see beyond the present and represent more than the individual defendant but the higher ideal of law. Confronting prejudice, whether racism or homophobia, and ignorance is an essential part of the make-up, it is what makes them so worthy. These 'men' are the representatives of justice rather than law. We see them prepared to take measures that are at odds with the process of law to achieve the 'right' result. This just outcome results in the cementing of the lawyer as an outsider, above both society's morals and the rules of the profession in search of a higher ideal. As Rosenberg notes of Lincoln:

> Ultimately, then, *Young Mr Lincoln* marks its hero as someone who works *within* but is not really *of* the legal machinery. In this sense Fonda's Lincoln bears passing resemblance to a similarly-coded 'legal' hero who came to prominence in books and on the motion picture screen during the 1930s, the lawyer-detective Perry Mason.[39]

It is apparent that Lincoln uses the law in different ways. In keeping with the binary themes within the film, at one moment Lincoln urges reliance on the due process of law whilst at other times rejects the formality of the legal process. Lincoln clearly exhibits the characteristic of the classic superhero screen lawyer; he defends the unpopular and with a remarkable twist breaks down the witness and reveals the true killer. He also reduces law to simplistic principles but he owns the interpretative key. It is Lincoln who single-handedly manages to produce a just result and save the two brothers from the gallows. He relies on his wits and belief in the truth and is self-mocking with respect to the extent of his legal knowledge. This is perhaps a crucial point, that it is the lawyers alone who can deliver justice. These films are telling us to have faith in the idea but not the system of law. Yet the system does end up producing justice whether for the plaintiff in *The Verdict* or the defendant in *Twelve Angry Men*. Perhaps more than an argument about

---

39 Rosenberg, op. cit., n. 25, p. 215.

37

idea versus processes, these films are telling us to have faith in the lawyers themselves. It is they who can see, and deliver, the path to justice.

The whole relationship between law, the lawyers, the legal process and justice, as played on the screen, is a complicated one. A good illustration of the complexities of the matter can be found in *Cape Fear*. Sam Bowden is being harassed by a former client, Max Cady, whom he had unsuccessfully acted for as a Public Defender. Bowden reveals the betrayal of Cady to a colleague;

Sam: Tom, 14 years ago in this case I had a report on the victim.
Tom: It was a rape case?
Sam: That's right, rape and aggravated sexual battery. Anyway I had a report on this victim and it came back that she was promiscuous and, er ... I buried it.
Tom: Phew. Anybody else know about it?
Sam: No, no no. I buried it, I mean I didn't show it to the client, I didn't show it to the prosecution ... but if you had seen what this guy had done to this girl ...
Tom: In every criminal prosecution the accused shall have the assistance of counsel for his defence.
Sam: Hell I know the sixth amendment, I believe in the sixth amendment. I mean that's why I left the Public Defender's Office, there was no way to serve the law in that capacity.
Tom: Some folks just don't deserve the best defence eh Sam?
Sam: No of course they deserve the best defence but if you had seen what he did to this girl ...
Tom: Buried the report ...
Sam: I mean if it was your own daughter Tom ... I mean ...
Tom: Buried the report ... Jesus, Sam.

As a result of Bowden's actions Cady is imprisoned for fourteen years. Whilst in prison he teaches himself law, finds out what has happened and returns to seek vengeance against Bowden and his family. Bowden's action is clearly contrary to the concept of due process and professional ethics though he is acting out of a higher ideal, the need to protect society from a dangerous rapist. Students on the film and the law module at Westminster find the Cady/Bowden relationship extremely problematic. Whilst at the outset a majority cannot countenance the behaviour of Bowden in ensuring that his client receives a prison term, by the time the nature of Cady is revealed (through a vicious sexual assault) the view is less certain. In a dramatic brutal final scene, Cady places Bowden on trial within the confines of a boat. Bowden's wife and daughter act as the judge and jury as Cady physically assaults and interrogates his former lawyer:

Max Cady: Can you please quote for me the American Bar Association Rules of Professional Conduct canon 7?
Sam Bowden: A lawyer shall represent his client ...
(Cady interrupts): A lawyer shall jealously represent his client within the bounds of the law.

38

Sam Bowden is shown as a weak and immoral figure, yet he was prepared to sacrifice his career in order that Cady should not escape justice. *Cape Fear* tells us that the process of law is flawed, and this is reinforced as Bowden is shown to be unable to lawfully restrict Cady's harassment.

Perhaps these films demonstrate why the (American) public seem to have such a love/hate relationship with the legal profession. Lawyers are shown as morally strong characters prepared to take great risk in defence of the concept of law or, more accurately, justice. Yet, the films portray the process of law as instrumental in the obstruction of justice. Justice thus becomes dependent on the lawyers themselves. We berate Bowden for the betrayal of his client but in the long term are grateful that he was prepared to ensure that Cady was imprisoned.

Many law films are concerned with the tension between law and justice and lawyers are given roles to ensure that justice prevails. Generally films are critical of rigid application of the rulebook, highlighting justice above certainty and authority. This issue is forcefully made within *Judge Dredd* (Danny Cannon, 1995) where the tension between the law and justice is made explicit – even Dredd comes to realize that his earlier rigid reliance is incompatible with the truth once his own wrongful conviction becomes apparent. It does seem that screen lawyers cannot lose as 'there is little critical lego-filmography, rose tinted spectacles rather than 3D glasses are the proffered for the viewing of these films'.[40] Even if we accept that the golden or heroic age has pased, our cinematic lawyers are still heroes. They may be flawed and more complex but they are still employed to unravel the complexities of the law but, most of all, to deliver justice, often despite the law. Lawyers need moral dilemmas to demonstrate their status and come out of the other side of the battle stronger and able to provide a lead for those around them. Part of this battle of wills is a trial with the formal process of law to ensure that the integrity of justice prevails.

---

40 Greenfield and Osborn, op. cit., n. 18, p. 120.

39

JOURNAL OF LAW AND SOCIETY
VOLUME 28, NUMBER 1, MARCH 2001
ISSN: 0263-323X, pp. 40–6

Cape Fear – Two Versions and Two Visions Separated by Thirty Years

GERALD J. THAIN*

This essay examines the changes between 1962 and 1991 that occurred in the context within which the two very different versions of Cape Fear *appeared. These two versions of the story of a threatened lawyer are emblematic of an altered perspective on law. The essay highlights the tension between art's role as a reflector of society and its values and its role shaping social views. The inference, from the different portrayals of Sam Bowden, that there has been a systematic decline in the lawyer's status and public esteem is not, however, borne out in the cinematic field. The situation has become one of moral ambiguity with the lawyer playing a more ambivalent role in society.*

ATTICUS FINCH AND *CAPE FEAR* I

The fictional Atticus Finch has become the icon of the 'legendary old-fashioned country lawyer' – a person of virtue, rectitude, and decency who represents all that is good about the practice of law, an image in sharp contrast to the frequent depiction of the modern lawyer as one whose sole motive is the acquisition of money and the commodities it can purchase. So common are references to Finch, hero of the Harper Lee novel *To Kill A Mockingbird* as the ideal lawyer that lawyers or law students being recognized for their public interest work are often described as an embodiment of Finch. When a film version of the novel was produced, it was no surprise that Gregory Peck was chosen to play Finch. Peck's strength as an actor has always been his ability to assure the audience that he stands as tall morally as he does physically; efforts by him to portray more complex or even villainous characters have been less satisfactory. His image calls to mind Abraham Lincoln far more readily than Captain Ahab (although he has played both roles).

* *University of Wisconsin Law School, 975 Bascom Mall, Madison, Wisconsin 53706-1399, United States of America*

Peck personified the role of Finch well enough to receive the Academy Award for best performance by an actor 1962, thereby overcoming both the general rule that portrayals of mentally or physically challenged characters are more likely to reap such awards than portrayals of virtuous protagonists and the specific strong competition in that year's Best Actor race (particularly from Peter O'Toole in *Lawrence of Arabia* and Marcello Mastroianni in *Divorce Italian Style*). It was a popular win by an actor well regarded by the public and his peers for playing a character whose very name has come to be a synonym for integrity.

The same year that Peck starred in *To Kill A Mockingbird* – 1962 – another, more generic picture starring Peck was released by the same studio, Universal. This picture was *Cape Fear*, based on a novel by John MacDonald (best known for his Travis McGee mystery series) in which a vengeful ex-con named Max Cady stalked the family of Sam Bowden because Bowden's testimony had been key to Cady's imprisonment. The role of Cady was played by Robert Mitchum, in another of his long line of persuasive performances, as an evil but clever force single-mindedly pursuing revenge.

In this picture (which I refer to as *Cape Fear* I hereinafter) Peck's character has many of the virtues of Atticus Finch, although he is not called upon to take a moral stand that pits him against his community. Sam Bowden appears as a decent, loving family man who performed his civic duty by giving truthful testimony against Cady; because Cady is canny enough to keep his overt actions within the letter of the law, Bowden eventually is forced to fight Cady to protect himself and his family. Of course, Peck's character eventually triumphs physically as well as morally in what may be characterized as a Hairbreadth Harry finale. The family unit is literally saved by the actions of its virtuous patriarch.

CAPE FEAR II

Few are the films, especially successful ones, that are not eventually remade and this fate befell *Cape Fear* in 1991. The passage of almost thirty years between the two versions unsurprisingly led to significant differences between them.[1] Some of these differences were essentially technological; the 1962 version (like *To Kill A Mockingbird*) had been shot in black and white while the remake was in colour. Others were due to directorial influence. The earlier version had been directed by J. Lee Thompson, best known as a competent craftsman, particularly of action films such as *The Guns of Navarone*; the 1991 version was directed by Martin Scorsese, widely regarded as the major American director of the last quarter of the twentieth century, even by those generally hostile to *auteur* theory. The most

1   R.K. Sherwin, *When Law Goes Pop* (2000) 171–81.

41

significant differences, however, were cultural. The differing approaches to telling what is essentially the same story seem to reflect a societal shift in viewing matters concerning the law and lawyers as well as other aspects of American society. In the course of approximately thirty years, the story of *Cape Fear* has become not the earlier version of unadulterated good versus evil pitting a good American family man against a violent and crafty evil-doer but a more complex story. And the 1962 story of vengeance being sought by one who was justly punished for crime becomes, in 1991, a story of retribution being sought by a criminal who was convicted because he was not provided with proper legal representation.

The key change in the two versions is that of Max Cady's reason for pursuing vengeance. In the 1991 version, Sam Bowden is not, as in 1962, the witness who testified against Cady; instead he is the lawyer who defended Cady at the trial. While serving as Cady's public-defender lawyer, Bowden held back evidence that might have changed the outcome of the trial-evidence of the victim's promiscuity. Presumably, this was due to Bowden's moral outrage at the conduct of his client, perhaps even a belief that such evidence should not have been admissible. What would an Atticus Finch have done in such a situation? Would he have followed the rule of law in the case while perhaps challenging it as a rule subsequent to the case? Or would he have resigned as a public defender then or later? Would he have found a capable replacement for himself as the defence counsel? Whatever the answer, it seems certain that neither Atticus Finch nor the 1962 film version of Sam Bowden would have engaged in deliberate withholding of evidence capable of leading to an acquittal of a defendant, no matter how despicable that defendant.

This change in the plot line also causes a change in our perception of Max Cady. The character is played in the 1991 version by Robert De Niro. Here, Cady becomes committed to his campaign of vengeance only after learning, while in prison, that Sam had not represented him to the full. Thus, his motivation makes him, to some degree, a sympathetic character, notwithstanding his sinister and violent conduct. His quest for revenge is something of a quest for 'justice' due to the circumstances of his conviction.

Bowden's character, played by Nick Nolte in the remake, differs from the 1962 version in that his family no longer is a loving and cohesive unit of father, mother, and daughter but that popular item of late-twentieth-century culture, a dysfunctional family. Sam Bowden has a mistress as well as a wife in this version. Cady's reappearance serves to disrupt and further disunite the family until the climax, where, in a houseboat on the waters of Cape Fear during a tremendous storm, the family eventually manages to unite to defeat and kill Cady in resisting his efforts to destroy them. It is not an easy task; Cady's character by the climax of this version is the type of almost superhuman villain resistant to many actions that would kill or incapacitate a physically normal person, a type of villain popular with film makers and audiences at least since the success of *Fatal Attraction* (1987). This contrasts

42

with the character in the 1962 version where Mitchum's portrayal is of a strong and cunning man but one clearly recognizable as having the physical limitations of a human being. By the end of the 1991 version of *Cape Fear*, the Cady character seems closer to the devil incarnate than a devilish villain.

CONTRASTING THE TWO VERSIONS

The two versions of *Cape Fear* surely reflect the changes occurring over three decades of American life and American popular culture. Although a number of changes in the 1991 version were Scorsese's, the key element of changing Sam Bowden from a witness against Cady to a defence counsel who did not present the strongest case for his client was in the script that was first presented to the director, according to Scorsese himself, who stated that he liked this change.[2] The Bowden family as a troubled one instead of the happy unit headed by Peck, in the 1962 version, was instigated by Scorsese. The director embarked on this project for Universal Pictures in return for Universal having backed Scorsese's *The Last Temptation of Christ* (1988) – a film that had been a pet project of Scorsese for many years but clearly one that would not be considered a likely commercial success.[3]

Both versions of *Cape Fear* apparently were satisfactory box-office successes. Indeed, the second version may have been the most financially successful film directed by Martin Scorsese. However, the later version tended to be compared unfavourably with the earlier one by a number of critics. A major complaint was that the role of Max Cady had become unrealistic in the new version. Many found that even an actor of De Niro's skill could not make them believe that the 1991 version of Cady was other than a created character whereas Mitchum's was more realistic. The change in the Max Bowden character was generally noted but this aspect of the later film did not lead to evaluation of it as a nuanced presentation of ethical dilemmas or the like; essentially the melodrama of the film and Scorsese's approach to its visual elements were the major focus. The 'gimmick' of using Peck, Mitchum, and Martin Balsam, actors who had all played roles in the 1962 film, in small parts in the 1991 version, also received some attention.

Now that nearly a decade has passed since the second version was released and both versions have been shown frequently on television (although, as usual the more recent film is more often shown) a view of the two films from the vantage of time seems appropriate. Seeing the two pictures, one finds the critical consensus of the years of release to hold up rather well. The 1962 version is a competent genre thriller, given credibility by the believability of Peck as an old-fashioned hero, a man of decency able

2   A. Dougan, *Martin Scorsese* (1998) 165–9.
3   D. Thompson and I. Chrishe (eds.), *Scorsese on Scorsese* (1996) 185.

43

to rise to the occasion when his beloved family is threatened with no good cause and even more so by Mitchum as a villain with a truly menacing presence. Their counterparts in the 1991 version, Nolte and De Niro, while generally regarded as actors of greater range than Peck and Mitchum, seem less satisfactory. Nolte's character seems more suited to an Ibsen play than to what remains a genre film while the script, if not De Niro himself, make his character's actions too 'over the top' to allow the willing suspension of disbelief necessary to a fully successful motion picture.

However, the limitations of the later film are matters of artistic success, not of failures to recognize a changing social climate. 1962 was a year of the Kennedy administration; indeed, the year of apparent triumph by the United States of America over its enemies in the Cuban missile crisis; certainly, that is how many viewed the situation at that time. In those pre-Watergate, pre-Vietnam war (in so far as the general public was aware), pre-Kennedy assassination, pre-riot days, idealism and optimism were widespread. The ability of an Atticus Finch to win the wars against racism, totalitarian ideologies, and other evils (if not necessarily individual battles such as the trial of Finch's innocent client in 'Mockingbird') was not doubted by most Americans. Indeed, government itself was viewed benignly by most. The travails of thirty years since that time to *Cape Fear* II has led to a public far more suspicious of authority of all kinds. Even if a rapist is sent to jail, it may have occurred only because a lawyer ignored the 'technicalities' of the law. Also, a vengeance-obsessed ex-convict may have a legitimate basis for anger at those within the legal system if not for the measures of revenge that he seeks. The so-called 1950s Ozzie & Harriet nuclear family either does not exist or is seriously impaired as a functional unit. The 1991 version of *Cape Fear* seems consistent with the sceptical movie-going public of its day just as the 1962 version is consistent with the optimism of its time.

In this comparison of the two films, I have asserted that the 1962 version holds up under critical analysis better than the 1991 version. Yet, the later version is, in many ways, a more interesting, if less successful, film in part because it blurs the lines between its 'hero' and its protagonist. It is also more interesting because a Scorsese film that is not a complete success is generally more interesting than a fully realized genre film.

Atticus Finch and his cousins such as the Peck characterization of Sam Bowden still exist, in fact and in fiction, notwithstanding the cynicism that so many today have toward the law. The world around them, however, has changed in ways that make it more difficult to ignore any warts on their portraits.

LAW AND *CAPE FEAR* – THE CHICKEN OR THE EGG?

Much attention has been given to the question of popular art and actual society. Does art simply reflect the society and its values or are the society's views shaped by popular art, especially those, like film and television, that reach a large audience? The correct, if intellectually wimpish, answer is that both occur - popular art is influenced by society as well as reflective of it and society is influenced by popular art. In comparing the two versions of *Cape Fear*, I have noted the way the two versions are representative of the times in which they were produced.

An interesting aspect of the widespread view of hostility towards lawyers is that it is largely directed to lawyers as a class. There is substantial reason to support the view that a high percentage of clients feel that their lawyer is honest, ethical, and trustworthy.[4] Some of the expressed hostility to lawyers surely comes from popular views of lawyers as predators, a view that ironically is not uncommonly presented by lawyers who are seeking, on behalf of their clients, to limit the scope of lawyer activity, such as those advocating for what they call 'tort reform'. Yet, as legal educators are well aware, demand for the legal education that is a prerequisite for practicing law continues to exceed the supply by a considerable margin. A cynic might say that this interest in the profession is because law practice is considered a door to potential riches but there is little doubt that a large number of law students see the profession as a mechanism for assisting people in need, especially those who traditionally are unrepresented or underrepresented before courts and agencies.[5]

The image of Atticus Finch, as noted earlier, is far from dead. However, this image of the lawyer may be more used within legal circles than outside them. The general public is more likely to view, say, Johnny Cochran, as the 'typical' lawyer. It is also likely to assume that the novels of John Grisham and the films made from his novels are realistic portrayals of legal practice rather than entertainments. Indeed, the president of the American Bar Association, in listing his aspirations for the future of the legal profession in an address at the annual meeting of the American Law Institute, listed among them the goal of seeing American lawyers recognized as practicing an honorable profession and noted that he did not expect to see this come to pass 'in his lifetime'.[6] Surely, this denotes the image that lawyers themselves largely believe they have in the public's mind.

Thus, today's popular culture may well depict a lawyer engaged in battling for a worthy cause, but the likelihood is strong that the battle will prove unsuccessful by almost any measure, as in the recent films *A Civil Action* and *The Rainmaker*, whereas Atticus Finch had had some measure of moral victory. It may be noteworthy that, in the most financially successful 'legal battle film' of 2000, *Erin Brockovich*, the heroine is a paralegal, not a lawyer (indeed, a key reason she is able to get vital facts from aggrieved

---

4   M. Galanter, *The Faces of Mistrust: The Image of Lawyers in Public Opinion, Jokes, and Political Discourse* (1998).
5   L. Schachter, 'Making It and Breaking It: The Fate of the Public Interest Commitment During Law School by Robert V. Stover' (1989) 88 *Michigan Law Rev.* 1874.
6   J. Podgers, 'Message Bearers Wanted' (1999) 85 *Am. Bar Association J.* 89.

citizens is because she is not a lawyer). The righteous cause depicted in the film triumphs only because of her persistence against the reluctance of her firm to bring the case. Her foul mouth and habit of wearing very revealing clothing are treated as admirable honesty on her part. Of course, there is a real Erin Brockovich and the film's portrayal of her is considered to be reasonably accurate. None the less, the perspective from which the story is told is different. Ms. Brockovich is not just the catalyst that starts an ultimately winning action against a major corporate power but, in essence, the antagonist of the company, with the lawyers for her cause playing rather minor, if necessary, roles in the struggle. The major lawyer for whom Ms. Brockovich works, depicted in the film by Albert Finney, is presented as a likable, somewhat easygoing individual, but one lacking the passion for justice that drives Erin Brockovich. No Atticus Finch is he!

The standard good versus evil of the genre film traditionally presented either good or bad lawyers. The 1991 version of *Cape Fear* presents a lawyer who is best labeled a protagonist rather than a hero and who is beset by moral ambiguity in both his professional and personal life. It seems significant that this occurs even though the lawyer was a public defender, generally a position considered filled by one of the 'good guys' in American liberal imagination. Perhaps the public defender is overworked, underpaid and without the resources of the opposition, but the position embodies the concept of equal justice under the law. In *Cape Fear* II, even a lawyer in this position is depicted as one whose moral compass is askew. If that is the case, then lawyers in more traditional practices surely are viewed as even less like Atticus Finch. This may be one of the 'lessons about law today that people learn from such sources as film and television'.[7]

7 S. Macaulay, 'Images of Law in Everyday Life: The Lessons of School, Entertainment and Spectator Sports' (1987) 21 *Law and Society Rev.* 185–218.

JOURNAL OF LAW AND SOCIETY
VOLUME 28, NUMBER 1, MARCH 2001
ISSN: 0263-323X, pp. 47–63

Myth and Law in the Films of John Ford

MICHAEL BÖHNKE*

This paper discusses the image of law, how it is created, the relationship of law and authority in its application and its effect on society as portrayed in the films of John Ford, one of America's important film-makers during the first three-quarters of the twentieth century. The focal point of this study is three films exploring the past of the United States of America. Young Mr. Lincoln *(1939), a biographical picture about the early years as a lawyer of the later president, and – as Ford is most typically associated with the making of Westerns –* The Searchers *(1956) and* The Man Who Shot Liberty Valance *(1962), which, as well as being two of his most acclaimed films, are also considered as highly important in the genre. The films are concerned with the establishment of law and the question of legitimacy. The two broad ways of the development of law are the subject of the first two films, presenting an imposing, unquestionable law-giver on the one hand and, on the other, the operation of custom, which shows the organic creation of social rules within a society. The third film confronts the two ways, showing the different assumptions about the inherent qualities of the law. Myth in this context has a dual function: as a reservoir of visual and/or content pattern but also on the narrative level causing calculated semantic effects. As Ford was a director with his distinct vocabulary of visual style and narrative terms, his films demonstrate a specific use of myth-making techniques, its connection with the inscription of certain values into law as well as a critique of this process.*

INTRODUCTION

I would like to explore the issue of how the law-making process is represented in a John Ford film and how law is established and for what purposes. What is the effect of the law on the societies in which it is implemented, what relation exists between society and those who bring the

* *Law Faculty, Ruhr-Universitat Bochum, Gebäude GC 8/135, D-44780 Bochum, Germany*

law? What role does violence play, as a reason to establish law, as a means of enforcing it, and as to its content?

John Ford saw himself primarily as a director of Westerns but as he was an *auteur* and not merely a genre director, he had his own approach to transcending the limitations of the genre with his films. His Westerns, situated in different locales, though mostly filmed in Monument Valley, range in time from the late eighteenth century to the late nineteenth century and cover all major topics important in that type of film. Even if Ford seldom used historical subjects his films can be assigned to certain periods or incidents, forming a kind of chronicle about the settlement of the West. His body of work is as complex as it is contradictory but a development is ascertainable, indicating increasing pessimism and uncertainty and also a revision (in part) of former attitudes.

Law was seldom the explicit topic of his films, but Ford was always interested in describing certain aspects of the functioning of society. For this purpose he often used the rural community to act as a microcosm embodying the tradition and the plain moral values of the pioneering life in nineteenth-century America. So the initial conflict lies between the law as written word (coming usually from the East) and those values and rules established in the community. Further, it represents the conflict between the natural law and codified legislation. It is also the conflict between the two forms of the genesis of law. On the one hand law is seen as imposed upon society by an authority standing high above and issuing downwards its commands; on the other hand, law is regarded as developing within society, being spontaneous and growing upwards, independent of any dominant will.[1] So Ford questions the legitimacy of law (tracing its reliance on religious faith and moral ideas) but also describes its formative effect on societies, bringing progress by transcending tradition.

FORD AND MYTH

John Ford was often called a mythical director and indeed his films were epic, often slow-moving, to the point of meandering, original and simplistic in their narrative, and include elements from ancient myths: the solitary hero torn between fate and determinism, the wise fool, the young man facing initiation, the sacrifice which must be made for the community. He most often deals with societies at an early stage of development, less complex and characterized by custom, service, and tradition. He uses the mythical narrative pattern of the hero's travel to express the shaping of character. His transcendental directing style evokes a spiritual element from the landscape, which is often the seemingly artificial, theatrical natural scenery of Monument Valley. Myth, however, contains not only (narrative) form but also a semantic dimension.

1 C.K. Allen, *Law in the Making*, (1964, 7th edn.) 1–2.

48

Ford uses myth, various techniques of formal or narrative pattern, to form a synthesis out of contradictions, to mediate a specific content. In this way myth, to Ford, is an indirect way of narration, depending on symbols as a common reservoir of previous knowledge. This process can be described using the structural myth theory of Claude Lévi-Strauss, who explained myths '... as a form of narrative mediation of cultural significant antagonisms.'[2] The 'master antinomy between culture and nature'[3] is set in a relational proportion, a process formulated first by Rousseau, who suggested a reintegration of culture in nature.[4] This mediation is performed by the Fordian hero, who is described by Gallagher as '... perceiving that myths (even defective) are necessary to sustain us, [he] seeks to mediate between myth (repressive order) and reality (chaos), in order, by purifying myth, to revitalise society.'[5] Thus, the Fordian hero operates as a 'Trickster', who brings mythical contradictions to light and then, gradually, mediates them.[6]

All of the three films to be dealt with here, are concerned with the 'birth' of a legal order, reflecting the questions of its sources and the way of its growth. In this way Ford uses the semantic figure of the Trickster in the first film, *Young Mr. Lincoln* to draw a picture of an ideal law that includes natural law. This shows the assumptions necessary to secure the power of law in a secular founding act – which is re-staged in a symbolic fashion. In addition there is an infusion of authority in this ideal law's visual representative. It signifies the natural law's endeavour '... to "justify" the means through the justness of the purposes ...',[7] to include the fundamentals and requirements of a developing civic society. In the second film, *The Searchers*, it is used to exemplify the ideal of the self-purifying power of a society marked by custom – abandoning both the authority of a single lawgiver and the presence of a natural law principle. In *The Man Who Shot Liberty Valance*, the two ways of creating and enforcing law clash, and myth is exposed as an element of establishing law that also hides its real sources.

In his Westerns Ford describes a state of society more simple and comprehensible but also subjected to far-reaching changes. His films deal with transitional periods in which individual as well as social relationships are shifting. Ford often describes a form of passage,[8] visualized fittingly with the symbol of the doorstep, distinguishing the old social system from the new. These changes are regarded as necessary for the process of civilization

2 R. Parr, *'Zwei Seelen wohnen, ach! in meiner Brust': Strukturen und Funtionen der Mythisierung Bismarcks (1860–1918)* (1992) 18.
3 C. Lévi-Strauss, *Mythologica Vol. III* (1976) 196
4 C. Lévi-Strauss, *Strukturale Anthropologie Vol. II* (1975) 45–56.
5 T. Gallagher, *John Ford: The Man and His Films* (1986) 479.
6 C. Lévi-Strauss, *Strukturale Anthropologie* (1967) 247.
7 W. Benjamin, *'Zur Kritik der Gewalt'* in *Walter Benjamin Gesammelte Schriften II.1*, eds. R. Tiedemann and H. Schweppenhäuser (1977) 180.
8 Gallagher, op. cit., n. 5, p. 384.

but also lead to personal wounds and losses. Superficially the transformation follows the line from chaos to order.[9] Ford, however, sees the former state just as a form of different order, an order, though clearly described as mythical, which is highly ambiguous. Only the certainty of the former preceding the latter is expressed without any value judgement. Thus Ford shows that no matter on what rational assumptions the positive law is based today, the founding act of law, it is subjected to a kind of mythical cause of (higher) authority – especially in the United States of America as a secular nation, lacking an absolute monarch. The figure worthy enough to impersonate the ideal of the law is, for Ford, Abraham Lincoln, who was described by someone who knew him as 'the greatest character since Christ'.[10]

FORD AND LINCOLN

Abraham Lincoln always stood at the top of Ford's hierarchy.[11] The most extensive depiction of Lincoln by Ford was his 1939 film, *Young Mr. Lincoln*, made during a stage in Ford's career when the view of the American past was still mainly affirmative. The film, however, is not a conventional portrait of Lincoln. It is more a parable in which the figure of Lincoln is used to perform special functions, ascribed to him. Superficially, *Young Mr. Lincoln* can be placed in the tradition of the then popular genre of biographical pictures (biopics) which spread during the second half of the thirties, usually painting idealized portraits of famous historical individuals.[12] From its content alone, however, *Young Mr. Lincoln* distinguishes itself from most other biopics by the fact that it did not depict any historically important incident in Lincoln's life, leaving the political dimension – with two exceptions – almost entirely aside. It is not another writing of a myth constructed around the historical person of Lincoln. Those myths were already in existence and referred to but absent from the film.[13] The central focus of the narrative is, rather, a definition of certain ideal qualities of American law, for which Lincoln is, in Ford's eyes, the best representative.

9 The master antinomy in Ford's films according to T. Gallagher (id., p. 476).
10 J. Richards, *Visions of Yesterday* (1973) 234.
11 Gallagher, op. cit., n. 5, p. 10.
12 An important (but unsuccessful) film about Lincoln had already been made in 1930 by D.W. Griffith. The beginning of the biopic wave in Hollywood can be dated from 1935 when German émigré film-maker William Dieterle made *The Story Of Louis Pasteur* and followed that success later on with portraits of Emile Zola, Benito Juarez, Paul Ehrlich, and Julius Reuter. While other Hollywood directors concentrated more on American personalities the fashion spread to other countries. And all those biopics were designed to feature a clearly recognizable contemporary message.
13 On the other hand it must be admitted that this foreknowledge is why Lincoln is chosen. It is his historical position (at least that in the folk memory) in combination with Ford's personal admiration as well as the authority arising from his tragic death that makes him the ideal protagonist.

The film was criticized for disguising historical facts in favour of 'a rewriting of the historical Lincoln figure on the level of myth'[14] in a famous article of the *Cahiers du Cinéma* first published in August and September 1970. In their structural analysis, the *Cahiers* emphasized that a constitutive narrative gap led to an overdetermination of the plot and a superseding of politics, thus producing the mythological (ideological) effect.[15] On the other hand the *Cahiers* recorded detailed characteristics ascribed to the law through mythical fashion (valued as a 'continuation of every idealistic depiction of the law as statement and procedure of a moralising condemnation of any violence.')[16]

In criticizing both the myth-making processes with regard to a) the quality of law and b) as to the suppression of history, the *Cahiers* not only confuse two different kinds of myths but also negate the specific qualities of Ford's *mise-en-scène*. Therefore two points must be taken into consideration: what function has the Lincoln figure in the narrative of *Young Mr. Lincoln* and what is the function of Lincoln in other Ford films?

The figure of Lincoln is indeed more often used by Ford than any other real-life character. He appeared in seven films made over a period of forty years.[17] With the exception of *Young Mr. Lincoln*, however, Lincoln is not the main character in these films; in fact he enjoys very little screen time and in *Sergeant Rutledge* he is not seen at all, only mentioned via dialogue by one of the black soldiers. The *Cahiers* said about these productions that 'every film refers to a single aspect of the composed personality or the complex historical role of Lincoln, which in this way appear as a universal term of reference applicable on different kinds of situation.'[18] In fact, in every film, Lincoln appears at a crucial point of the story and with a specific function in the narrative. More importantly, on the formal side, a kind of sublimation is evident: in the early films Lincoln was impersonated by an actor, in later ones, like *The Man Who Shot Liberty Valance* and *Cheyenne Autumn*, a portrait is enough to mediate a certain content.[19] Thus Lincoln

---

14 W. Fluck, *Young Mr Lincoln: Der Text der Cahiers du Cinéma und der Film von John Ford* (1978) 11.
15 id., pp. 12–3.
16 id., p. 43.
17 The films were: *The Iron Horse* (1924), *The Prisoner Of Shark Island* (1936), *Young Mr. Lincoln* (1939), *Sergeant Rutledge* (1960), *The Man Who Shot Liberty Valance* (1961), the Civil War episode in *How The West Was Won* (1962), and *Cheyenne Autumn* (1964).
18 Fluck, op. cit., n. 14, p. 11.
19 In *Cheyenne Autumn*, for instance, the US Secretary of the Interior, Carl Schurz (Edward G. Robinson), hesitant of letting the Cheyenne nation go home to Dakota or to relocate them with military force back to the Oklahoma reservation, looks, in a beautifully composed shot, at a Lincoln photograph, his own face mirrored in the glass in front of the picture, asking his dead friend what to do. Naturally Schurz decides against military violence in favour of the humanitarian resolution.

51

becomes more and more an icon, a symbol used by Ford to represent certain abstract terms like idealism, human rights, equality or consciousness.[20]

The *Cahiers* concede the specific function of Lincoln in these films but insist that in *Young Mr. Lincoln*:

> Lincoln himself becomes the protagonist of the fiction and for that reason can't be inscribed as a Fordian figure but for the sake of a certain amount of distortions and mutations (referring to the narrative first and from this to the historical truth).[21]

This distinction, however, seems only plausible if one ignores the use of *dramatis personae* by Ford as mere symbols '... deprived of individuality in favour of embodying the virtues of a society ...'[22] and that those '... tendencies toward stylization match his inclination to treat people as archetypes and quotidian events as sacred ritual'[23] so that often the key figures are not only alienated from their contemporaries but from the narrative itself.

A contemporary film critic noted that:

> If names like Ann Rutledge, Stephen Douglas, Mary Todd and John T. Stuart weren't given to the characters, 'Young Mr. Lincoln' would pass simply for the story of a young lawyer in the frontier days of New Salem and Springfield, Ill. ...

but on the other hand 'discovered' the '... many holes, dramatically and historically.'[24] So, if Ford uses the process of myth-making to connect values with the figure of Lincoln, he also distances the recipient from that figure and stresses aspects that would not let this figure appear 'real'. Instead he constantly isolates it from the rest of the people, falling back on Christian iconography and symbolism, to underline the symbolic content of the ideal.

The accentuation of the signifying quality of the visual signs, an extension of meaning on the level of iconography is stressed a second time through the reduction of the narrative level, which has been described as a 'breakdown of the fabula':[25]

20 The use of the image of Lincoln (as well as the Lincoln image) became a standard in American courtroom films. Not only that Lincoln portraits or sculptures can be found in countless courtrooms or lawyers' offices the presentation ranges from Lincoln on a coin in the opening credits of *To Kill A Mockingbird* (1962), in which Gregory Peck appears as a lawyer with 'Lincolnish qualities', to *A Few Good Men* (1992), in which the Lincoln Memorial can be perceived in the background just at that moment when the careless lawyer (Tom Cruise) decides to fight for justice.

21 Fluck, op. cit., n. 14, p. 11.

22 J. Baxter, *John Ford* (1971) 19.

23 Gallagher, op. cit., n. 5, p. 478; note also the quote of Jean Marie Straub calling Ford the most 'Brechtian' of all film-makers, on pp. 477 and 494–5.

24 V. Wright, *Lincoln in Fancy* in Fluck, op. cit., n. 14, p. 183.

25 H. Bitomsky and M. Müller, '*Gelbe Streifen Strenges Blau: Passage durch die Filme von John Ford*' (Part one, 1978) 258 *Filmkritik* 283, at 287.

52

The gaps, the incompleteness, the paradigmatic insertions injure the fabula in a way that it can't function as one anymore. That means it fails as a metaphorical simile for something outside of itself.[26]

From this dialectic Ford derives an allegorizing effect: '... the incarnation of the Law and of America.'[27] So the Lincoln figure in *Young Mr. Lincoln* is not so much a glorification of a historical figure but a humanization of a symbol and its repositioning on a historical person. In other words, it is not merely Lincoln who becomes mythical but the law itself. This narrative process of abstraction, is effected by a form of visual presentation that often leaves the Lincoln figure in the centre of the frame, or in a generally domineering position, but primarily alone, unable to establish contact to those around him. In this way *Young Mr. Lincoln* marks a kind of starting point in Ford's examination of law, its development, use, and social functioning.

YOUNG MR. LINCOLN

The first part of the film describes the founding myth: after Lincoln (Henry Fonda) received, amongst other books, *Blackstone's Commentaries* in exchange for some goods from a pioneer family, the scenery switches immediately to a medium-close shot of Lincoln reading the commentary, humbly remarking 'Law!'; he repeats this exclamation accompanied by dissolve which shows him lying in the forest, his long legs leaning against a tree stump in a surrounding of a peaceful landscape. In this rather peculiar position he is discovered by Ann Rutledge. Next the two are wandering under old oaks alongside the river and Ann is trying to persuade Lincoln to finish his education in Jacksonville college. Suddenly Lincoln throws a stone into the river and [dissolve] the sun-drenched water transforms into a grim one with ice floating on it. Lincoln, alone now on the same way as before, reaches a little graveyard with a tombstone bearing the name of Ann Rutledge. While he is putting the first spring flowers on the grave he speaks with Ann about his future. He grabs a bough declaring if it falls to her direction he will go to study law, if not, he will stay in the village. The bough falls on Ann's side but after a moment of silence he concedes that he may have directed it to her direction.

This sequence shows the emergence of American law. First Lincoln is gifted the law book from the illiterate pioneer family, glad to see the book in good condition ('the law is indestructible'[28]). Thus Ford demonstrates the '[...] handing over by the people of the custody of the Law to their chosen Leader',[29] the establishing of a form of representation that is not dependent

26 id.
27 Richards, op. cit., n. 10, p. 275.
28 Fluck, op. cit., n. 14, p. 20.
29 Richards, op. cit., n. 10, p. 278.

on a federal government. It places the natural law as its basis, presenting nature as the fountain of ideal order. To Ford it is nature and, therefore, the natural law which reveals the divine rules and the Lincoln figure encapsulates the contradiction between secular law and divine power. '... Law and innate intuitive knowledge are one with nature ...'.[30] The reference to history, however, and the future role Lincoln would have to play, break into the abstract idealism of this parable, giving the whole narrative a new direction and infusing it with a mythical quality of the law that supersedes legitimacy through authority.

The supposed historical role of Lincoln as the mediator between the natural law of the Declaration of Independence and the Constitution, which added the previously unmentioned protection of right of property to the rights of the individual,[31] is already suggested here, when he reads – in the above-mentioned scene – in *Blackstone's Commentaries*:

> The law is the right of a person to life, reputation and liberty, the right to acquire and hold property. Wrongs are violations of these rights.

In this way he subsumes the right of ownership under the basic principles of the natural law. The subordination of this law under the authority of natural/ divine rules constructs a fiction of justice, which dissolves the tension between justice and its '... execution in the form of law, legitimacy or legality ...'.[32] The law establishing and justifying authority, as a mythical authority,[33] avoids the question of the inherent violence of the law in form of a natural law, which assumes the justness of all natural causes.[34] In this respect it disguises '... power as the principle of all mythical establishment of law.'[35]

Secondly the reference to the right to hold property, in conjunction with the election speech at the beginning of the film, has a mediating effect on economic and political topics. The election speech, containing protectionism of customs duty and the national bank (the programme of the Whig Party in opposition), which 'is exactly the programme of the developing American capitalism ...'[36] is contrasted with the Lincoln figure as an incarnation of 'populist'[37] values standing for a Jeffersonian ideal of an agrarian individualism and against centralism and 'big business'.[38] This contradiction is solved by an avoidance of any further recourse by the Lincoln figure to politics, rather, establishing a moral order superior to all politics through the

---

30 Gallagher, op. cit., n. 5, p. 167.
31 D. Gerhard, *Abraham Lincoln und die Sklavenbefreiung* (1965) 7.
32 J. Derrida, *Gesetzeskraft: Der 'mystische Grund der Autorität'* (1991) 44.
33 Benjamin, op. cit., no. 7, p. 199.
34 id., p. 180.
35 id., p. 198.
36 Fluck, op. cit., n. 14, p. 15.
37 See, for ideology of populism, Richards, op. cit., n. 10, pp. 222–33.
38 Fluck, op. cit., n. 14, pp. 83–4; see, also, Richards, id., p. 231.

'... intimate relationship to law and a (natural and/or divine) knowledge about good and evil ...'.[39] Lincoln thus embodies moral purity unaffected by political decisions or interests. In this way the *Cahiers* are right to assert that '... the whole film is a superseding of politics through morality.'[40] This is an element common in many a Ford film along with the moral integrity and even purity of the usual Fordian hero. This fact is important in that way, as all qualities of law later on must be seen against the background of this moral ideal.

After Lincoln received the law from the pioneer mother, a series of oppositions is introduced into the narrative: country versus city, high society versus lower class, education versus simple-mindedness, chaos versus order. In every case Lincoln (= the law) works as a mediator and – in the last case – as an authority, illuminated with a sparkle of almost divine determinism and faith. The Christ parallel is stressed with Lincoln's arrival in Springfield, riding on a mule and by his quoting of the Sermon on the Mount to tame a lynch mob.[41] So the primary social function of law is here to unify society thus following the natural rights approach which makes its origin not a case of particular interests but of all relevant power. The function is furthermore to establish the authority of the law in society. This is performed by the Lincoln figure in the second part, to a degree, and, fully, in the third part of the film.

After Lincoln reached Springfield he had to handle his first case of two feuding neighbours, arguing about debts and compensation. Since one of them did not pay the sum due he got a beating from the other. That is why he demands compensation of the same amount as the debt. Lincoln declares the claims as nearly the same leaving a small difference, which he demands as his pay, threatening his sceptical clients with physical violence ('Did you fellas ever hear 'bout the time I butted two heads together?'[42]). In appearing as a crafty, mischievous mediator ending the conflict, a real Solomon, he expresses the ideal order of law in finding a fair balance, a judicial insight that comes to him quite naturally.

In this way Ford stresses the connection between law and force (power) and the different, albeit conjunctive, quality of its introduction and its practice. He shows:

> that law is always a power which one has granted, which is authorised, which is approved and justified, a power, which is through its use justified or justified through its use ...[43]

This dual function of the law, being accepted because of its origin from a higher authority and as an instrument of social organization containing an

39 Fluck, id., pp. 15–6.
40 id., p. 21.
41 Richards, op. cit., n. 10, p. 278.
42 A.J. Place, *The Non-Western Films of John Ford* (1979) 53.
43 Derrida, op. cit., n. 32, p. 12.

55

authority of organized force is also shown in the third part of the film while the progress of the second part laid emphasis on the unifying function of the Lincoln figure. It places him in Fourth-of-July celebrations of the plain folk and later in a ball in the elegant house of his future wife, Mary Todd, thus proving that he is a man of the people but also one who can cope with the protocol of high society.

The third part, at least, contains a great courtroom scene with Lincoln defending two brothers accused of murder. The killing took place in the evening of the Fourth of July and two young men are arrested for the deed. They turn out to be the two sons of the pioneer family, the Clays, who happened to hand the law book to him a long time ago (the sons were only little boys then). An attempt at lynching the two young men by the townspeople is prevented by Lincoln, again demonstrating the influence of law on social and on individual behaviour, as well as the power lying in its enforcement. The trial starts with nearly all, except Lincoln (the law), against the Clay family. This trial sequence again shows Lincoln acting with incontestable authority and as the great unifier. The authority is also expressed on the formal level, placing Lincoln in the center of the frame or letting him stand or move in a way that he is dominating the scenery. The unifying quality is emphasized in the course of the trial with his refusal of a questionable plea bargaining to save one brother but having the other sentenced to death. 'Because Lincoln is Right he can accept no compromise ...'.[44] He furthermore demonstrates 'in the selection of the jury ... that only the quality of the people can bring justice'.[45]

Principally, however, this sequence clearly shows the kind of quality law must have to be enforced and expressed like this. Lincoln, shown so far as, despite his profession, not being dependent upon logical, rational, knowable precepts,[46] defines his standpoint against that of the pedantic prosecutor with the sentence 'I may not know much about the law. But I know what's right and what's wrong.' So again Ford takes up the theme of the force inherent in the law. He shows that:

> there is no applicability or enforceability of law without force, no matter if it is immediate or not, if it is physical or symbolic, outer or inner, compelling or regulative force, if it's brutal or in a subtle way discursive and hermeneutical and so on.[47]

He also presupposes that the force of the law is only right (and adequate) in the service of justice. He finds this justice in the rigorous moral idealism of the natural law. So if the conflict in the courtroom scene is that of the rational legal authority of the positive law versus the enforcement of the natural law, Ford is opting for the latter, because 'the reference to the means

44 Richards, op. cit., n. 10, p. 275.
45 A. Sinclair, *John Ford* (1979) 91–2.
46 Place, op. cit., n. 36, p. 54.
47 Derrida, op. cit., n. 32, p. 12.

56

of force, seems not to be questioned by the advocates of natural law, because they are justified through the natural purposes.'[48]

Ford surrenders in a glorious victory the natural-law principle: Lincoln wins the case, frees the two brothers from the charge, convicting the real murderer in the witness stand and winning public acclaim of the people, acceptance in high society, and the thanks of the family, whom he has saved. In the true apotheosis of the last few shots he locates his subject, Lincoln, in history, ending with the final frame of the Lincoln Memorial.

The finale again emphasizes that *Young Mr. Lincoln* shows Ford at his most supportive of myth. Criticizing the positive law not through the social circumstances from which it is derived, not by exposing their '... structures, which conceal but also reflect the economic and political interests of the ruling social forces' but by pitting an ideal against it that he himself must have seen as impracticable, belonging to a bygone age, may not be a clear '... denunciation of the ideology of the narrative (at least at this point in his career) ...'.[49] That he lets this ideal of the past win, that he himself sees as passed,[50] may justify an accusation of being unhistorical (and may have inspired the critique of the *Cahiers*). In the year 1939, however, when *Young Mr. Lincoln* was made, the past had become a variable good, and numerous 'historical' films were made to serve other ideologies than that of Ford's moral idealism. So, all in all, Ford raises questions about the origins of law, of authority and enforcement, but only later on would he find the distance to regard former ideals critically.

THE SEARCHERS

The film *The Searchers* is certainly not a film about law in the sense of courtrooms, trials, lawyers, prosecutors, and judges. It is a Western situated in a remote, god-forsaken part of Texas (albeit filmed in Monument Valley) after the Civil War. Surrounded by wasteland, single families live on small farms distant from one another. The landscape is bleached, living is hard, and thinking is simple. If Ford was directing his films to be a kind of recreation of ancient myths, *The Searchers* is the closest he comes in realising this intention.

In all this, the film seems the complete opposite of the themes shown in *Young Mr. Lincoln*, no bucolic countryside where people living in ideal commitment along with nature, no evocation of a pantheistic spirit to base a

---

48 id., p. 71.
49 Place, op. cit., n. 42, p. 58.
50 That Ford didn't use the evocation of past times to construct a continuity where there is none, but treats it as bygone and irrecoverable, is expressed in the grave scenes, which are a recurring element in his films, notably in *Young Mr. Lincoln*, *My Darling Clementine* (1946), and *She Wore A Yellow Ribbon* (1949). See, also, Richards, op. cit., n. 10, p. 270.

natural law theory on, and no blessed lawgiver, with the right to unquestioned authority. With the very beginning (showing the lonely silhouette of Ethan Edwards riding to the homestead of his brother), Ford demonstrates that even if such a lawgiver had existed his communication would not have reached this place.

> [The] ... settlers were more or less left to their own devices. The societal and juridical procedures give evidence for that (election of judges, sheriffs, the joint pursuit of crimes, as posse, lynch-law, vigilante committees etc.[51]

So *The Searchers* is, speaking about law in John Ford's films, essentially a film about custom. Again this abstract content is visualized by the central figure, in this case Ethan Edwards (John Wayne). It differs from *Young Mr. Lincoln*, however. Ethan is not law's embodiment but a catalyst provoking actions and thus making the unseen social assumptions of the small white community around him visible. Since many Ford films describe periods of transition, his protagonists operate in situations between subsistence and change.[52] The film presents a society which has not differentiated its institutions. A kind of head is Samuel Clayton (Ward Bond), who is the minister but also the captain of the vigilante force. The life is uniform, marked by the ritual and carried out between baptizing, marrying, and burying. With the appearance of Ethan, existing order begins to waver. He disturbs a funeral service as well as wedding preparations, constantly questioning the authority of Clayton, asking about what function he is performing in certain situations.

So Ethan is the figure of the essential loner, and in this way recurrent in his purpose as well as in his character in numerous Ford films. The loner has to fulfil a societal task, but he is not adapted for this. He '... has to pay with a loneliness that paradoxically closes a gap in society.'[53] With the loner figure, Ford describes the relation between liberty and order as an antinomy between the individual and the community in a time, where the balance between individual rights and social responsibilities on which communities depend, has not been established.

The Odyssey of Ethan and Martin, however, leads to an individuation process, which, as a kind of initiation, promotes young Martin to an equal member of society. It is also an encounter with cultural extremes, with different systems of organization and order. Now Ford describes those self-regulatory societies, depending on customary rules and sanctions, again in symbolic fashion – in a formal pattern, which has become one of the most prominent in the cinema of John Ford: the 'doorway-shot'.[54] It serves as a

---

51 H. Bitomsky, '*Gelbe Streifen Strenges Blau: Passage durch die Filme von John Ford*' (part three, 1980) 284 *Filmkritik* 341, at p. 375.
52 Gallagher, op. cit., n. 5, p. 245.
53 H. Bitomsky, '*Gelbe Streifen Strenges Blau: Passage durch die Filme von John Ford*' (part two, 1979) 267 *Filmkritik* 95, at p. 106.
54 Doorways play an important part also in *The Man Who Shot Liberty Valance*, *The Last Hurrah*, and *The Sun Shines Bright*, all films dealing with political and/or

frame of this film, being his very first and very last shot, and is constantly used throughout the plot. The first shot begins with a black screen and then a door, covering a small space in the middle, is opened, light streams in, and a woman steps out of the darkness onto a sunlit porch.

The beginning, which became famous, is a kind of reverse establishing shot, because instead of introducing the landscape with a long shot and a pan, it introduces with its darkness/light symbolism the main theme in a Manichean fashion. It establishes the master antinomy of this film between inside and outside, setting in motion pairs of contradictory elements beginning with that of nature versus culture, continuing with individual versus group, blood relationship versus social relationship, white versus native American culture, authority versus freedom, civilization versus violence and so on. More so, together with similar shots of doorsteps, openings in Indian tepees, or cave mouths, the camera always placed behind the openings underlining the surroundings, it creates an effect of framing which is a simple but fitting symbol of cultural alliance and the inherent regulations of specific societies.[55] With the diversity of these shots, Ford states that each culture is marked but also restricted by values, and again makes a step towards natural law, by applying this symbol to nature. As nature, however, is 'hard' this time (somebody is always muttering about 'bad land' or blaming '*this* country') its 'law' serves as the basis of Ethan's racism. In this way Ethan is depicted as acting irrationally, fit for survival in nature but not really belonging to civilization. Through Ethan, the film '... persistently questions seemingly linear cause and effect patterns ...'.[56] Ethan's behaviour, however, also reveals the irrational assumptions of the others and by (unjustly) doing so, he initiates the self-regulatory process of society.

This process is represented first by Martin. He is portrayed as half-illiterate, vested with a general consciousness of right and wrong,[57] that let him stay with Ethan in a redeeming function. Secondly it is represented by, primarily two, women out of their neighbourhood, Mrs. Jorgensen and her daughter Laurie. As in *Young Mr. Lincoln*, where the mother hands the law book over to Lincoln, establishing the equivalent of mother – law – nature,[58] the women in *The Searchers* appear as the taming and civilizing factor and

juridical topics. At the end of *Young Mr. Lincoln*, after Lincoln has won the case, one can see him stepping alone through the door of the courthouse, whose surrounding blank wall covers the whole frame. One can hear cheering of the people but Ford did not cut to the crowd, but remains on this shot and then fades out. See, for 'doorways' also, W. Luhr and P. Lehman, *Authorship and Narrative in the Cinema* (1977) 154–7.

55 It could also indicate the transitory view on myth and law when related to the Platonic cave simile (see Platon: *The State*, Seventh Book, 514a–518e), Plato's sceptical view on myth (see, for instance, L. Coupe, *Myth* (1997) 104–5), and his tracing back of the nature of justice to reason (see N. Bowie and R. Simon, *The Individual and the Natural Order* (1977) 58).

56 Luhr and Lehman, op. cit., n. 54, p. 86.

57 Allen, op. cit., n. 1, p. 88.

58 Fluck, op. cit., n. 14, p. 22.

59

also show persistence in their attitude towards the land, which their men otherwise would have left. The women are also marked with signs of formal education, Mrs. Jorgensen being a former schoolmarm, while her husband, albeit wearing glasses, when a letter arrives cannot read it himself and has his daughter Laurie read the letter out loud. Laurie will marry Martin, and thus the couple, again on the symbolic level, represent the balancing out of the former contradictions, demonstrating that Ford at this point of his career is still optimistic that the next generation will do better than the former. The integration is completed by leading Debbie back into the bosom of the family. As her own family was destroyed, however, she is to live with the Jorgensens. So the re-establishment of the family unity, again using the doorway symbol, is the last evidence of the self-regulating process of society and also of the rejection of Ethan, who with his racist view caused the former disturbance. In the end the family is unified, but it cannot be the restoration of the former one, matched by blood relationship (the only relationship Ethan accepts, once stating that he has no relatives anymore, as when he is presuming that his niece may have slept with a native American). A new one, however, will come into being, through marriage and adoption, customary acts to which Ethan will not adapt, riding away, again a loner.

As in numerous post-war films Ford expresses in *The Searchers* a sense of cultural dislocation, either depicted as a clash of different cultures or a rapid change within a single culture[59] (the latter describes the conditions in *The Man Who Shot Liberty Valance*) showing the polarized cultures of the whites and the native Americans. In this film Ford also reveals the racism and assumptions of cultural superiority which were usually suppressed or unquestioned in other Westerns, even in Ford's former work. He shows that custom which defines itself in dissociation from other cultures is eager to place itself above the other. This latent pattern is brought out by the openly racist Ethan, and the real conflict in this film is whether the society is affected by it or whether it is able to overcome it. So Ford, again exposing himself as a moralist, shows, that even if custom is of lesser importance today for the creation of positive law, there may be some kind of enduring custom which must be rooted out of society.

THE MAN WHO SHOT LIBERTY VALANCE

The film, *The Man Who Shot Liberty Valance*, was often described as an old man's work, even as a 'testament',[60] and indeed it marks not even a doorpost to the last stage of Ford's directoral career (he made only three more feature films, plus some minor work), but gave the Western genre, along with Sam Peckinpah's *Ride The High Country* (1961), a last new turn, beginning the

---

59 Luhr and Lehman, op. cit., n. 54, p. 149.
60 J. Hembus, *Das Western-Lexikon* (1995, 3rd edn.) 411–13.

60

final period of the classical age of this genre. It is more, however, than a summation of former themes and concerns. It is not the great sentimental reminiscence, which some critics expected, panning and patronizing the film upon initial release.[61] It is a further development of Ford's vision of the Old West, depicted as a way of life, that stopped existing a long time ago.

In a way, the two main characters of the former films are now brought together. The Ethan figure at the end of *The Searchers*, having confronted his racist attitude, is still not capable of adapting to the changing reality of society. He seems to be like a forerunner of Tom Doniphon (also played by John Wayne), while the lawyer and later senator Ransom Stoddard (James Stewart in place of Henry Fonda) is a kind of secular (and rational) Lincoln. It is easy to see the conflict arising from the meeting of those opposing characters, who represent different sides of the development of custom and law, in their relationship to society. With the introduction of a third figure, however, named Liberty Valance[62] (Lee Marvin), the two otherwise natural antagonists become partners for a while, with Doniphon constantly protecting Stoddard (= the law). Liberty Valance, representing the allegorical principle in this film, is '[. . .] rather unique in Ford: a singular example of an absolute one-dimensional character: pure unadulterated violence and chaos without hint of redeeming feature.'[63] Certainly this figure is a new element, which adds to the change of key Ford expresses in this film, making it more sombre and claustrophobic than any other Western he made before.

The change of tone is obvious; instead of idealism now resignation reigns. The all-justifying idealism of the higher order in *Young Mr. Lincoln* is gone, as is the idea of a self-regulating society, that would deal with wrongdoing. Not that there is no development in the film. The establishment of literacy and law take place. They are, however, outshone by the technical progress and a more advanced form of organization. In general, a new calculus is set producing new winners and losers by replacing a '. . . rough equality of all men in a state of nature [through] . . . social stratification based on unequal distribution of property.'[64] With this film Ford also comes to the conclusion that the ideal of natural law is not adequate for dealing with the increasing differentiation of modern society. He also shows that customary law, as a popular evolutionary law, does not come to terms with the legal interpreters acting only as the representatives of the people and deriving the law from the characteristic customs of the community alone.[65] Instead, law is interpreted and applied by specialists, dealing with the abstract contents of another, the juridical discourse.[66] Ford shows these different spheres, being situated in

61 L. Maltin (ed.), *Movie and Video Guide 1993 Edition* (1992) 774.
62 For the meaning of this and other 'speaking names' in the film, see Gallagher, op. cit., n. 5, pp. 392–3.
63 id., p. 396.
64 H. Nash-Smith, *Virgin Land: The American West as Symbol and Myth* (1970) 62.
65 Allen, op. cit., n. 1, pp. 112–3.
66 id., pp. 114–5.

different spaces; rational legal authority, personified in Ransome Stoddard, is a product of the East. Stoddard, being completely different from the townspeople in the West in culture, manner, thinking, would not adapt to this society as would the old Westerner Doniphon to these upcoming 'modern' times. The difference is that Stoddard has actually the power to change society by establishing education and law. He only could do so with the help of the locals, having the wish to live in better circumstances. Stoddard and the people, however, do not share the same assumptions about the law. This time Ford shows that the law is not an ideal untouched by the convenience of the ruling class but serving the interests of particular groups. This is demonstrated with the second political meeting, which has nothing to do with the people of Shinbone, but comprises a lot of phoney rhetoric and political fuss. It is this meeting, however, where Stoddard begins his real political career, which will make him a Senator on the legend that he is the man who shot Liberty Valance.

So the final irony is that both men are 'the man who shot Liberty Valance', Tom, who really did it, and Ranse, whom everyone regards as the one who did it. This demonstrates that '... in the public realm, figures and events that possess a defining importance can be infused with fabrication.'[67] It also shows that that fabrication consists of a mediation of contradictions. Again these contradictions are embodied in one character, that of Ransom Stoddard, but this 'embodiment' is a fraud. To establish law in Shinbone, Ranse did not only have to teach the 'abc' but he also had to be recognized as one of the people. As the man who shot Liberty Valance, he is able to 'perform' the dual task, being the well educated lawyer from the East, but also the true Westerner, by killing the ruthless outlaw in a shootout. By showing the real circumstances, lying behind this enforcement of the law Ford reveals the connection of violence and misrecognition.[68] The system which has not grown out of society but is imposed on it, is an order of its own, requiring new 'doorways' to enter it. In '... establishing a certain authority for that law, however, Ranse has at the same time undermined its legitimacy.'[69]

CONCLUSION

In the symmetrical way Ford often directed his films, he returns to the starting point with *The Man Who Shot Liberty Valance*, again questioning the way law is established and enforced. Again it is the value inherent in the law, and the authority necessary to gain its acceptance that is the main topic

67 C. Ryan, 'Print the Legend: Violence and Recognition in The Man Who Shot Liberty Valance' in *Legal Reelism*, ed. J. Denvir (1996) 23.
68 id.
69 id., p. 26.

of his examination. What, however, formerly belonged to the sphere of ideal commitment to justify its creation and application is now the result of convenience and the interests of particular groups. That this results in a changing attitude to myth as a quality of Ford's direction is fairly obvious. Myth was something of a reality in *Young Mr. Lincoln*, hence the film is not realist, being a kind of parable about the ideal of law. If, however, natural law is no longer applicable, due to the development and differentiation of society it is replaced by a rational legal system (raising the question of cause and effect). Ford expounds the mythical element of law, which seems to be the element of mediation, but he concedes, that in a rational legal system the myth is referring to former values which have ceased to exist.

JOURNAL OF LAW AND SOCIETY
VOLUME 28, NUMBER 1, MARCH 2001
ISSN: 0263-323X, pp. 64–78

The German Courtroom Film During the Nazi Period: Ideology, Aesthetics, Historical Context

PETER DREXLER*

This essay examines the films of the Nazi period concerned with questions of justice and the administration of the law. It traces the ways in which law films developed prior to the Nazi era. It notes the apparent paradox of the Nazi obsession with questions of justice, law, and legality which are found in their strictly controlled film output. The use of film as a mass propaganda weapon affected legal subjects and this can be seen as a means of creating consensus. This centred on the role of the state in creating a system which allowed the individual to be integrated into the mythical folk community. Those who threatened this social cohesion were depicted as threats to the common sense of ordinary people and this stretched from propaganda films into comedies.

INTRODUCTION

The Nazi period offers a rich field for a study of the representation of law in film. Between 1933 and 1945 about 1,100 feature films were released, and a substantial number of these are more or less explicitly concerned with questions of justice and the administration of the law. But this is a problematic which has attracted little critical interest from both law and film historians.

I was first confronted with this issue a few years ago, while collecting material for a paper on German *Gerichtsfilm* (courtroom film) 1930–1960 that had been commissioned for a conference.[1] I was surprised to find that there existed no critical study on the subject. More irritatingly, the German

---

* *Department of English and American Studies, University of Potsdam, Karl-Liebknecht-Strasse 24-5, D-14476 Golm, Germany*

1 P. Drexler, '*Der deutsche Gerichtsfilm 1930–1960. Annäherungen an eine problematische Tradition*' ('German courtroom film 1930–1960: an approach to a problematic tradition') in *Verbrechen – Justiz – Medien. Konstellationen in Deutschland von 1900 bis zur Gegenwart* (*Crime – justice – media. Constellations in Germany from 1900 to the present*), eds J. Linder and C.M. Orth (1999).

word *Gerichtsfilm*, as it occasionally cropped up in manuals and film histories, appeared to be an extremely elusive and fuzzy term, with no precise definition and with no clear demarcation from related terms such as *Kriminalfilm, Detektivfilm* or *Gerichtsmilieufilm* (films with a legal setting), and often subsumed under other categories such as *Propagandafilm, Problemfilm*, or *Tendenzfilm*; in short: nothing to pin it down as an identifiable genre with a history and a canon of established texts. The reasons for this critical neglect and terminological confusion, as I found out, are quite complex.

Everyday use of the word *Gerichtsfilm* seems to raise no serious problems. When you confront colleagues or students with the term, they will tell you that this is a type of film which is mainly set in a courtroom and predominantly concerned with legal procedure. They invariably come up with titles of American feature films such as *Witness for the Prosecution, Twelve Angry Men*, or *Judgment at Nuremberg* or of popular American and German TV courtroom series, the latter often oriented towards American models.[2]

Much of this attraction derives from elements of American legal procedure that have become staple features of the American courtroom film: spirited exchanges between the prosecution and the defence, aggressive cross-examination of witnesses, trial by jury, the role of the judge as a kind of referee in a match between contending parties, the examination of evidence in the courtroom, and other 'dramatic' elements which have ensured the lasting popularity of this film genre.

The 'undramatic' character of German legal procedure, which is inquisitorial rather than adversarial and therefore cinematically less attractive, may account for the low generic profile of German courtroom film from its beginnings in the 1920s. Even films which can serve as key examples to establish a German tradition of this genre, such as Richard Oswald's *Dreyfus* (1930), Wolfgang Liebeneiner's *Ich klage an* (*I Accuse*, 1941), Erich Engel's *Die Affäre Blum* (*The Blum Affair*, 1948), Wolfgang Staudte's *Rosen für den Staatsanwalt* (*Roses for the Prosecutor*, 1959) and *Der letzte Zeuge* (*The Last Witness*, 1960), Hark Bohm's *Der Fall Bachmeier – Keine Zeit für Tränen* (*The Bachmeier Case – No Time for Tears*, 1984), Roland Suso Richter's *Nichts als die Wahrheit* (*After the Truth*, 1999), cannot be termed courtrooom films in the American sense because in many of these films the courtroom is not the main locus of action and conflict, but usually provides the setting for one or several climactic scenes in a narrative which is otherwise concerned with various aspects of

2 This is a point which has recently been made by S. Machura and S. Ulbrich, who argue that German cinema and television audiences in their viewing habits as well as in their everyday perception and knowledge of the law and of courtroom procedure are deeply influenced by U.S. productions: '*Recht im Film: Abbild juristischer Wirklichkeit oder filmische Selbstreferenz?*' ('Law in film: realistic representation of the law or filmic self-reference?') (1999) 20 *Zeitschrift für Rechtssoziologie* 168.

65

legal procedure and criminal investigation. 'Legal film', then, would seem to be a more appropriate term for this German variant of courtroom film, but I shall stick to the latter term because it has become common usage.[3]

THE EMERGING PARADIGM OF GERMAN COURTROOM FILM: THE LESSONS OF THE WEIMAR PERIOD

To understand the ideology and the aesthetics of the courtroom film during the Nazi period, and further, to understand the obsession with questions of justice, law, and legality which permeates Nazi film as a whole, we must examine its historical antecedents: film culture and film politics of the late 1920s and the early 1930s. Weimar film, in particular during the years immediately preceding the Nazi takeover, reflects the social conflicts and political upheavals of the time in a wide spectrum of *Tendenzfilme* that seek to solicit support for a variety of causes. In many of these films the law figures as a symptom or as a symbolic representation of a corrupt state of society. This is most obvious in films with a communist background such as Fjodor Ozep's *Der lebende Leichnam* (*The Living Corpse*, 1929), Slatan Dudow's *Kuhle Wampe* (1932), Hans Tintner's *Cyankali* (1930), or Piel Jutzi's *Mutter Krausens Fahrt ins Glück* (*Mother Krause's Trip to Happiness*, 1929), which contain dramatic courtroom scenes, in which the law is represented as an instrument of class justice and social oppression.

Some of the most famous films of the late Weimar period, Fritz Lang's *M* (1931), Richard Oswald's *Dreyfus* (1930), and Hans Behrendt's *Danton* (1931), offer interesting examples of a close interrelation of political and legal discourses, which can be read as ominous signs of the times, that is, approaching fascism. All of these films evoked highly controversial responses because of the issues they addressed and the cinematic means they employed, and this becomes particularly evident in their highly effective use of courtroom scenes.

Oswald's film reconstructs the famous case of the Jewish captain Alfred Dreyfus who was sentenced to lifelong deportation for high treason in 1894 and acquitted eleven years later, after a bitter political and legal struggle that deeply divided France. Reviving this notorious case of a political miscarriage of justice in the politically charged climate of the early 1930s was clearly a signal, a plea for the republic, against militarism,

---

3 Another reason for the obscurity and critical neglect of German courtroom film is that German film historians, unlike their British and American colleagues, shun the category of genre, which they associate with the standardizing tendencies of Hollywood film. See, for example, J. Schweinitz, '"Genre" und lebendiges Genre-bewußtsein. Geschichte eines Begriffs und Probleme seiner Konzeptualisierung in der Filmwissenschaft' ('"Genre" and concrete awareness of genre. On the history of a term and its conceptualisation in film studies') (1994) 3 *montage/av. Zeitschrift für Theorie & Geschichte audiovisueller Kommunikation* 99.

66

totalitarianism, and anti-Semitism, and the parallels to the then current political situation were unmistakable.[4] Oswald conceived the film as a theatrically 'staged' historical document, designed to bring the past back to life and call it to account before the 'judgment seat of the present',[5] arranged in a series of miniature scenes and large historical tableaux. The latter are remarkable especially for their extended courtroom scenes, which carry the political message of the film. The most impressive and pathetic of these is the trial against Émile Zola, after his famous 'J'accuse' article in the journal *L'Aurore*. The French novelist is played by Heinrich George, a prominent actor with communist sympathies, who later played equally prominent roles in films of the Nazi period (including courtroom films!). He has the most memorable appearance when he defends himself against the accusation of libel and turns the courtroom into a tribunal of a higher justice which will one day prove him right: 'Condemn me, gentlemen. One day, the Republic will thank me for defending its honour.'

In a similar fashion *Danton* expresses a political message for the present in the confrontation of two conflicting attitudes toward the revolution: that of Danton and his adversary, Robespierre, (that is, humane, democratic versus totalitarian, terrorist) in a series of theatrical tableaux, from the storming of the Bastille to Danton's execution, and again, the political message is effectively expressed in two long courtroom scenes (the trial of Louis XVI and that of Danton).

In comparison with these historical films Fritz Lang's *M* contains a far less direct and tangible reference to contemporary issues, even though in the film's conception Lang had been inspired by famous contemporary murder cases (Haarmann, Kürten) and despite the 'humane' concern for the sex offender in the famous underworld tribunal scene by his 'defence' who argues for his diminished responsibility (s. 51 of the German penal code) and ensures that he is tried before a regular court. What is remarkable about *M* is the ambivalence of its legal, and implictly political discourse. In its sympathies the film oscillates throughout between the forces of order and those of anarchy. The most obvious instance is the hunting down of the murderer by the combined efforts of the police and the criminals. The use of parallel editing gives this sequence an air of complicity. This ambiguity is also intensified with the abrupt transition from the underworld tribunal to the courtroom in the final scene, where the judge prepares to read the verdict to an audience of women mourning their dead children. With this open ending, *M* points to a corruption of values, which throws a sombre light on Germany on the eve of fascism.

4 For the highly emotional and controversial reception of this film, see H. Korte, *Der Spielfilm und das Ende der Weimarer Republik* (*Feature film and the end of the Weimar Republic*) (1998) 267–78.
5 G. Dahlke and G. Karl (eds.), *Deutsche Spielfilme von den Anfängen bis 1933* (*German feature films from the beginnings to 1933*) (1988) 227.

I have singled out these films because they indicate an extraordinary awareness of the narrative potential of legal procedure for cinematic representation. This applies above all to their use of the courtroom as a locus of dramatic confrontation and conflict to make a political statement or expose a critical state of society. Can we though call them courtroom films? Contemporary reception appears to have focused on other – more obvious – thematic aspects.[6] From the evidence of these and other *Tendenzfilme* of the period, then, we must conclude that legal procedure and courtroom scenes are not elements defining a film genre but rather transgeneric categories which represent the law as a thematic complex at the interface of political culture, social debate, and civil society, which is regularly invoked or questioned as a symbolic agency of order and legitimacy.

There are, however, other films during the late Weimar period with a more specific legal focus; and they constitute the matrix of an emerging genre of courtroom film. A comparatively large group of these is directed towards specific reforms of the penal code or of legal practice, for example, incest: *§ 173 Blutschande* (s. *173 Incest*, James Bauer, 1929); perjury (s. 154): *Meineid* (*Perjury*, Georg Jacoby, 1929); abortion (s. 218): *Das Recht der Ungeborenen* (*The Right of the Unborn*, Adolf Trotz, 1929); circumstantial evidence: *Voruntersuchung* (*Examination of Prisoners*, Robert Siodmak, 1931); prison reform: *Geschlecht in Fesseln* (*Sex in Fetters*, Wilhelm Dieterle, 1928). Other films are based on spectacular court cases, for example, the Scheller-Krantz-case of 1927/1928: *Jugendsünden* (*Sins of Youth*, Carl Heinz Wolff, 1929); *Jugendtragödie* (*Youth Tragedy*, Adolf Trotz, 1929), and *Verirrte Jugend* (*Lost Youth*, Richard Löwenbein, 1929).

To assess the scope and generic character of this large body of films would require massive research. Histories of Weimar cinema, which are mostly concerned with the 'canonical' films of the period, are quite unhelpful on this subject.[7] For an assessment of the enormous bulk and variety of German film production during these years Gero Gandert's work is relevant. The first volume of his manual *Der Film der Weimarer Republik* (1993), designed to document the annual production and reception of German film between 1919 and 1933, focuses on the momentous year 1929, which also marks the transition from silent to sound film. Of the 219 German feature films released during that year, there are more than thirty with a marked legal content. Judging from the critical reception as documented by Gandert, most of these films can be dismissed as banal, melodramatic, or sensational, designed to exploit a popular interest in contested legal issues or

6 In the case of *Dreyfus*, for instance, the 'espionage' and 'documentary' aspects were used as generic terms. See Korte, op. cit., n. 4, pp. 267, 273; in the case of *Danton*, the term 'historical film' was used (Korte, id., p. 294).

7 S. Kracauer, for instance, in his famous history of Weimar film, *From Caligari to Hitler: A Psychological History of the German Film* (1947) ch. 12, has only a few dismissive remarks on these films, which he thought only served as a kind of 'safety valve' for social discontent.

in contemporary *causes célèbres*, but their very bulk and the regularity with which they feature courtroom scenes and elements of legal procedure indicate that by the end of the 1920s there existed a large matrix of feature films, in which the law and its administration figures as a critical focus of political, legal, sensational, and melodramatic discourses.

The advent of sound film is another factor that may help to explain the popularity of courtroom subjects during these years. In his comprehensive history of film Jerzy Toeplitz has an instructive chapter on the use of theatrical models in the early 'talkies'.[8] He singles out crime stories and courtroom scenes as ideal vehicles for the creation of suspense and dramatic effects through concentration on dialogue and on single, isolated settings. This vogue was also supported by the existence of courtroom plays, which easily lent themselves to adaptation. This temporary return to theatrical models led to an early vogue of 'talkie trials' in the United States of America, which mark the origins of the popular genre of American courtroom film. Toeplitz briefly discusses parallel developments in German film of the late 1920s and early 1930s, concentrating on the criticism of 'photocopied theatre' in Oswald's *Dreyfus*, which he interprets as typical of German criticism of 'theatricality' in early sound film. Siegfried Kracauer, the acutest film critic of the Weimar period, is a case in point. Examining his reviews from 1929 to 1932, when sound film made its breakthrough in Germany, one notes that his most scathing criticism was reserved for the 'stageyness' of many productions making use of the new technology,[9] notably those dealing with crime or courtroom subjects.[10] Two reviews, in particular, deserve attention because they contain the gist of his critical argument and a rudimentary recognition of the generic character of courtroom film. In his review of Gustav Ucicky's legal comedy *Hokuspokus* (1930), which was based on a play by Curt Goetz, he takes issue with the closeness of the filmscript to the dramatic original, and with the courtroom setting of most of the action, which he denounces as 'theatre dragged onto the screen'.[11] In contrast, Fjodor Ozep's *Der Mörder Dimitri Karamasoff* (*The Murderer Dimitri Karamasov*, 1931) is praised as the first German sound film which can bear critical comparison with the masterpieces of silent film because the literary subject – the crime story and legal plot of the novel – has been adequately translated into filmic language and dialogue has been subordinated to visual expression.[12]

8 J. Toeplitz, *Geschichte des Films* (*History of Film*) (1987, reprint) ch. 38.
9 Reprinted in appendix 2 of the German translation of *From Caligari to Hitler*, *Von Caligari zu Hitler. Eine psychologische Geschichte des deutschen Films* (1979) 409–567.
10 See, especially, id., pp. 437–42, 464, 480–3, 498–500.
11 id., p. 438.
12 id., pp. 480–3. It is noteworthy that Kracauer in this review singles out the prototype of American courtroom film, *The Trial of Mary Dugan* (1928) as a negative example, because of its reliance on dialogue and its exclusive setting in a courtroom.

69

Weimar film, it can be said in conclusion, in many ways prepared the ground for the courtroom films made in the Nazi period, cinematically, by providing narrative models and generic conventions of representing the law, and thematically, by focusing on issues which lent themselves to a variety of political, sensational, and satiric uses.

PROPAGANDA AND ENTERTAINMENT: REPRESENTATIONS OF THE LAW IN NAZI FILM

The Nazi takeover of 1933 marks a decisive break in German film culture as far as total political control of the whole process of film-making is concerned. This is a well known story, often recounted, from Gerd Albrecht's positivistic account *Nationalsozialistische Filmpolitik* (1969) to Eric Rentschler's lucid study *The Ministry of Illusion: Nazi Cinema and Its Afterlife* (1996). 'Film played a cenral role in the operations of the Ministry of Propaganda,' Rentschler argues:

> serving as a mass mobilizer and an ideological weapon. The NSDAP sought to permeate all sectors of daily life. It 'coordinated' institutions and organizations, purging the film world of Jews, socialists, Communists, and anyone else it deemed objectionable or untrustworthy. The Ministry of Propaganda evaluated film scripts, oversaw activities in the various studios, checking each finished production carefully, determining how films were to be advertised and reviewed, deciding which works warranted official recognition. Almost every feature made during the period must therefore be understood as the reflection of party structures and strategic priorities.[13]

This break, however, did not entail a radical change in film aesthetics and subject matter. More recent studies have stressed the aspect of continuity between Weimar and Nazi cinemas,[14] pointing to the fact that the vast majority of films released between 1933 and 1945 were 'unpolitical' generic productions, following established formulas, almost half of them comedies and musicals, and only about 100 of them manifest propaganda films. But it is precisely in the deceptively 'unpolitical' character of this massive output of entertaining, escapist films, as more recent studies on the aesthetics of Nazi film have shown, that the main political essence and ideological thrust of Nazi film is to be located.[15]

13 E. Rentschler, *The Ministry of Illusion: Nazi Cinema and Its Afterlife* (1996) 8.
14 Apart from Rentschler's study, see, especially, Korte, op. cit., n. 4, and K. Kreimeier, '*Von Henny Porten zu Zarah Leander. Filmgenres und Genrefilm in der Weimarer Republik und im Nationalsozialismus*' ('From Henny Porten to Zarah Leander. Film genres and genre film in the Weimar Republic and in National Socialism') (1994) 3 *montage/av. Zeitschrift für Theorie & Geschichte and audiovisueller Kommunikation* 41.
15 Again, Rentschler's study must be mentioned. See, further, S. Lowry, *Pathos und Politik. Ideologie in den Spielfilmen des Nationalsozialismus* (*Pathos and politics. Ideology in the feature films of National Socialism*) (1991) and K. Witte, *Lachende*

70

Representations of the law in these films, as we shall see, have an important function of creating consensus, both in 'unpolitical' and in propaganda films. Generally, many films of the Nazi period bespeak an immense preoccupation, in fact obsession, with questions of justice and legitimacy, and in this they mirror the perverted Nazi habit of justifying and legitimating the most monstrous political measures, from the *Ermächtigungsgesetz* (law of emergency) of 1933 to the *Sonderstrafrechte gegen Fremdvölkische* (special laws against aliens) and *Reichsbürgerrechte* (citizenship laws) of the 1940s, which prepared the way for the murder of the Jews.

Representation of the law in film, as we have seen in the case of Weimar cinema, is rarely concerned with a realistic depiction of legal procedure or with a serious critique of existing laws. This is even more so with Nazi film, which uses the law in various functions: to demonstrate the 'humane' and 'benevolent' character of the political system, or to lead the erring individual back into the *Volksgemeinschaft* (folk community), to propagate the efficiency and security of the law system, thus glossing over the actually existing perversion of the law, or, by contrast, to denounce foreign law systems for propagandistic purposes.

Film historians have neglected this important field of ideological conditioning, partly because the representation of law in many films is quite imperceptibly interwoven with other issues, partly because – for example, in the case of openly propagandist films – the political issues addressed have been the central focus of critical attention. Above all, the legal problematic in most of these films has not been considered worth separate consideration, let alone reflection of their generic status.[16]

Alfred Bauer's manual, *Deutscher Spielfilm Almanach 1929–1950* (1950) lists a growing number of *Gerichtsmilieu*-films during the period under consideration. Whereas from 1933 to 1937 only about one film a year came under that category, in the years 1938 to 1945 some four to five films were listed annually. However vague that category may seem, it indicates a growing attention on the part of the Ministry of Propaganda to the ideological uses of legal subjects in feature films. This is certainly the case with the production of crime films, as Drewniak points out (who makes no distinction between crime and courtroom films).[17] After 1938 this took the form of an increasing political control of the production of crime films,

---

Erben, Toller Tag. Filmkomödie im Dritten Reich (*Laughing Heirs, Wonderful Day. Film Comedy during the Third Reich*) (1995).

16 G. Albrecht in his *Nationalsozialistische Filmpolitik. Eine soziologische Untersuchung über die Spielfilme des Dritten Reichs* (*National Socialist film politics. A sociological survey*) (1969) 164 ff., lumps together films dealing with '*Rechtspflege und Kriminalität*' (crime and the administration of the law). B. Drewniak in *Der deutsche Film 1938–1945. Ein Gesamtüberblick* (*German film 1938–1945. A survey*) (1987) 423–32, uses the term 'Kriminalfilm' to cover the entire field. Rentschler, op. cit., n. 13, p. 7 only mentions 'detective films and adventure epics'.

17 Drewniak, id.

71

which were supposed to foreground the investigatory function of the police in their 'service for the people'. Frequently, this required the consultation of police authorities in the production of crime films. This growing concern may also account for the increased focus on legal subjects and legal procedures in crime films, which were to emphasize the model function of the Nazi system of criminal justice and hence came under the influence of the Ministry of Justice. From 1943 onward, according to Drewniak:

> every film script which had been submitted to a production company had to be sent to the press officer of the *Reichsjustizministerium* for inspection, if it was concerned in any respect with questions of the law and its administration.[18]

It can be inferred from such measures that the increase of *Gerichtsmilieu*-films after 1938 indicates a growing need to legitimate and stabilize the system through films.

The *Gerichtsmilieu*-films of that period can be roughly categorised as follows:

(i)   legal comedies, for example, *Der Maulkorb* (*The Muzzle*, Erich Engel, 1938); *Kleines Bezirksgericht* (*Little District Court,* Alwin Elling, 1938); *Das Ekel* (*The Creep*, Hans Deppe, 1939); *Der Gasmann* (Carl Froelich, 1941); *Venus vor Gericht* (*Venus in the Dock*, Hans H. Zerlett, 1941), and *Ich bitte um Vollmacht* (*I Request Power of Attorney*, Karl Leiter, 1944);

(ii)   hybrid films containing both elements of crime investigation and courtroom procedure, such as *Der Fall Deruga* (*The Deruga Case*, Fritz Peter Buch, 1938); *Dr. Crippen an Bord* (*Dr Crippen on Board*, Erich Engel, 1941); *Der grosse Preis* (*Grand Prix*, Karl Anton, 1944), and *Der Verteidiger hat das Wort* (*The Counsel for the Defence's Address*, Werner Klingler, 1944);

(iii)   legal melodramas such as, for example, *Ich verweigere die Aussage* (*I Refuse to Give Evidence*, Otto Linnekogel, 1939); *Roman eines Arztes* (*A Doctor's Story,* Jürgen von Alten, 1939), and *Die schwarze Robe* (*The Black Robe*, Fritz Peter Buch, 1944);

(iv)   'problem' (that is, propaganda) films with courtroom scenes such as *Jud Süss* (*Jew Süss*, Veit Harlan, 1940) and *Ich klage an* (*I Accuse,* Wolfgang Liebeneiner, 1941); and

(v)   a singular instance of an American-type courtroom film, *Sensationsprozess Casilla* (*Sensation Trial Casilla*, Eduard von Borsody, 1939).

This wide spectrum of films focusing on legal subjects and courtroom procedure indicates an acute awareness of the propagandistic potential of the law, and this applies to both openly propagandistic and to 'innocuous' and merely 'entertaining' films.

---

18 id., p. 429.

72

One of the most effective measures of exerting political control over the production and reception of film was a highly differentiated rating system,[19] and the rating *'staatspolitisch besonders wertvoll'* (politically especially worthwhile) would suggest that films which were distinguished as such, were films with a political tendency and singled out to convey an 'educational' message in confirmation of the Nazi *weltanschauung*. In many cases these films were produced, and this applies above all to the initial phase of the Third Reich, when the regime needed to stabilize itself, to support and explain the necessity of a number of new laws and regulations: for example, the *Reichsarbeitsdienstgesetz* (law introducing compulsory labour service for young men), the *Gesetz für den Aufbau der Wehrmacht* (law introducing general conscription), and the *Gesetz zum Schutze des deutschen Blutes und der deutschen Ehre* (law for the protection of German blood and honour, that is, the Nuremberg Race Laws), all passed in 1935. According to Klaus Kanzog, the following films were made in support of these laws: *Ich für dich – Du für mich* (*I for You – You for Me*, Carl Froelich, 1934), *Hermine und die sieben Aufrechten* (*Hermine and the Seven Upright Men*, Frank Wysbar, 1935), *Der höhere Befehl* (*The Higher Command*, Gerhard Lamprecht, 1935), *Pour le Mérite* (Karl Ritter, 1938), *D III 88* (Herbert Maisch, 1939), and *Jud Süss* (*Jew Süss*, Veit Harlan, 1941).[20] What is remarkable about these openly propagandist films is that in a substantial number of them the law is invoked as an authority or tribunal to arbitrate the contending norms and ethical positions they thematize in the framework of Nazi legal ideology. Quite often this takes the form of highly dramatic courtroom encounters in which the political message of these films finds its clearest articulation.[21]

One film, which deliberately was not given the rating 'politically especially worthwhile' but 'only' that of 'artistically especially worthwhile' (*'künstlerisch besonders wertvoll'*) in order to camouflage its propagandistic

19 See K. Kanzog, *'Staatspolitisch besonders wertvoll'. Ein Handbuch zu 30 deutschen Spielfilmen der Jahre 1934 bis 1945* (*'Politically especially worthwhile'. A handbook of 30 German feature films of the years 1934 to 1945*) (1994) and U. von der Osten, *NS-Filme im Kontext sehen! 'Staatspolitisch besonders wertvolle' Filme der Jahre 1934–1938* (*Looking at NS-films in context. 'politically especially worthwhile' films of the years 1934–1938*) (1998).
20 Kanzog, id., p. 33. Kanzog mentions a number of other films which were made to support administrative and political measures, for example, *Verräter* (*Traitors*, Karl Ritter, 1936), which supported the founding of the *Volksgerichtshof* (People's Court) in 1934 as a special court dealing with political offences.
21 See, for instance, *Der alte und der junge König* (*The Old and the Young King*, Hans Steinhoff, 1935), *Das Mädchen Johanna* (*The Girl Johanna*, Gustav Ucicky, 1935), *Wenn wir alle Engel wären* (*If We All Were Angels*, Carl Froelich, 1936), *Patrioten* (*Patriots*, Karl Ritter, 1937), and the already mentioned *Verräter, Pour le Mérite*, and *Jud Süss*.

message, was Wolfgang Liebeneiner's *Ich klage an* (*I Accuse*, 1941). This film had been commissioned by the government with the intention of soliciting acceptance in the population for a law regulating 'euthanasia' and thus legalizing the ongoing practice of exterminating those 'unfit to live', that is, people suffering from mental illnesses.[22] In the 'euthanasia' bill the legalization of the offence *'Tötung auf Verlangen'* (mercy killing) had been coupled with that of the elimination of the mentally ill. This double objective is subtly woven into the propagandist argument and into the plot of the film. *Ich klage an* is about a young woman, Hanna Heydt, who is suffering from multiple sclerosis. In the terminal stage of her illness, she entreats two doctors to give her a lethal injection: the family doctor, Dr Lang, who refuses, and her husband, who finally complies with her wish. Dr Lang, whose decision is based on ethical and legal considerations, it turns out, has for the same reasons saved the life of a child suffering from meningitis who is now reduced to an existence of vegetating 'blind, deaf, and idiotic' in an asylum. Shaken by the consequences of his 'failure' after a visit to the asylum and the confrontation with the child's despondent parents, Dr Lang undergoes a dramatic change of heart. Professor Heydt, Hanna's husband, now faces a charge of murder. At the trial several witnesses are examined, but no light is shed on the deed of Professor Heydt, who remains silent about his motives. Dr Lang makes a belated appearance in the witness stand, still shocked by the consequences of his treatment of the child whom he has 'saved'. He confesses his double moral 'guilt' in that case and in the case of Hanna Heydt. This statement clears the accused of the charge of murder and opens the way for a commutation of the charge of murder into that of a mercy killing (s. 216 of the penal code). Professor Heydt, however, now gives up his reticence and turns the court into a tribunal against the existing state of legislation by delivering a passionate address to the court:

> I accuse a statute which prevents doctors and judges from fulfilling their duties towards the people. For that reason I do not wish that my case be hushed up. I want my verdict. It will be a signal, it will be a clarion call.

Here the film ends, leaving the audience to ponder about the existing state of the law. This is a very effective finale to a film which skilfully orchestrates the audience's sympathies from the very beginning. The open ending in the manner of Fritz Lang's *M* and the rhetoric of the accused who turns the tables on the court with his 'I accuse' in the manner of Zola's famous harangue in Oswald's *Dreyfus* show that Liebeneiner has learned the lesson of Weimar film.

---

22 See the documentation of the genesis of this film in D. Traudisch, *Mutterschaft mit Zuckerguß? Frauenfeindliche Propaganda im NS-Spielfilm* (*Sugar-coated motherhood? Misogynist propaganda in NS-feature film*) (1993) 102–6.

TWO VERSIONS OF JUSTICE: *SENSATIONSPROZESS CASILLA* AND *DER VERTEIDIGER HAT DAS WORT*

This applies not only to Weimar models but also to other traditions. Eduard von Borsody's *Sensationsprozeß Casilla* is a singular case in the history of Nazi film because it perfectly imitates and parodies the genre of American courtroom film, which by the 1930s had become established as a popular genre.[23] Released during the last weeks before the outbreak of World War II, the film is an interesting document of Goebbels's culture war against Hollywood.[24] Heinrich George, who had eloquently argued the cause of liberty and democracy as Émile Zola in Oswald's *Dreyfus*, now plays a cunning American attorney, Vandergrift, who defends a German citizen in a United States court against the charges of kidnapping a child. Witnesses who are either unreliable or bribed, an ambitious and corrupt prosecutor, an overbearing, erratic judge, a gullible jury, aggressive and unfair cross-examinations of witnesses, fabrication of evidence, and a sensational coverage of the case in the media – all this adds up to a devastating panorama of American society, where public opinion is made by the press and the law degenerates to a marketable commodity, which is only accessible to those who can pay for it. This is the gist of the defendant's final address to the court, which nearly seals his fate. It is only through a retrial that the clever attorney can save him from the death penalty.

Sensationsprozeß Casilla is also remarkable for its intimate knowledge of American law and courtroom procedure, and its ability to exploit those elements of the American system that would make it appear most vulnerable and alien to a German audience: the 'negotiable' character of justice, the adversarial character of legal procedure, and the power of the media in shaping public opinion.[25]

In 1944 Heinrich George again played the role of a lawyer, this time a German lawyer, Justizrat Jordan, in Werner Klingler's *Der Verteidiger hat das Wort*. The subject of this film is the murder of a woman, as it turns out the divorced wife of Justizrat Jordan's prospective son-in-law, the accused. The professional ethics of the German lawyer contrasts strongly with that of his unscrupulous American counterpart in *Sensationsprozess Casilla*. He only takes up a case when he is convinced of the innocence of the accused.

---

23 M. Kuzina, *Der amerikanische Gerichtsfilm. Justiz, Ideologie, Dramatik* (*American courtroom film. Law, ideology, drama*) (2000) 16.

24 See M. Spieker, *Hollywood unterm Hakenkreuz. Der amerikanische Spielfilm im Dritten Reich* (*Hollywood under the swastika. The American feature film during the Third Reich*) (1999).

25 There are other films of the period, where foreign law systems are criticized, for example, *Dr Crippen an Bord* (*Dr Crippen on Board*, Erich Engels, 1942), *Der Kaiser von Kalifornien* (*The Emperor of California*, Luis Trenker, 1936), *Zu neuen Ufern* (*To New Shores*, Detlef Sierck, 1937), *Der Fuchs von Glenarvon* (*The Fox of Glenarvon*, Max W. Kimmich, 1940).

75

'Justice and law' he considers to be something 'holy', a 'service for the community'. The trial itself, as it unfolds in the final scenes of *Der Verteidiger hat das Wort*, with its sober dignity and static calm, contrasts sharply with the hectic atmosphere in the American courtoom of *Sensationsprozess Casilla*. The judge, a humane, almost fatherly figure, who has a firm grasp of the proceedings, a prosecutor who is persistent but fair, a brilliant counsel for the defence, whose summing-up of the case leaves no doubt about the innocence of his client and convicts the real murderer. All this presents an entirely falsified state of criminal justice under National Socialism, which is in sharp contrast to the grim reality during the last years of the war. At this time, tens of thousands were convicted and executed under the jurisdiction of *Sondergerichte* (special courts) under the statutes of an increasingly dehumanized criminal law.

MUZZLED LAUGHTER: THE USES OF LEGAL COMEDY

> Is there any government in the world which rewards those who teach people to laugh and present them with a smile? ... Three years ago, many people in Germany thought that now they had no more reason to laugh. They were right! ... The humour of these times [i.e. the Weimar years] was artificial, the jokes were obscene, the merriment full of innuendo. In our new Germany you can have a real laugh.

This is a passage from a review of Carl Froelich's popular legal comedy, *Wenn wir alle Engel wären* in the *Lichtbild-Bühne* of 19 October 1936.[26] It is quite revealing because it offers a good description of the function of laughter in the innumerable film comedies made during the Third Reich. The laughter evoked through these films is very much a controlled reaction, a 'muzzled' laughter, to borrow the title of one of the most popular comedies of these times, *Der Maulkorb* (*The Muzzle*). Laughter, thus understood, means a temporary loosening of control, which can be the source of various complications, pranks, and misdemeanours, to let off steam, as it were, but finally, the lid is firmly placed on the kettle again and order restored. Legal comedy is the ideal medium to produce this sort of laughter.

The typical heroes of Nazi legal comedy are ordinary people who, through foolishness, ignorance, or carelessness, get into conflict with the law. Invariably, they end up in a courtroom, where justice is administered leniently, and punishment takes the form of ridicule and correction. Carl Froelich's *Der Gasmann* is a good example. In this film Heinz Rühmann, one of the most popular comedians of the time, is cast as a minor official who inadvertently finds himself in possession of a large sum of money. He fails though to report this to the authorities and subsequently plunges into a

---

26 Quoted by F. Courtade and P. Cadars, *Geschichte des Films im Dritten Reich* (*History of Film in the Third Reich*) (1975) 268.

76

series of amorous and financial adventures, which terminate in a law court. It turns out, however, that he has, mainly through foolishness and timidity, committed no actual crime, and he is cleared when like a *dea ex machina* a mysterious lady appears in the witness stand, the mistress of the owner of the money, who wants to stay anonymous, to give evidence. This clears the accused, and the case dissolves in general laughter. Nevertheless there is a constant threat of punishment, which permeates the whole film, and this also applies to the representation of the law. The initial strictness of the judge and the prosecutor during the trial gradually give way to good humour and leniency, thus indicating that the law with all its severity is a just and humane institution, which can distinguish between human weakness and criminal behaviour.

There are several other legal comedies which conform to this pattern. Erich Engels's *Der Maulkorb* is about an over-solicitous prosecutor who investigates an offence which he himself has committed while in his cups and has entirely forgotten: he has put his dog's muzzle on the head of a statue of his sovereign after a convivial evening with his friends. In court, when the truth comes out, he is saved, however, by a series of accidents and legal tricks. Carl Froelich's *Wenn wir alle Engel wären* again features Heinz Rühmann as a minor civil servant who through his own carelessness and ignorance faces a charge of theft and is saved in the nick of time by the sudden appearance of a witness who exonerates him. There are rare cases when somebody does receive a sentence in a legal comedy. This though usually takes the form of a mild punishment, designed to correct and 'educate' the culprit, as in Hans Deppe's *Der Ekel*. In this film a notorious grumbler is charged with insulting an official and sentenced to a short term in prison, which will give him time to think over his role in the community.

SOME CONCLUSIONS

Legal comedies of the Third Reich show us the discrepancy between the reality of the law and its presentation in film at its most glaring because they suggest a 'normality' and ordered state of society which is regulated by transparent and humane administrative acts and procedures. They acknowledge the potential of chaos and anarchy in everyday life and its laughable and ridiculous aspects. They allow escapades or subversive fantasies of wish-fulfilment, but only to the point where such behaviour becomes a danger to the supposed interests of the community. It is this double character of the law, the humane and reassuring presence of order, and the constant threat of the power to control and punish, that makes legal comedy so effective as a medium of ideological control. In a general sense, this applies to the whole spectrum of films with legal subjects that were made during the Third Reich. The ubiquity of the law and its agents in Nazi films[27] conveys an idea of its presence in everyday life, which appears to be self-evident and suggests a 'natural' state of things. In this function, these films present anything but a realistic or documentary evidence of the actual state of the law during the Third Reich, but a perverted image and a camouflage of its reality.

To get a glimpse of this reality we must turn to other films, for instance *Verräter vor dem Volksgerichtshof* (*Traitors before the People's Court*), a documentary of the trial of the officers and civilians involved in the attempt on Hitler's life on 20 July 1944. At Hitler's order, this film was to be shown in all German cinemas, in order to deter, intimidate, and morally destroy the opposition. This, however, proved impossible because of the psychopathic, farcically authoritarian conduct of the trial by the president of the Volksgerichtshof, Roland Freisler, who from the beginning gave the accused no chance to defend themselves and left no doubt about the death sentences they would receive. Since this would not have deceived even the most gullible and uncritical audience about the true character of this trial, the film was declared a *'Geheime Reichssache'* (Official Secret) and only given screenings to selected circles of party officials.[28]

It is this discrepancy between the reality of the law and its representation in film which makes it necessary to study the courtroom films of the period because it helps to understand the nature of Nazi rule and its fascination for many, a power which was not just the cynical and brutal exercise of force and terror, but one that was asssisted and made possible by the power of images.

27 I suspect that there are hundreds of films of various genres made during the Third Reich that feature elements of legal procedure or contain courtroom scenes. Here is a random selection of three films from my own recent viewing. *Der Fuchs von Glenarvon* (*The Fox of Glenarvon*, Max W. Kimmich, 1940), a historical propaganda film set in Ireland, contains a highly dramatic scene of 'popular' justice, in which a traitorous English Justice of the Peace is condemned to death by the Irish peasants he has betrayed. *Paradies der Junggesellen* (*Bachelors' Paradise*, Karl Hoffmann, 1939), a musical comedy in praise of marriage, begins and ends with a courtroom scene. *Zu neuen Ufern* (*To New Shores*, Detlef Sierck, 1937), a melodrama set in Australia, has the heroine in the dock of an English law court in an early scene of the film, facing a charge of forgery, which she has not committed.

28 H. Kramer, *'Filme zur NS-Justiz'* (*'Films about the NS system of justice'*) (1984) 17 *Kritische Justiz* 301–3. It is interesting that this article, written by a jurist, only covers documentary films and feature films about the state of the law during the Third Reich that were made after 1945.

78

JOURNAL OF LAW AND SOCIETY
VOLUME 28, NUMBER 1, MARCH 2001
ISSN: 0263-323X, pp. 79–96

The Social Issue Courtroom Drama as an Expression of American Popular Culture

MATTHIAS KUZINA*

Drawing on recent works of commercial Hollywood cinema and topical made-for-television movies, this paper explores the cultural implications of two distinct varieties of the American courtroom picture: the problem film in the guise of a legal drama and the trial movie which may take the form of a social issue film. Both types merge into a category that overtly abounds with liberal stances and humanitarian attitudes, films that portray actual or – only rarely – fictional excesses of rigid conservative orthodoxy, movies that have also succeeded in capturing the interest of the public on both sides of the Atlantic. Further, the aesthetics of the documentary tradition related to this generic strain is examined in such a way as to cast light on the quality of critical reflection and certain ideological inferences thereof.

INTRODUCTION

Up to now the courtroom drama has been considered one of the most popular American film genres, and the social issue variant seems to be held in high repute by many critics and viewers.[1] The courtroom genre can – tentatively – be subdivided into ten basic groupings, which are interrelated: courtroom 'whodunits', legal thrillers, historical courtroom dramas, true crime courtroom dramas, lawyer films, courtroom satires and courtroom comedies, court-martial films, social issue courtroom dramas, hybrid courtroom dramas, and jury room dramas. There are special forms such as dramatized

* c/o Law Faculty, Ruhr-Universitat Bochum, Gebäude GC 8/135, D-44780 Bochum, Germany

1 The following is partly adapted from my doctoral dissertation *Der amerikanische Gerichtsfilm: Justiz, Ideologie, Dramatik* (2000), which is an interdisciplinary study concerning the American courtroom drama (film and television) of the last five decades: 77 movies are categorized (the index of titles encompasses both feature length films and selected TV series); particular attention is paid to the evolution of the courtroom genre in terms of the social reality depicted and the legal culture referred to.

documentaries, courtroom films that address issues of political justice, various types of non-fiction feature films, and movies that are peripheral to this genre.[2] As for the average tele-feature and theatrical film about legal procedures as narrative-based cultural practices,[3] the dramatic action often manifests itself as an eclectic amalgam of courtroom scenes and marginal events taking place in other social spaces.[4] Michael Crichton's female lawyer film *Physical Evidence* (1988), which incidentally shows no social issue motifs whatsoever, is a case in point. Legal dramas follow particular conventions that are more or less specific to American culture; they are prone to the perpetuation of stereotypes, whether the centre of interest be the miraculous comeback of a burnt-out lawyer, the abuse of the legal system to secure the acquittal of a guilty client, a prosecutor's fight for justice, or the unexpected, emotional confession of a conscience-stricken person on the witness stand.[5] The dialectical approach to judicial questions and the theatricality inherent in the gradual resolution of the conflict can be regarded as minimum requirements for the classification of legal narratives, besides the locale of the courtroom.[6] Unless the particularities of the adversary

2 For an overview on law films outside the courtroom, see S. Greenfield and G. Osborn, 'Film, law, and the delivery of justice: The case of Judge Dredd and the disappearing courtroom' (1999) 6(2) *J. of Crim. Justice and Popular Culture* 35. In his study *Law in Film: Resonance and Representation* (1999), D.A. Black also adopts a very broad perspective and considers the reflexivity of films about law, which he designates as 'stories about the process of storytelling, or *narratives about narrative*' (p. 55).

3 That is to say, 'a series of ritually constructed, conventionally verisimilar narratives' (Black, id., p. 58).

4 Many crime films and thrillers include a courtroom sequence as a subsidiary narrative element.

5 The formulaic plot patterns are easily identifiable. Bennett and Feldman specify the well-known, reassuring Perry Mason story type:

> in which the great lawyer agrees to take a hopeless case and build a defense against all odds. The evidence against the client is so damaging that even the lawyer suffers doubts about his faith in the client's earnest claims of innocence. We suffer through the maze of dead ends before the trial. The prosecution case is ironclad. The trial only makes things worse. Each witness contributes to the inescapable conclusion that the defendant must have committed the crime. Then something occurs to the lawyer – perhaps as a result of something a witness said, or a remark the client made, or a change of heart on the part of a conspiratorial witness, or a stroke of genius on the lawyer's part. A new interpretation for the facts begins to emerge. Indeed, a new 'story' takes shape. A key witness is recalled. The new version of the crime is unfolded through a brilliant line of questioning. The witness is trapped. The web of circumstances is unraveled. Justice is done. Reality and Justice become reconciled.

W.L. Bennett and M.S. Feldman, *Reconstructing Reality in the Courtroom: Justice and Judgment in American Culture* (1981) 35.

6 Compare N. Rafter's definition of the genre in *Shots in the Mirror: Crime Films and Society* (2000) 93. Black points out that the 'courtroom setting might serve as a narrative hub from which various flashbacks and stories emerge, even if the courtroom itself does not remain on-screen for more than few minutes' (op. cit., n. 2,

80

system of the Anglo-American (criminal) trial – different truth claims, opposing courtroom participants, and the juxtaposition of testimony – are aptly and coherently represented in the fabric of the story, the films concerned do not correspond with the notion of the American courtroom drama as formulaic art or an expression of broader cultural significance.[7]

In the late twentieth century, in the wake of the advancement and proliferation of made-for-TV movies, reality-based stories and socio-psychological subject matters have gained ground and became an integral part of popular culture. Courtroom films that centre around current social problems are widely appreciated by the general audience, albeit with a tendency to arouse controversy.[8] Mick Jackson's *Indictment: The McMartin Trial* (1995), which clearly illustrates the enforcement of law at the expense of justice, is a prime example of the emotive quality of the present-day social issue courtroom drama: an upright defence attorney strives to prevent the American legal system from being misused by publicity-seeking bigots, who – as representatives of the State of California – wish to combat the societal malaise of child abuse by persecuting innocent suspects. Jackson's film follows the longest, most expensive criminal trial in American history. The accused are exposed to the wrath of the female prosecutor, a fanatical social worker, the community, and the news people. Despite or perhaps because of its blatantly critical stance on the administration of justice in the context of the pressure of public opinion, this made-for-pay-TV movie (HBO) received a hostile reception in the press.[9] Though there was no denying that the

p. 66). The first part of Peter Levin's TV true crime courtroom drama, *Precious Victims* (1993), is an extreme example of such fragmentation.

7 For a comprehensive study of popular story formulas in American literature, see J.G. Cawelti, *Adventure, Mystery, and Romance: Formula Stories as Art and Popular Culture* (1976). The 'Hollywood Formula' is discussed in P. Roffman and J. Purdy, *The Hollywood Social Problem Film: Madness, Despair, and Politics from the Depression to the Fifties* (1981). D.R. Papke elucidates the cultural significance of the American trial in 'Law in American Culture: An Overview' (1992) 15 *J. of Am. Culture* 3.

8 C.B. Rosenberg states that '[t]oday, television legal drama has matured to take in almost everything that is a matter of societal debate – the death penalty, gay rights, abortion, adoption, gang violence, drugs, mass murder, race relations, children's rights, sexual harassment, and disability rights, among many others.' 'Foreword' in *Prime Time Law: Fictional Television as Legal Narrative*, eds. R.M. Jarvis and P.R. Joseph (1998) x.

9 See, for example, J. Millman, '"Indictment" handles McMartin Case with hands of Stone' *San Francisco Examiner*, 19 May 1995; G. Bellafante, 'Television: Chronicle of a Witch Hunt' *Time* [Domestic], 22 May 1995. Bellafante complains about 'an aggressively prodefense point of view', an allegation that is unfounded. The critically acclaimed fact-based account of the McMartin trial, featuring James Woods as defence attorney Danny Davis and Henry Thomas as prime suspect Ray Buckey, lends itself to some scrutiny. See Kuzina, op. cit., n. 1, pp. 238–41. Screenwriter Abby Mann was previously criticized for resorting to 'liberal stance pronouncements' in his TV adaptation *The Marcus-Nelson Murders* (1973), a landmark in television history. See 'The Marcus-Nelson Murders' *Variety*, 14 March 1973.

81

charges against the defendants were the product of mass paranoia, two major American networks that were originally curious about the projected tele-feature decided to hedge the question of guilt.[10]

Many social issue courtroom dramas focus on (violent) crimes that government authorities and state institutions such as the police are investigating. This sub-genre most closely refers to the acknowledgement of or disrespect for the liberties protected in the Bill of Rights. The narratives always culminate in a (criminal) trial or other legal inquiry, and the juridical question of guilt or sanity is invariably intertwined with public policy questions, with ethical codes or social values relating to American society. In point of fact, some of these films delve into the complexities of the prosecution of (assumed) juvenile delinquency; others ponder on the availability of procedural justice; others denounce the practice of discriminating against minority groups and indigent people; still others expose laws and practices that put handicapped or stigmatized persons, homosexuals, rape victims, and the powerless at a disadvantage. Thus, they are characterized by an integration of judicial and socio-political issues.[11] Beneath the surface, this sub-genre is about the problem of the congruence between official action and declared rule which is worth striving for and which constitutes what is called 'the internal morality of the law'.[12] Factual social-issue courtroom dramas often demonstrate how the principles of legality have been shattered. In their contribution to the study of the American problem film from the 1930s to the rise of McCarthyism, Peter Roffman and Jim Purdy hold preaching a social message as the salient feature of this category.[13] The didactic mode is recognizable in documentaries such as *Rape Culture* (Cambridge Documentary Films, 1978) and in lawyer films such as *Sworn to Silence* (Peter Levin, 1987). The defence of a guilty or discourteous client is no longer a taboo subject for film-makers,[14] and in R.L. Joseph's notable case its relevance to the

---

10 'Criminal Injustice' *Chicago Tribune*, 18 May 1995.
11 For analyses of social issue courtroom dramas proper – *Dummy* (Frank Perry, 1979), *Gideon's Trumpet* (Robert Collins, 1980), and *Philadelphia* (Jonathan Demme, 1993) – see Kuzina, op. cit., n. 1, pp. 221–26, 234–36.
12 L.L. Fuller, *The Morality of Law* (1969, rev. edn.) 81 and throughout.
13 Roffman and Purdy, op. cit., n. 7, p. viii. The authors argue that 'the problem film combines social analysis and dramatic conflict within a coherent narrative structure. Social content is transformed into dramatic events and movie narrative adapted to accommodate social issues as story material through a particular set of movie conventions.'
14 Compare G.R. Newman, 'Popular Culture and Criminal Justice: A Preliminary Analysis' (1990) 18 *J. of Crim. Justice* 261, at 267. For details of the film and the ethical statements given, see Kuzina, op. cit., n. 1, pp. 186–8. There is no widespread acceptance that criminals deserve the protection of legal rights. B.K. Crew writes: '[The] notion that lawyers who defend immoral clients must themselves be immoral resonates with a popular conception (or better, misconception) about law. A naive view of law, common in American culture, is that law is, or ought to be, equivalent to morality.'

dissemination of social ideals and to the detection of dominant ideologies should not be underestimated.[15]

THE GENESIS OF SOCIAL ISSUE FILMS

The precursors of contemporary social problem films are to be found in the era before World War I, when one- or two-reelers were produced to entertain the broad masses of the urban working class: 'The comedies, melodramas, and occasional westerns about labor conflict, tenement poverty, or political corruption reveal through fantasy an America torn with ideological conflict.'[16] It is not surprising that silent cinema came to criticize cases of partiality in legal proceedings and a legal system that seemed to be heavily dependent on economic interests. Edwin S. Porter's *The Kleptomaniac* (1905) represents an early example of the criticism of ideology in this popular culture medium. The film

> offered a scathing portrait of the American legal system and its treatment of the poor. Its heroine, a penniless woman of the tenements, stole a loaf of bread to feed her daughter, and was sentenced to jail. A parallel story within the plot revealed a wealthy woman acquitted for shoplifting luxury items from a department store. Court scenes when the two are brought to trial resembled a virtual assembly line of justice – as marshals herded the accused before the judge like so many cattle. Yet the wealthy were brushed out of the courtroom with a sympathetic wave of the hand. One privileged woman clicked her heels in delight as the judge dismissed her case.[17]

The Kleptomaniac concerns the nature of class conflict in America and the subjugation of the interests of the poor in general and the impotence of the individual in particular. Those taking advantage of their positions of power were once labelled 'criminaloids'.[18] In the words of Sloan, Porter's film suggests that 'the nation's "criminaloids" [...] stretched even to those in judicial robes'.[19] Notwithstanding the political message expressed, the film was not deemed provocative. As Sloan points out, no effective national

('Acting Like Cops: The Social Reality of Crime and Law on TV Police Dramas' in *Marginal Conventions: Popular Culture, Mass Media and Social Deviance*, ed. C.R. Sanders (1990) 137.) *Sworn to Silence* was written by Robert L. Joseph. The script was inspired by Tom Alibrandi and Frank H. Armani's *Privileged Information* (1984).

15 The concept of ideology referred to in this paper is from the German philosopher Karl Jaspers who defines it as 'a complex of thoughts or ideas, which for the thinker represents as absolute truth an understanding of the world and his/her situation therein that is really a self-deception, a stratagem to justify, disguise and evade [the reality of the world], one way or another, to his/her present advantage'. (*Vom Ursprung und Ziel der Geschichte* (1949) 169 (my translation).)

16 K. Sloan, *The Loud Silents: Origins of the Social Problem Film* (1988) 3–4.

17 id., p. 18.

18 The sociologist Edward A. Ross coined the term in 1907. See Sloan, id., pp. 15 and 17.

19 id., p. 18.

censorship existed at that time.[20] A melodrama entitled *Was Justice Served?* (D.W. Griffiths, 1909) exposes the dangers inherent in trial by jury when the defendant has a prison record. The jury system, which entails – as the Anglo-American mind conceives it – 'one of democracy's most sacred myths',[21] is neither lacking in inherent weaknesses nor (outside the United States of America) famous for its assumed reliability. The question posed in the movie's title is, of course, purely rhetorical, and could be utilized for recent social issue courtroom dramas as well. 'Had it not been for an act of fate', Sloan comments, 'the legal system would have sent an innocent man to jail.'[22] In the silent era, the social conscience film also paid attention to the intricacies of penal reform, the suffragette movement, and other reformist ideas.

During the 1920s, the output of social problem films bore no resemblance to the one in the era of progressivism: the interest in social criticism dwindled, when the American spirit of optimistic materialism and prosperity paved the way for the prominence of light entertainment and comedy.[23] A new cycle of social problem films – movies dealing with institutions of social control that are characterized as being ridiculous and with legal practitioners that are identified with unscrupulous, manipulative individuals (shysters) – was initiated by the calamity of the Great Depression. The actual economic breakdown, which affected the entire nation and the nation's culture, was aesthetically transformed into a moral breakdown, which in turn was reflected in a cynical view of the American politico-juridical scene:

> The legal establishment is likewise hopelessly inept, something to beat. If the police manage to arrest a gangster, a mouthpiece lawyer is immediately able to secure his release.[24]

The shyster cycle embraces such films as James Flood's *The Mouthpiece* (1932), William Dieterle's *Lawyer Man* (1932), and George Archainbaud's *State's Attorney* (1932), each of them presenting a protagonist who is characterized as:

---

20 id., p. 19.
21 J.J. Desmarais, 'Twelve Angry Men' in *Magill's American Film Guide*, ed. F.N. Magill, vol. 5 (1983) 3460.
22 Sloan, op. cit., n. 16, p. 42. This holds for one of the greatest legal dramas of all time, Sidney Lumet's *Twelve Angry Men* (1957), which does not represent a microcosm of the social whole, since women are deliberately excluded. Its happy ending, a Hollywood convention, is contrived. As Desmarais puts it: 'What if there had been no Henry Fonda?' (Desmarais, id., p. 3461). *We the Jury* (1996), a gripping TV movie by Sturla Gunnarsson, represents a complete reversal of Lumet's script: a celebrity accused of first-degree murder is finally found guilty after moderate interventions by a female juror. According to this jury room drama, liberal concerns are no longer of prime importance.
23 See Roffman and Purdy, op. cit., n. 7, p. 10.
24 id., p. 17. The authors refer to the courtroom scenes in George Hill's *The Secret Six* (1931) and Howard Hawks' *Scarface* (1932).

84

the perfect wish-fulfillment figure for the Depression, able to survive – indeed, flourish – amid the chaos. [...] For the shyster lawyer, the courtroom is a stage. Here he is not merely actor, but also author and director. Judge, jury, witness, and the law itself are props shuffled around as the shyster sees fit.[25]

With the introduction of the Motion Picture Production Code (Hays Code) in 1930, which stressed the inviolability of the law, cultural realities were altered. A world-view that accentuated the notion of America as 'the home of the brave and the land of the free' was imposed on the movie audience: 'Wealth, status, and power are possible in America, the land of opportunity where the individual is rewarded for virtue.'[26] The messages conveyed and attitudes reflected could be traced to the ideological fixations of those in power, with moral values that belonged to the dominant social order. It was almost impossible for Hollywood film-makers to effectively reduce the aspirations of the American Dream to the absurd. Anti-Semitism was scarcely hinted at as a phenomenon pertinent to the United States, since the producers quite seriously 'insisted that any sympathetic portrayal of Jewish problems would only provoke more anti-Semitism'; they 'refused to deviate from an upper middle-class WASP image of America that was more in keeping with audience aspirations.'[27] However, *Counsellor-at-Law* (1933), William Wyler's adaptation of a screenplay by Elmer Rice, deals with an ambitious Jewish lawyer who is caught in a whirlpool of prejudice and rancour. Mervyn LeRoy's *They Won't Forget* (1937), on the other hand, makes no reference to the subject matter the story is based on: the notorious Leo Frank trial – charges of anti-Semitism permeated the lengthy court procedure that was called 'the American Dreyfus case' – and the Frank lynching.[28]

In the late 1930s, the juvenile delinquency film evolved as a sub-genre of the problem film, and the depiction of the social milieu was slightly more substantial than the dramatization of criminality itself. Legal proceedings were later integrated into the social consciousness film: Nicholas Ray's *Knock on Any Door* (1949) reflects on the culpability of a young murderer, who – due to unethical tactics employed by the district attorney – eventually

---

25 id., pp. 31, 32. Ultimately, the critical tone exhibited in these movies was downgraded by Hollywood-like twists to the plot: with innocuous resolutions for their own sake, the motion picture industry has always been able to reassert traditional values. The shyster genre was transcended by John Ford's *Young Mr. Lincoln* (1939). See N. Rosenberg, 'Perry Mason' in *Prime Time Law: Fictional Television as Legal Narrative*, eds. R.M. Jarvis and P.R. Joseph (1998) 120–1.

26 Further: 'Stereotypic values celebrate Americana in terms of home, motherhood, and community, puritan love and work ethic.' (Roffman and Purdy, op. cit., n. 7, p. 6.) See, also, R. Sklar, *Movie-Made America: A Cultural History of American Movies* (1975) 173–4.

27 Roffman and Purdy, id., p. 235.

28 id., p. 171. See J. Leonard, 'Broadcast Views' *New York*, 25 January 1988; L. Stone, 'The Murder of Mary Phagan: Georgia Breach' *The Village Voice*, 28 January 1988.

cannot be saved from the electric chair.[29] Mark Robson's *Trial* (1955) places the courtroom procedures (a Mexican-American student is erroneously charged with first-degree murder) in relation to pro- versus anti- communist politics.[30] John Frankenheimer's *The Young Savages* (1961) opposes a D.A. who wants to make political capital out of the conviction of three youths to his liberal-minded assistant, who in the end does not allow opportunistic considerations to affect the conduct of the murder trial.[31] These theatrical features are not devoid of clichés. They played an important role in the formation of the social issue formula concerned, even though they do not stand out from the classics of the American courtroom drama. Roffman and Purdy argue that in the 1950s and the 1960s, social consciousness was 'no longer a dominant cultural motif'.[32] As for the courtroom picture, social issues were essentially relegated to the background. Television programming caused a resurgence of the problem film.[33] Youth-oriented social issue topics were successfully adopted by prime time TV movies that fall into the docu-drama category. They in no way follow the *Perry Mason* formula. Since the 1970s, they have, among other themes expanded in the contemporary courtroom film, increasingly been concerned with corrupt institutions of law and order, with the right to representation by counsel, with miscarriages of justice, with the fallibility of the legal system (through the misapplication of capital punishment), with subtle or overt forms of racism, sexism, and preferential treatment and, hence, ideological decisions made by courts.

THE SIGNIFICANCE OF THE COURTROOM SEQUENCE

All social issue courtroom dramas do in one important respect allude to the due process guarantee contained in the Fifth and Fourteenth Amendments to the United States Constitution, which requires that all government actions be in accordance with the rule of law. Television movies either show that the ideals of equality and democracy are subject to deterioration or comment on

---

29 See P. Bergman and M. Asimow, *Reel Justice: The Courtroom Goes to the Movies* (1996) 172–7; Roffman and Purdy, op. cit., n. 7, p. 145.
30 Bergman and Asimow, id., pp. 142–7.
31 See Kuzina, op. cit., n. 1, pp. 218–20; G. Pratley, *The Films of John Frankenheimer: Forty Years in Film* (1998) 18–21. Also consider the characterization of the D.A. in Micki Dickoff's television drama *In the Blink of an Eye* (1995), which paints a frightening portrait of the implications of a politicized judiciary and the concomitant perversion of the course of justice.
32 Roffman and Purdy, op. cit., n. 7, p. 297.
33 In American popular culture, *The Defenders* (CBS, 1961–5), a first-rate series about a father-and-son defence team, marks the very epitome of liberal legalism. See D.R. Papke, '*The Defenders*' in *Prime Time Law: Fictional Television as Legal Narrative*, eds. R.M. Jarvis and P.R. Joseph (1998) 3–20. A 'creative treatment of profound social issues' was also attributed to David E. Kelley's intriguing TV series *Picket Fences* (CBS, 1992–6). See D.E. Abrams, '*Picket Fences*' in *Prime Time Law*, id., p. 144.

the erosion of human rights or deplore the disintegration of morale.[34] In Paul Wendkos's *Presumed Guilty* (1991), a re-creation of a spectacular real-life incident, documentary techniques are combined with dramatic enhancement. A twenty-year-old named Bobby McLaughlin is mistaken for a killer and – after an unfair trial if not a scandalous judicial examination – faces a sentence of at least fifteen years in prison. The convict is thereafter nearly destroyed by a system that measures its effectiveness in terms of the severity of punishment instead of the conclusiveness of evidence. Only after a prolonged and bitter struggle to exonerate the protagonist from the capital crime the overzealous prosecutor has charged him with is the verdict quashed. The story-line of this television movie is symptomatic of the shortcomings of many a courtroom drama. A running time of 94 minutes hardly suffices to illustrate the judicial scrutiny from the preliminary hearing to the presentation of the evidence and – secondly – the appellate procedures in the aftermath of the sentencing.[35] Rather, the typical legal drama conveys the impression that the court of appeals does not matter that much; that remedies to individual predicaments are provided by outside agents instead of the legal profession or forces within the law; social issue topics can at best be touched on. *Presumed Guilty* exhibits a mere tinge of authenticity.[36] Prior to the last courtroom scene, which takes place in 1986, a short TV interview is incorporated into the ordinary chain of events that – in reality – led up to a sensational compensation for wrongful imprisonment, namely $1.93 million. The stylistic device of television reportage serves to highlight the involvement of the mass media, not to mention the significance of reflexivity.

In its last sequence, Michael Switzer's fact-based tele-drama *Cries from the Heart* (1994), also known as *Touch of Truth*, turns out to be a courtroom film. An autistic seven-year-old boy, who is unable to communicate verbally, is sexually abused by his male guardian at an establishment for the

---

34 *A Death in Canaan* (1978) by Tony Richardson concentrates closely on the denial of basic human rights: The police heinously coerce a highly suggestible adolescent into confessing to the act of slaying his mother, so that there is a striking discrepancy between the law as declared and as actually administered. In *Breaking the Silence* (1991) by Robert Iscove, a young man who has been physically and psychologically maltreated by his parents is charged with patricide. Iscove handles the social issue subject with great subtlety (the story is fictitious). In *Moment of Truth: Murder or Memory* (1994) by Christopher Leitch, a female therapist talks a teenager into believing that he committed a murder – without realizing that she hypnotizes him. There are numerous filmic examples of susceptible male youths or young adults involved in crimes, and the factual (human interest) stories dramatized by Richardson and Leitch attract attention to malfeasance in governmental institutions and the inaccessibility of objective reality respectively.

35 In McLaughlin's case, dating back to 1979, it took seven years until justice was to prevail over indifference, unfairness, and illegality.

36 *In the Blink of an Eye* appears to be its perfect fictional counterpart: on account of the practices of the district attorney's office, the wrong man is finally executed and an innocent woman is incarcerated for fifteen years to satisfy the public's need for revenge. See n. 31 above.

handicapped, where the child learns to communicate via the computer. Although the prosecution's case does not seem to be watertight – there is no positive evidence against the guardian – a criminal charge is brought against him. It is up to the jury to decide whether the child can be trusted completely. In cross-examination, the autistic boy suddenly blows his top. Since Switzer's film conveys an optimistic mood (the script leads the viewer not to suspect the boy's truthfulness), the jury gives the right verdict. While the courtroom scene in *Cries from the Heart* revolves around the efficiency of the machinery of law, a malfunctioning legal system is portrayed in Andy Wolk's *Criminal Justice* (1990), which emerges as an intense drama about a fictional case based on circumstantial evidence. An unemployed young black man is charged with robbery and assault. The proceedings that follow hardly cover questions of guilt or innocence; it is only a matter of time before the suspect agrees to enter a plea of guilty. As one critic puts it: 'In pursuit of the deal, the truth becomes irrelevant.'[37] Interestingly, there is absolutely no disclosure about the real perpetrator of the crime in this made-for-cable TV movie. Due to the overburdened big-city court system, cases are scarcely ever resolved in the presence of the jury. The director places much emphasis on verisimilitude and idiosyncratic detail (obviously not on the dreariness of legal minutiae); he thereby puts the suspect in a strange world in which there is no scope for a civil liberties perspective: 'The object in that world is not to dispense justice but to dispose of cases.'[38]

Supplementary courtroom scenes are indicative of problem films in the guise of legal dramas. An out-of-court settlement is presented in John Badham's theatrical film *Whose Life is it Anyway?* (1981), which was adapted from Brian Clark's stage play of the same name. An artist who becomes quadriplegic after an accident fights for the right to die – that is to say, for disconnection from life-support equipment. In a somewhat biased hearing – the matter is presented in a way that shows favour towards the standpoint of the paralytic – he is declared mentally competent. The legalization of physician-assisted suicide is still an issue of great contention in the western world,[39] which has only rarely been taken up by film-makers.[40]

---

37 'Criminal Justice' in *Variety*, 3 September 1990.
38 D. Margolick, 'This Courtroom Is a Long Way From "L.A. Law"' *New York Times*, 2 September 1990.
39 In 1997, Britain's Parliament rejected 'by 234 votes to 89 the seventh attempt in 60 years to change the law on assisted suicide despite polls showing 82 per cent of British people want reform'. D. Humphry, 'A Twentieth Century Chronology of Voluntary Euthanasia and Physician-assisted Suicide, 1906–2000' (1999) <http://www.finalexit.org/chronframe.html>.
40 A more sensational account of euthanasia is given in Steve Gethers's *Mercy or Murder?* (1987), a social issue docudrama about the case of *Roswell Gilbert v. Florida* (1985). Emily Gilbert is a 76-year-old victim of Alzheimer's disease and osteoporosis. When her husband cannot endure her pain any longer, he takes Emily's life. Roswell Gilbert awaits trial for murder. This TV movie aims at a realistic rendering of the prosaic quality of the legal process – though not of the courtroom

88

Likewise, there are hardly any serious American movies that deal with the credibility of rape victims in court in a non-ideological manner: public policy and the legal system do not provide for an intellectually, politically or morally enlightened approach to this subject in courts of justice and popular culture media alike. Lawrence M. Friedman notes that 'rape was always among the least-reported, least-prosecuted, and least-punished of the major crimes'.[41] *The Accused* (Jonathan Kaplan, 1988) is not just about legal neglect, namely the female Assistant D.A.'s vain attempt to bring the victim's assailants to trial for rape (she settles for a charge of reckless endangerment); it is about how society brands rape victims as blameworthy and about the iniquitous mentality that disregards violence against women which finally leads to the 'institutional oppression of the rape victim'.[42] Screenwriter Tom Topor states: '[R]ape is the only crime I can think of where the victim's word is not accepted.'[43] For the cinema audience, the verbal account of a male eyewitness is backed up with the enactment of brutal gang rape, while the victim's testimony lacks legal pertinence and narrative authority. In other words, the male witness embodies the sole 'agent of the truth'.[44] Drawing on Althusser,[45]

procedures themselves. The figure of the emotionless, unrepentant offender, the focal point of the drama, does not typify an easy object of identification. For obvious reasons, the jury does not know as much about Emily's suffering and her husband's state of mind as the viewer (the preliminary in-depth visual rendition of the past by far surpasses any present-time attempt to verbalize the circumstances surrounding the killing), but no effort is made to morally or legally exculpate the protagonist, who is found guilty of first-degree murder and sentenced to life in prison. For an overview of the ongoing discussion about mercy killing see S.P. Freedberg, 'Murder or mercy?' in *St. Petersburg Times*, 31 January 1999.

41 L.M. Friedman, *Crime and Punishment in American History* (1993) 217. See, also, S. Chermak, 'Crime in the News Media: A Refined Understanding of How Crimes Become News' in *Media, Process, and the Social Construction of Crime: Studies in Newsmaking Criminology*, ed. G. Barak (1994) 104–5. In their description of the film *Rape Culture* (1978), the editors of a listing of social issue films highlight the notion that 'rape is part of an accepted way of life'. See *Reel Change: A Guide to Social Issue Films*, ed. P. Peyton (1979) 84. Christina Hoff Sommers claims that there is no such thing as a 'patriarchal rape culture' and questions the assumption that rape is a manifestation of misogyny. In her controversial indictment of the 'feminist establishment', *Who Stole Feminism? How Women Have Betrayed Women* (1994), she challenges the idea that rape plays a role in maintaining patriarchy. She brands American society as extraordinarily violent, but doubts that violence is peculiarly misogynist (see pp. 222–3 and ch. 10).

42 M. Cook, 'Criticism or Complicity: The Question of the Treatment of Rape and Rape Victim in Jonathan Kaplan's *The Accused*' (1991) 24/25 *CineAction!* 80, at 82.

43 As quoted by P. Burne in 'The Accused' (March 1989) 72 *Cinema Papers* 53.

44 B. Nichols, 'Sons at the Brink of Manhood: Utopian Moments in Male Subjectivity' (1989) 4 *East West Film J.* 27, at 37. See, further, P. Fleck, 'The Silencing of Women in the Hollywood "Feminist" Film: *The Accused*' (1990) 9(3) *Post Script* 49, at 54–5; C. Clover, *Men, Women, and Chain Saws: Gender in the Modern Horror Film* (1993) 149–50; Cook, op. cit., n. 42, pp. 84–5.

45 L. Althusser, 'Idéologie et appareils idéologiques d'Etat' in *Positions 1964–1975* (1976).

89

Patrice Fleck even goes so far as to refer to *The Accused* as a covert vehicle of 'indoctrination to patriarchy'.[46] Fleck persuasively argues that the make-up of the movie itself hinges on the veiling of intentions, and it is very likely that those responsible for the realization of this movie – being captivated by patriarchal ideology – fell victim to their own ideological thinking.

Nuts (Martin Ritt, 1987), adapted by Tom Topor, Darryl Ponicsan, and Alvin Sargent from Topor's 1980 off-Broadway play, proves to be one of the more prominent examples of a theatrical courtroom drama which takes the form of a social issue film. As a result of outstanding direction and highly imaginative performances, it can be regarded as one of the most riveting fictional law movies American popular culture has so far brought about. It does not include any distinguishable trial sequence, since the court proceedings span almost all of the film. The composition of the courtroom scenes conforms to the particular requirements of the genre: a call-girl who killed a client in self-defence desperately fights to prove her sanity. She can count on a public defender who is intellectually and emotionally superior to the prosecuting attorney, and – what a surprise – the court finally declares her mentally fit to stand trial so that she can later be vindicated from the charge of homicide.[47] This movie looks behind the façade of bourgeois society that wants to get rid of people who do not adjust 'adequately'. *Nuts* not only denounces the judicial-psychiatric establishment, but formulates an indictment of middle-class complacency in so far as there is reason to believe that some people happen to turn a blind eye to parental sexual abuse, which has often been – at least in theatrical movies – neglected. In that hypocritical world, the rebels against indifferent society are committed to psychiatric institutions where they are put under sedation.[48] The proposition that the fairness of the process should also be available to *personae non gratae* seems to run counter to American ideologies. *Nuts* is indeed a social issue courtroom drama *par excellence*.

Judgment Day: The Ellie Nesler Story (1999), directed by Stephen Tolkin and starring Christine Lahti, is another trial movie in which the meticulous delineation of criminal justice themes (that is, the workings of the legal

46 Fleck, op. cit., n. 44, p. 49. According to the French Marxologist Louis Althusser, the arts and the law belong – amidst other institutional systems, rituals, and praxises – to Ideological State Apparatuses, in which prevalent ideologies manifest themselves. It is a trusim that even the Hollywood woman's film is not immune to the incursion of ideas that promulgate the interests of the dominant segment of society. See, also, n. 15 above.

47 Judge Stanley Murdoch, played by James Whitmore, has been aptly characterized as 'that rare movie justice, a man of Solomonic wisdom who belongs on the bench'. R. Kempley, 'Nuts' *Washington Post*, 20 November 1987.

48 For this stance on society and the law, some media commentators criticized the movie in such a way as to punch below the belt. See T. Milne, 'Nuts' *Monthly Film Bulletin*, February 1988. Compare J. Maslin, 'Nuts' *The New York Times*, 20 November 1987; J. Kozak, 'Nuts' *Boxoffice*, February 1988; A. Kohn, 'Therapy Gone Awry' (1988) 22 *Psychology Today* 64.

90

system) and the development of social issue motifs are contemporaneous. It tries to retell the true story of a woman who shoots her son's alleged molester in the courtroom and subsequently pleads not guilty by reason of insanity to a first-degree murder charge.[49] Short courtroom scenes, which are scattered all over the dramatic texture of the movie, are suitable devices to trigger off extensive flashbacks. Again, the meta-narrative quality and suggestiveness of visual evidence dominates. The director seems to hold the opinion that Nesler has no choice but to take the law into her own hands. Regrettably, the authorities are unable to make provisions for Nesler's seven-year-old son who cannot testify when he has to face his tormentor in court. What is typically American – not merely a popular-culture stereotype – is the public reaction to this case of 'vigilante justice'. There is a polarization between Nesler's supporters and the opponents of vengeance, but the sentiment expressed by the former group predominates. *Judgment Day* does not miss a chance to interpret the killing of the malefactor as an act of heroism: Nesler is cheered by the crowd, but does not escape the verdict of the jurors who decide that she was sane during the killing. She is found guilty of manslaughter and receives a ten-year prison sentence. That the legal plausibility of the conviction and the appropriateness of the penalty are not really questioned ultimately limits the persuasive power of this film.[50]

THE REPRESENTATION OF LAWLESSNESS IN DOCUDRAMAS

When it comes to dramatizing the problem of institutional corruption in the American judicial system and revealing functionaries' propensity for ideological reasoning, film-makers' efforts have sometimes been remarkably effective. Police lawlessness has been particularly pernicious in the United States of America.[51] Therefore, lawless conduct by law enforcement officers, or rather the disparity between judicial action and statutory law, has been a

49 *Judgment Day* is in some respects reminiscent of *While Justice Sleeps* (1994) – the director hides behind the pseudonym of Alan Smithee – in which an equivalent frame of reference is made use of: because of loopholes in the law, a molester cannot be prevented from terrorizing his victim by legal or non-violent means. However, this fictional telefilm comes close to the celebration of the revenge formula, especially since the psychic condition of the victim's mother, played by Farrah Fawcett, is not that credible (as distinct from *Judgment Day*).

50 Interestingly enough, the 1993 trial in Sonora (California) was in fact dubious – certainly more questionable than the action of the movie suggests. In 1997, Nesler was granted a retrial of the sanity hearing because of juror misconduct. See M. Yi, 'Mother in "vigilante" debate is released from prison, apologizes' *Seattle Times*, 2 October 1997.

51 Fuller, op. cit., n. 12, pp. 158–9; A.M. Dershowitz, *Reasonable Doubts: The O.J. Simpson Case and the Criminal Justice System* (1996) 55–6, 94–5 and throughout.

distinctive cinematic motif.[52] Among the latter-day 'criminaloids' on the screen are politically zealous district attorneys and members of the police force striving for personal power. Experts who may give opinions as evidence have also come in for severe criticism. Errol Morris's stylized non-fiction film, *The Thin Blue Line* (1988), is about Randall Dale Adams, who was falsely accused of shooting a police officer and convicted of the crime through perjured testimony, prosecutorial misconduct, and the quasi-negation of the rule of law. In the words of the director, the film 'doesn't chronicle a murder investigation after the fact – it is a murder investigation'.[53] The manner in which Morris laid bare the weaknesses of the criminal justice system and thereby examined the categories of legal judgement was unprecedented. In particular, the reliability of testimonial evidence and the legality of adjudication procedures were questioned; the arbitrariness of the employment of capital punishment was challenged.[54] The Randall Adams story need not be embellished for the sake of dramatic impact. *The Thin Blue Line* towers head and shoulders above many fictional 'law' films both in (formal) sophistication and (emotional) impact. As Nichols writes:

> Morris demonstrates that a documentary need not guarantee that a re-enactment present the official version of 'what really happened.' Instead, Morris shows how policemen and prosecutors, those accused and those accusing others, construct the past they need, burdening it with all the specificity of detail and motivational logic that customarily serves as a guarantor of judicial certainty.[55]

It is only in the last two decades that film-makers have increasingly turned to non-formulaic legal narratives.[56] One of them concerns the case of Vincent Simmons, a black man who was forced to represent himself and subsequently found guilty of two counts of aggravated rape. He was actually sentenced to

---

52 On the picture of policing in popular culture, see Crew, op. cit., n. 14; C. Crawford, 'Law Enforcement and Popular Movies: Hollywood as a Teaching Tool in the Classroom' (1999) 6(2) *J. of Crim. Justice and Popular Culture* 46.

53 As quoted by J.J. O'Connor in 'The Film That Challenged "Dr Death"' *New York Times*, 24 May 1989. Dallas psychiatrist James Grigson, the initial subject of Morris's film project, acquired international notoriety as 'Dr Death'. Law professor Richard K. Sherwin contends that *The Thin Blue Line* has become a 'cultural symbol'. See R.K. Sherwin, *When Law Goes Pop: The Vanishing Line between Law and Popular Culture* (2000) 109 and ch. 5.

54 See, generally, E. Martin, 'Towards an Evolving Debate on the Decency of Capital Punishment' (1997) 66 *George Washington Law Rev.* 84, at 124 (fn. 209).

55 B. Nichols, '"Getting to Know You ...": Knowledge, Power, and the Body' in *Theorizing Documentary*, ed. M. Renov (1993) 179–80.

56 In 1982, the political documentarian Emile de Antonio dramatized the trial of American peace activists known as the Ploughshares Eight, in which the real defendants portrayed themselves. For longer comments on the film, *In the King of Prussia*, and the re-enactment of the trial, see R. Lewis, 'Filming the Ploughshares Eight: The Perils of Peace Filmmaking' (1998) <http://www.unc.edu/sycamore/98.1/antonio.html>.

100 years in prison. A fairly subjective reality is captured in Jonathan Stack and Liz Garbus's feature documentary collaboration about Simmons and five other inmates of the Louisiana State Penitentiary at Angola, the largest maximum security prison in the United States. *The Farm: Angola, USA* (1998) shows how 45-year-old Simmons, after serving one-fifth of his sentence, pleads his innocence before a parole board, offering exculpatory evidence.[57] After thirty-five seconds (!) of deliberations, the three-man board turns down Simmons' appeal. This sequence, which lasts barely eight and a half minutes, but is one of the best remembered of the film, is partly taken up by a different quasi-documentary representation revolving around Simmons's plight and the victims' distress. In Jonathan Stack's *Shadows of Doubt: State vs. 85188* (1999), set in small town America, the action crystallizes around two opposing poles, but the director avoids the traditional formula of the good/evil conflict. To begin with, Stack focuses his attention primarily on the adversarial mode in the verbal reconstitution of antecedent 'truth'. He hardly uses flashbacks to authenticate the alleged crime, but relies on what a jury member, the district attorney, policemen, and others are able to recollect.[58] Unable to provide new evidence, the director is quite reticent about the putative crime, and the viewers cannot be sure whether the sisters who purport to be victims of rape accuse the wrong man. Whenever a short dramatic recreation is shown,[59] actors are absent. Point-of-view-shots emphasize the subjective quality of what is being recounted and constructed both verbally (off-camera) and pictorially. Thus, this documentary leaves much room for speculation.[60]

The Thin Blue Line and *Shadows of Doubt* are well-crafted films about the rigidity of the criminal justice system and about the impact of ideological

---

57 One of the twin sisters originally stated that she could not possibly identify the perpetrator because all black men looked alike to her. See, also, A.S. Lewis, 'The Farm' *The Austin Chronicle*, 9 November 1998.

58 Accordingly, *Shadows of Doubt* does not use the trial transcripts as the basis for its script. The 'courtroom sequence' comprises 87 shots with an average length of almost ten seconds. It begins with a close-up of a newspaper headline: 'Testimony Begins in Simmons Case'; Olivia Simmons Eggins's statement that she didn't go to the trial is heard as a voice-over. The location of the former trial is shown in shot 5 (the empty jury box), shot 7 (the defendant's table), shot 11 (the judge's bench and the witness box), shot 31 (the defendant's table), shot 45 (the judge's bench and the witness box), shot 81 (the empty jury seats; the Stars and Stripes in the background), and shot 87 (the empty jury box), which marks the end of this sequence. Here the off-screen jury comes into play.

59 Shots 15 to 18, shot 20, shot 24, shot 26, shot 28, shots 37 to 39, various flashbacks in shots 47 to 80.

60 Joe Berlinger and Bruce Sinofsky's *vérité* style non-fiction social issue film, *Paradise Lost: The Child Murders at Robin Hood Hills* (1996), which covers the trial of three teenagers accused of the brutal murder of three boys in rural America, was criticized for insincerity and obscuration. See C.J. Hogan, '*Paradise Lost*' *Cineaste*, December 1996; P. Arthur, 'Media Spectacle and the Tabloid Documentary' *Film Comment*, January/February 1998.

thought on American society. How can the courts guarantee due process whilst those engaged in trial procedures are thoroughly influenced by populist calls for capital punishment or racist overtones? It is stunning that eminently convincing pleas for a more humane legal culture have not yet succeeded in stripping legal bureaucracy of some of its reactionary proclivities. Suffice it to say that there are formidable non-American drama-documentaries concerning the functioning of legal institutions within the framework of social issues.[61]

CONCLUSION

The American (criminal) trial has been a superb source and setting for drama.[62] Ideally, under the adversary system 'each side tries to win by all legal and ethical means'.[63] The pursuit of truth, however, must be reconciled with the principles of lawfulness and fairness. Since courtroom films often dramatize a fictive conflict between the demands of legal reasoning and pushing through a morality that seems most opportune, movies hardly ever aim at an adequate assessment of the significance of probative facts. In the real courtroom, the reconstitution of truth is more problematic. Truth itself is too equivocal a concept; the notion of truth as being beyond absoluteness is hardly intelligible to the layperson.[64] Alan M. Dershowitz describes the multi-layered process:

> The truth is that most criminal defendants are, in fact, guilty. Prosecutors, therefore, generally have the *ultimate* truth on their side. But since prosecution witnesses often lie about some facts, defense attorneys frequently have *intermediate* truth on their side. Not surprisingly, both sides emphasize the kind of truth they have more of.[65]

Fictional movies are mostly concerned with the search for truth from a single perspective through an adversarial contest and – in a criminal justice context

---

61 Charles McDougall's *Inquest* (1996) is particularly impressive. On the Hillsborough Family Support Group's initiative, Jimmy McGovern wrote a script about the football stadium disaster occurring in 1989 and the dubious legal proceedings that followed. See P. Scraton, 'Policing with Contempt: The Degrading of Truth and Denial of Justice in the Aftermath of the Hillsborough Disaster' (1999) 26 *J. of Law and Society* 273.

62 See ch. 4 of M.S. Ball, *The Promise of American Law: A Theological, Humanistic View of Legal Process* (1981).

63 Dershowitz, op. cit., n. 51, p. 43.

64 Bennett and Feldman comment on legal objectivity: 'The judgments made in criminal trials can be regarded as objective only in the sense that they reflect the use of a uniform and agreed-upon set of legal procedures and judgment practices.' (op. cit., n. 5, p. 32.) In the American courtroom drama, the objectivity in legal judgment conveyed in the resolution of the trial usually contradicts the notion that there is no definitiveness of 'truth'.

65 Dershowitz, op. cit., n. 51, p. 35.

94

– the conviction of the real culprit, whereas dramatic recreations tend to focus on the manipulation of truth, on the subjectivity of legal storytelling, on institutional injustices and procedural inadequacies.[66] The ubiquity of the formulas employed in fictional forms of American popular culture has to do with the dualism of virtue and depravity, which is not confined to tales of crime and to the legal film:

> The good–evil morality called for a clear-cut, gratifying plot resolution – the Happy Ending, in which evil was destroyed and the good rewarded.[67]

In the Hollywood movie, there is ordinarily a world of difference between the hero and the villain, so that immoral (and illegal) means to achieve righteous ends may appear to be justified. To be sure, there are less blundering dramatic conventions and more sophisticated instances of character configurations. In *We the Jury*,[68] Kelly McGillis is Alyce Bell, a pious woman whose morals cannot be doubted, a devoted wife and mother who puts things right when other members of the jury are on the wrong track: When all is said and done, order is restored. The characterization of the central figure perfectly fits the (filmic) image of the ideal juror; the script borders on the affirmation of American legalist ideology, according to which, in the pursuit of truth, the jury cannot err.[69]

Fact-based social issue courtroom dramas, with a few exceptions, deal with the implementation of civil rights in the United States of America. Social issue documentaries frequently do without conventional lawyers' manoeuvres and do not depend on what has impudently been labelled 'courtroom histrionics'.[70] In *Shadows of Doubt*, for instance, the regular courtroom setting – the theatrical space in which the protagonist and the antagonist commonly confront one another – is virtually non-existent: viewers have to content themselves with a few glimpses of the vacant courtroom, which serves just as a legal icon, an authenticating background site, that is. The trial story nevertheless allows a dramatic aura to flourish, and contradictory accounts of the incident are clearly presented orally. Whenever moviemakers do not refrain from critiquing the machinery of justice in the United States – thereby primarily, though not necessarily, falling back on real cases – the resultant filmic depiction of law

---

66 In the latter case, truth often defies comprehension.
67 Roffman and Purdy, op. cit., n. 7, p. 5.
68 See n. 22 above.
69 See the essay of the editors of *Cahiers du cinéma*, 'John Ford's *Young Mr Lincoln*' in *Movies and Methods: An Anthology*, ed. B. Nichols (1976) 493, at 519. Because of the natural representativeness of the trial ('[I]t is America itself which constitutes the Jury', id.), there is a marked overlap between the jury room drama and the social issue courtroom drama.
70 J. Denvir, *Legal Reelism: Movies as Legal Texts* (1996) xiii. See also Bergman and Asimow, op. cit., n. 29, p. 225.

counterbalances the idealized notion of the judiciary (and the administration of justice) that has been pervasive in the American collective psyche. The repercussions of ideological thought identifiable in social institutions such as the legal system are striking, regardless of whether the cinematic construction of society, law and justice refers to singular imperfections – they might as well be representative of widespread phenomena.

96

JOURNAL OF LAW AND SOCIETY
VOLUME 28, NUMBER 1, MARCH 2001
ISSN: 0263-323X, pp. 97–116

Patterns of Courtroom Justice

JESSICA SILBEY*

Any one film can sustain a myriad of compelling intepretations. A collection of films, however, sharing formal and substantive qualities, reveals a common effect more than a diversity of meanings. This essay traces the shared formal and substantive qualities of a group of films, as I name them 'trial films'. It documents this genre of film by identifying the genre's norms of viewing and identification. It also investigates peculiar hybrid discourse of the trial film genre that combines both filmic and legal discursive practices to show how trial films cultivate support for the American system of law through its constitution of a specific viewing audience. In so doing, I broach the following questions: how do images of law in film help sustain the power and legitimacy of legal institutions? How does the study of film genres, like the courtroom drama, reveal the way law lives beyond its formal processes?

I. THE GENRE AND ITS VIEWER-SUBJECT

What will follow in this essay will be the identification of the 'trial film' genre. Specifically, I look at the space of the courthouse and courtroom and how, in film, they signify legal processes and law's promise of justice. In practice, the trial is a ritualistic aspect of the law that is often overlooked (and, in fact, a stage in the litigation process that is rarely reached) but that is crucial to the law's binding of its practice with its ideals in culture. I would dare to say that the trial, for many people, is the symbol of law in action. How, then, does it garner meaning in these films?

My answer is two-fold. First, trial films, as a group, contain identifiable patterns of narrative structure, cinematic features, and character development that manifest assumptions, embolden expectations, and reproduce ideological notions of legality. These patterns – marks of a genre – induce specific expectations of law in the films' community of viewers,

* *Law Clerk to Hon. Levin Campbell, US Court of Appeals for First Circuit; (from August 2001) Associate in Litigation, Foley, Hoag and Eliot LLP, Boston, Massachusetts, United States of America.*

expectations of their own subjective and authoritative role in making meaning and meting out justice within the American legal system. Second, in order for these patterns to be influential (as I argue that trial films are in the production of popular legal consciousness), as embodied by the trial film genre, these patterns constitute and encourage the identification of a specific kind of film viewer, what I call the trial film's viewer-subject. This viewer-subject is one end-effect of the trial film genre: an experience through which the spectator (inscribed by the filmic text) interacts with the social viewer (audience member) and is asked to assume certain positions within and by the film in order to make sense of it. This viewer-subject is one way trial films help sustain the power and legitimacy of legal institutions.

The trial film's viewer-subject mirrors the concept of the liberal legal subject (the subject of legal liberalism) and his central role in the pursuit of justice.[1] In a three-stage process, the trial film encourages its viewer-subject both to believe in his crucial contribution to the law's success and to critique the law's all-encompassing constitutive capabilities. Normally (that is, generically), this critical position is incorporated into the film's story of law and results in an affirmation of both law's capacity to include those who dissent from it and film's capacity to incorporate its viewers in its worldmaking. The trial film deliberately choreographs the viewer-subject's participation in and critique of law to produce and sustain the ideology of liberal legalism: an understanding that law's recursive structure sustains its authority and power, but also an insistence on the possibility of (as the liberal legal subject claims to embody an example of) individual resistance and agency despite law's engulfing presence. In other words, the viewer-subject of trial films, as constituted by the discursive strategies of film and law, is encouraged to expect justice through law by virtue of his unique contribution to the system (the filmic system of meaning and the legal system of justice), and yet also to insist that justice reside apart from the law's institutionalized processes.

II. THE VIEWER-SUBJECT'S JOURNEY TOWARD JUSTICE

1. Step one: framing patterns, static symbols, and establishing shots

Most initially striking among trial films are the consistent establishing shots setting the scene in the house of law. Much of the time, these shots are at the beginning and end of the film, like a frame, the law as the skeleton that structures the story.[2] Other times, these shots are only in the film as the trial

---

1 I deliberately use the masculine pronoun here. One of my arguments, made elsewhere, is that the dominant viewer-subject of the trial film is male, that is, the liberal legal subject as constituted by trial films is gendered masculine. J. Silbey, 'The Subjects of Trial Films' (PhD., University of Michigan, 1999) ch. 5.

2 See, for example, the discussion of *And Justice for All* (Norman Jewison, 1979) that follows.

98

process is introduced – after the discovery of the crime, or upon introduction of the attorney, judge, jury member or witness who is to be central to the law's functioning in this case.[3] In either instance, usually an initial shot sequence pastes together a complex experience of what will be the legal experience – grand and opulent, pregnant with promise, disorienting and mysterious, somewhat ominous and potentially threatening. The result of this initiation into the legal system that will, from then on, structure and flavour the film's story, is a double relation to the law: on the one hand detached and alienated and on the other hand involved and invested. In both relations, however, the viewer-subject is led, as if by hand, through the corridors and doors of the courthouse making the law – however distant, noble or flawed – the context in which the conflicts of the film must be resolved. The space of the courthouse seems inevitable, and in this way, the viewer-subject is made to urge a resolution of this double relation in the terms given to him: by his own occupation of the legal process and toward the law's overdetermined goals of order and justice.

The baptism most often begins with either shots from outside the courthouse looking up at the glare and height of its cupola or head-on shots of a statue, monument or engraving outside the building; it inevitably includes a wide-angle shot of the front steps and tall pillars of the courthouse, the viewer-subject placed at the edge of government property about to touch down on government soil. The statues might be lady liberty, as in *Inherit the Wind*,[4] or a shot of the monument commemorating the battle of Iwo Jima, as in *A Few Good Men*.[5] The monuments and statues salute the purpose of the building they introduce; they seem to say that the nation's rule of law that provides our freedom is worth the fights of the past. This, in turn, implies that the fight that will follow is also worth the freedom it ostensibly will enable. The fight for freedom means little, however, if there are no visible individuals in whose name the fight goes on. For this reason, the absence of people in these establishing shots is, at first, ominous. It is not difficult, however, to fill the absence with our own desire to infuse these monuments with the freedom and justice they promise. The empty stairs and the tall pillars facing us directly are, thus, like a newly-laid carpet beckoning the viewer-subject into the house on the hill. When, soon after, the steps inevitably teem with crowds, the ominousness has faded and the goodwill sustained by the liveliness and energy surrounding these monuments has taken its place. The diminutive size of the people on the exaggerated steps of courthouse is both comforting, as the strength of the building and its enduring quality protects us as we hover, and daunting, as we recognize our potential insignificance among the crowds standing in the building's shadows.

3 See, for example, *Adam's Rib* (George Cukor, 1949).
4 *Inherit the Wind* (Stanley Kramer, 1960).
5 *A Few Good Men* (Robert Reiner, 1992).

This sequence highlights the differences between the inanimateness and permanence of stone, and the lively, however temporary, presence of individuals. It also points to the mutual dependence of such opposites – the stone walls are made significant by the individuals who are housed by them, as the individuals are made immortal by the stone that is carved in their name. The law is somewhere in the middle here, in the binding relation – both animate and inanimate – as it is both the house on the hill and the people that built it there. There is a grandeur about these sequences, a triumphant tone that always comes with gleaming gold, blue skies and the bustle of people busy with life's work. It suggests that law's entrance should be followed by a fanfare as something to be revered and appreciated. If such a sequence were to be shot in dreary conditions – aberrant weather over dilapidated buildings – the grandeur of the structure would remain, only it might be tainted, hinting at corruption, foreshadowing a fall. The expectation of opulence and great-heartedness remains, however, only in its disappointed form. In either instance, the experience of this initial shot sequence of the courthouse is the beginning of a relation between the glory and pride that attaches to an unfaltering legal system and the individuals who call to it in challenge and need.

Like a dose of reality, once inside the glorified house of law, the camera's object and its stalwart gaze often change rapidly. The steps continue inside, but instead of being covered by a welcoming carpet, they are dizzying as the camera hangs from the cupola suggesting that here the law is untouchable and precarious. Made to look up at the height of the dome, the viewer-subject cannot help but compare it to the steeples and rotundas of churches and cathedrals as it reaches for the sky and is coloured like the heavens in blue and gold. Less significant and less stable than before, the viewer-subject nevertheless considers law as a faith, as other-worldly and as indispensable to our organization of social life. When we are brought further into the inner domain of the courthouse, twisting stairs and corridors project a sense of claustrophobia with their shadows and dead ends; labyrinthine hallways are either ghostly empty or they are too crowded, with no room to move. Either way, the necessity of faith has strengthened as trepidation and confusion encroaches. The viewer-subject, initially in awe of the monument to law and grateful for its enduring promise, grows concerned about his original naïvety. Within these walls, a balance must be achieved that is not inherent in their structure. Invested in the law's foundation, and already infused with expectations that past successes will carry into the future, the viewer-subject is caught in the middle of its contradictions, between the concrete force of law's daily life and its goal of lasting justice.

The establishing-shot sequence ends in a courtroom combining the experience of our initiation with the inner sanctum of the house of law. It is both reminiscent of the courthouse hallways – disordered and confusing in the diversity of individuals who populate the room and whose chatter is unintelligible to us – and of its front entrance, grandiose and belittling in its wooden panelling, symmetrical galleries, raised judge's bench and haloed windows. The usual symmetry with which we are introduced into the courtroom, however – from behind the gallery, down the centre aisle, focusing on the judge's bench and the United States flag adjacent – cures some of the residual anxiety from outside the room. This is where little battles are fought in the name of the bigger ones, and here, it looks as if order reigns and we have a place within it. Often the judge is introduced just after our entrance, or sometimes the judge sits awaiting our arrival, banging the gavel shortly thereafter, as if court could not begin until we got there. In harmony with the judge's timing, we feel that this is where the film begins – our introduction to the courthouse aside – with the individual case before an individual judge calling the court to order.

In the shot sequence of these images lie competing feelings of order and disorder, vertigo and claustrophobia, reverence and alienation, humanity and immortality, realism and idealism, defeat and triumph. The constant juxtapositioning of these images challenges the viewer-subject of the film to make sense of their dichotomous relationships. Entirely engulfed by the law's monument in stone, marble, gilt, and wainscoting, we must make sense of these contradictions within the space provided. Our expectations have been established by this entrance; we are awake to the possibility of fault and corruption while we remain wary, however hopeful, of the impact of a specific verdict on our faith in the law's ability to achieve an enduring order and justice. Our entrance cued the battle cry. And it is in the courtroom, we expect, the truth of law's potential will be revealed. Common to all the films I have studied, with some minor deviations, these shots map the viewer-subject's initiation into the house of law and set out the ensuing fight that will judge law and the persons who are brought before it. As a part of the trial film genre, these scenes, repeated over and over, form part of a cultural consciousness – a common spatio-temporal experience – that, with each repetition, represent a feeling and reaffirm a claim to law's relation to justice in terms of that individual journey before the law for the viewing audience who belongs to this particular cultural co-ordinate.

(a) *And Justice For All*
The opening montage sequence of *And Justice For All*[6] begins with the juxtaposition of the wide sunny steps of the courthouse building and its narrow dark halls in the entry way. The hallways are made of marble, lit by antique sconces; the hallways are vacant and shiny. Inside, the camera focuses on a series of informational signs that mark the judge chambers as well as rules of courtroom decorum and schedules. Other signs direct the process for legal complaints, body searches, and security measures. Some signs are permanent, painted on doors, written on plaques; others seem fleeting, hand-written on blackboards and scraps of paper. Indication of

6 *And Justice For All* (Norman Jewison, 1978).

101

activity is everywhere, as the signs are supposed to organize that activity, but the building is empty. The initial glory of the sunny courthouse and the marble hallways gives way to the mundaneness of signs prohibiting gum-chewing in the courtroom. The scene ends with a chorus of school children fumbling over the pledge of allegiance, their last phrase 'and justice for all' to the beat of distinctly 1970s music, and the camera focusing on a painting above the judge's bench depicting Jesus addressing angels at his resurrection. The children suggest the promise of the future, but their garbled pledge threatens a naïvety; the painting screams of sacrifice and redemption, but also threatens the lives of those that come before the judge in court.

Placed in the context of the characters of this film about a Baltimore public defender, Arthur Kirkland (played by Al Pacino), who sees himself as a little man fighting for other little men against what he experiences as a corrupt justice system, this opening montage is a sarcastic indicator of an American ideology: surrounded by all the signs of justice – some glorious, some mundane – the promise of law is at worse superficial and at best idealistic, nearly impossible to experience or achieve. Like many religions, this quest for justice is about rules and redemption, sacrifice and resisting revenge. So in the beginning, while Arthur Kirkland believes deeply in the promise of law, he also realizes that sometimes law's rules need to be broken to achieve that promise of justice. This is a paradox he is willing to live with, that he actually lives to maintain – like the dichotomous senses of our initial entrance into the courthouse – until too many people are needlessly harmed at the hands of the internally flawed system. Without the glimmering possibility of their redemption, Arthur, no longer able to make sense of the contradictions, seeks revenge. He does so by challenging the very foundation of the system the film set up from the beginning – the courtroom as a majestic and orderly place, however filled with ordinary people full of faults – and calls into question the futility of his role, the intention of law, and throws the court into chaos.

This chaos is preordained from the beginning of the film. After the opening montage, we return again to the courthouse, this time on the shoulder of Arthur Kirkland as he leaps the stairs of the building two at a time, weaves in and out of the crowded hallways, and eventually lands in court, before the suicidal Judge Rayford (played by Jack Warden), where Kirkland will successfully plead for a continuance for his client accused of forging lottery tickets. His agility and liveliness is in direct contrast to our introductory glimpse of him, not a minute before, slumped against the wall of a crowded, filthy jail cell where he spent the night for contempt of court. He is our hero, the man who, while part of the law, having internalized its procedure and its ideals, nevertheless fights like a solitary crusader with the legal contradictions that too often resolve themselves in favour of the system and not its subjects. As Arthur identifies with his clients, the viewer-subject is made to identify with him, following him to his ultimate test: whether or

© Blackwell Publishers Ltd 2001

not to defend a judge who is guilty of rape and who is remorseless. Caught between his defender sensibilities that recognize the honesty that defending the guilty infuses into the justice system and his awareness that this powerful judge has taken advantage of those defender sensibilities for his own loathsome gain, Arthur Kirkland must decide whether to adhere to a central legal tenet that everyone, even an admitted rapist, is entitled to a fair trial, or to throw the trial and with it his legal career.

The establishing shot of the film set up this conflict between the glamour of the courthouse façade, the workaday atmosphere of its inside, and the insinuation of mythical (and potentially mistaken) sacrifice at its finale. The ending shot concludes this conflict: we see Arthur Kirkland close-up sitting dazed at the top of the courthouse steps, under the pillars, squinting in the sunlight, having just been carried out of court by the bailiffs because he purged himself of his client's guilt in open court before the jury. The scene is triumphant – in the sun, at the top of the stairs; we are proud of Kirkland's courage despite the mistrial he just caused, and we feel relieved that everyone, not only counsel, knows the truth of the judge's guilt. We also recognize that he is still (as are we) within the stronghold of the law, for good or for bad; despite the centrality of Kirkland (in this last shot and throughout the film) and despite our satisfied sense of vengeance made possible by his heroic *coup de grâce*, the kind of momentary chaos and vigilante justice Arthur inspired is nevertheless recovered into the possibility of an ordered justice as attorneys and clients climb the stairs for another day at the courthouse.

(b) *Class Action*

Class Action[7] begins with a panorama of the San Francisco skyline, the morning sleepy rush-hour and a montage of monuments in the city parks, and a shot of a courthouse cupola and the United States flag blowing in the wind. We enter the courthouse, up the steps and under its dome. Shot from above, the cupola is imposing and the camera is wobbly indicating a sense of unrest to come. Echoing through the halls, we hear the murmur of arguments over a syncopated pounding of gavels. Through the fracas we hear clichéd phrases oozing from the courtrooms, clichés otherwise envisioned from the outset: 'justice is blind not deaf', 'appeals to emotion have no place in the courtroom of law', 'the court of justice, like Alice and Wonderland, is filled with non-sequiturs; it makes no sense, until we give it sense'. All of these clichés imply the inevitability of that individual voice that will infuse the empty halls and towering heights with meaning; they also imply the prerequisite, that before such an infusion, these monuments to law and national pride are barely significant as they stand alone.

Grandiose and clichéd from the beginning, this film goes on to narrate the eternal rivalry of justice (that individual voice) with the rule of law (the

---

7 *Class Action* (Michael Apted, 1991).

constellation of monuments) through the conflicted relationship of two attorneys – an overbearing, adulterous father who works as a civil-rights attorney, and his self-righteous and bitter daughter who works for a rival corporate law firm. The film traces the work on one case by father and daughter, each researching for opposing sides an automobile company that is being sued for knowingly profiting from deadly malfunctioning cars. At the core of the case, and the film, is the schism between head and heart, professional and personal, law and justice that drives apart daughter and father. We watch as the daughter (played by Mary Elizabeth Mastrantonio), desperate for a place 'where [her father] can't make the rules', fights her father (played by Gene Hackman) and his every move in and out of court – a place where she thinks the rules make the game even. We watch as she has the authority of legal precedent behind her, as she uses it to take revenge for her father's adultery and as she rests on the brink of legal victory, until she realizes that justice lies on the other side.

Her mother's overdetermined sacrificial death by heart attack on the glorious courthouse steps awakens her daughter to the fact that law does not make a game fair, it must be made fair by the players. So when she serendipitously learns that her firm has knowingly conspired to cover-up their client's legal liability, she vows to right the scales of justice with the legal upper hand she has been dealt. In this way, she not only mirrors the tension from the establishing shot of the film, but settles it in favour of that individual voice. Despite the legal precedent, and despite her oath as an attorney to represent her client to the best of her ability, the daughter colludes with the father, the opposing counsel, in exposing her client as the fatally reckless corporation it was accused of being. Her firm is humbled by the loss, but not out of business; and she remains a lawyer, although not in the corporate firm. Thus, the game of law continues to be played, according to the rules that remain always already in place, by a self-righteous individual who believes in the power of his or her voice to alter the game for the better, if only for a moment.

(c) *Twelve Angry Men*

Twelve Angry Men[8] begins with an upward scan of the courthouse façade which widens as it climbs, overwhelming the screen. Inside the courthouse, the camera hangs from the ceiling, first dwarfing the inhabitants it shelters, and then slowly demonizing them as it draws closer – too close – to return them to a human size. Then we are inside the courtroom; it is miniature compared to the atrium outside. A fishbowl close-up of the judge's gavel and his hand as it fiddles with a pencil suggests a bored, depleted man who is nevertheless supposed to stand for law's wisdom. With a sigh, the judge monotonously intones the criminal burden of proof and discharges the responsibility of its application to the jury of twelve men before him.

8 *Twelve Angry Men* (Sidney Lumet, 1957).

Humanity is grossly mundane here, made especially so in contrast to the courthouse's exaggerated granite and cathedral heights. With a last scan of an already exhausted jury, the camera fades from a pitifully drawn, young face of the defendant charged with a capital crime to the jury deliberating room, which, unlike the opening shot of the courthouse, is claustrophobic and sweltering; mounted fans don't work and the doors are shut, apparently locked from the outside. The jury is slated as either prisoners or animals. Either way, their contribution to law, like the judge's, cannot be inspiring. Posed with this monstrous picture of law's house inhabited by pathetic members, the opening of this film suggests nothing but the emptiness and defeat of justice. There is no hint of law's promise here, except in its absence.

The end of the film, however, is a complete reversal of this opening sequence. Positioned from the stifling and dark coat closet, the camera follows each juror out the door of the deliberating room, pans to the table filled with paper and dirty ashtrays – indication of a busy life and passing time – and fades into a shot of the front of the courthouse looking down from under the immense pillars. The camera then zooms slowly to focus on Henry Fonda's character, a juror, who stands below – humanized this time, not demonized, by the camera's proportional treatment. On the steps of the courthouse, Henry Fonda's character exchanges names with a fellow juror (played by John Fielder) for the first time. Both, then, walk away and down the steps into the waning light of day. The camera remains on the steps, focusing the viewer-subject on the centre screen in between the columns hanging like a chandelier looking out at the day and re-establishing the house of law as enlightened and inviting.

This ending is a summation of the events of the film that chronicles the day of a jury deliberation in which one man (played by Henry Fonda) convinces eleven others to change their 'guilty' vote to 'not-guilty' based on a new (and according to the film, better) understanding of the rule of law and its ideal of equal justice for each individual. Set up originally as a system of disinterested people and disorganized parts, law is (re)made by a group of twelve men by virtue of their argument, the conflict between individual and group desires, and the clarification that results. This film initially questions the jury system by portraying a tyrannical majority as the decision-making body, an imbalance between group dynamics (the imposing structure) and the individual voices (the dwarfed shots of people inside the structure, parts without the whole). That we never know people by name in this film accentuates this imbalance; law is an impediment to the ability to stand as an individual among many with the same rights and allowances, to be known by name without prejudice or malice and without foregoing impartiality. At the end, however, the balance between house and member is repaired; through the trial process, the film restores the activity and the ability to know each other by name and as citizens of the same house, and the viewer-subject is made to live comfortably beneath its columns.

105

These framing patterns – particularly the opening shot sequences of the films – form part of the filmic codes through which the expectations of law and justice are established and fulfilled (and sometimes broken) during the viewing experience. These expectations are integral to the relationship between the viewer-subject and the film that is enabled by the trial film genre as it develops throughout the one film and across many others similarly coded. In these beginnings, the viewer-subject is positioned ambivalently, wary of the edifice that towers before and above him, as well as hoping for its shelter as a haven of order and righteousness. In the end, that ambivalence has lessened as the viewer-subject has been made to identify with the film's marginal legal subject who nevertheless triumphs at the heart of law's ritual process, thus recapturing the gloriousness of the opening and keeping at bay its gnawing anxiety. The trial process becomes a metaphor not only of the justice that law can enact, but of the struggle through which a determined individual must journey in order to participate in that justice he has learned to demand from the law. These framing patterns are only the skeleton of the trial film experience, however – the outline of the film's story – that will fill out and grow complex from the subsequent transitions and developments in the film's narrative and form.

2. Step two: position, relation, and perspective

If the above framing patterns were all that was remembered of the trial film, the journey to justice would be the development from legal edifice to legal hero – a story of the individual who triumphs over the inanimacy of legal monuments and infuses them with the promise of individual determinism and freedom for which they were arguably erected to praise. This is a crude summary of the experience of the trial film, however. Once inside the courthouse and drenched with the details of the particular conflict whose resolution the legal process promises, these framing patterns are revealed as merely the stage on which more complex and subtle relationships with the law are played. These relationships within law's theatre are constant throughout the genre; just as there are limited opening and closing shots for the trial film, so there are limited predetermined relationships that are made by the camera between the viewer-subject and the legal process that unfolds during the film.

Most of these relationships are positions and roles that blossom in the courtroom and are constituted through the trial process in the form of persistent camera movement and technique that hones and manipulates the viewer-subject's understanding of the merits of the case at hand. For example, inevitably, the camera positions the viewer-subject as an actor in the courtroom – in the jury box, on the witness stand, behind the judge's bench, over the shoulder of the trial attorney – and often in a position which, at that moment, is potent with critical decision-making duties. The viewer-subject is in the jury box when counsel makes closing remarks, for example, or he is on the witness stand when counsel asks questions that are crucial for

106

the revelation of the truth of the case. In this way, the trial's promise as a cohesive and satisfying process lies in the confluence of these positions as inhabited by the viewer-subject.[9]

The camera will also cue the revelation of clandestine relations between characters in the film, relations, which once outed by the trial process, enable a just conclusion. By framing the film's characters in a single head shot, for example, and then cutting swiftly from one character to another, the camera discloses the psychic relationship between the thoughts, lives, and situations of the highlighted persons within the courtroom, encouraging the viewer-subject to declare the pertinent connections relevant for the trial at hand. This kind of relational composition is common in many films as a form of suturing device,[10] but in trial films they are the imperative contrast to the initially inhuman shots of monuments, façades, stairs, flags, empty hallways and courtrooms. Now, filled with faces – often close-ups of emotional expressions and gestures – the house of law is imbued with the significance of individual human lives as represented by the uncovered relationships between people in a court of law.

Finally, the camera also acts as a perspective lens, zooming and reverse-zooming, panning and rotating, providing a sense of coherence and omniscience within the courtroom, that is, able to see the situation from many angles and with a multi-faceted perspective of time and space. The camera takes on the representation of the ideal of justice – for example, providing distance for objectivity, close-ups for intimacy and emotion, zoom shots for pointed commentary – in order to evaluate the case from all possible positions and to put the problem in a reasonable situational context. In its more technical manoeuvres, the film camera is not mimicking the human eye but accomplishing those perspectives only capable of a machine that hangs from a ceiling or can pivot through 360 degrees. In this way, the ideal of justice as a form of perspective is only imaginable as a combination of the human with his technological or institutional supplements. Law's promise is thus imagined not only as a disclosure of the viewer-subject's privileged knowledge based on the camera's reinforcing and revealing connections in the courtroom, but also as incorporating the ideal of a superstructure, a justice system powered by a community of individuals and their institutional by-products of rules, roles, stages, and props.

As an example, take *The Verdict*.[11] At the climax – the trial toward which all of the film's energy has been directed – the camera hangs back from the

---

9 M. Ball, 'The Play's the Thing: An Unscientific Reflection on Courts Under the Rubric of Theater' (1981) 28 *Stanford Law Rev.* 104.

10 Suture as a concept originated in psychoanalytic theory with Lacan's student Jacques-Alain Miller. It was incorporated by film theorists, initially by Jean-Pierre Oudart, to describe the production of the subject through film, particularly in terms of the subject as produced by the exchange of gazes through the filmic discursive practices. See J.-P. Oudart, 'Cinema and Suture' (1978) 4 *Screen 18* 35–47.

11 *The Verdict* (Sidney Lumet, 1982).

activity in the courthouse, easily losing sight of and focus on the central character of the film, Francis Galvin (played by Paul Newman). He fades into the woodwork behind the plaintiff's table, is lost around the labyrinthine corridors of the courthouse, is blocked by the balconies and the columns inside the building. He is the underdog in this case of medical malpractice, an alcoholic plaintiff's attorney who has seemingly during the course of the film tragically bungled what would have been his first winnable case in over three years. The lack of the camera's focus on Galvin suggests his own weakness and his ambivalence toward the legal system which we learn has cost him his job and his integrity due to corrupt colleagues from years past. He has become a pawn of the system, a stereotype of an ambulance-chaser, and as such, his figure and his lifestyle are completely dominated – taken over – by the structure of the courthouse.

The trial drags on for several days and straddles a weekend. With each witness, Galvin's case grows weaker and the anticipation of the trial's outcome bodes only tragedy. During the examination of these witnesses, the viewer-subject is made to simultaneously participate in and judge the trial's progress by being placed in critical roles and by cueing key relationships between the characters. Galvin's expert witness, for example, has been bought off by the defence to flee the jurisdiction and Galvin is instead stuck with an incredible general practitioner to counter the reputations of the world-renowned obstetricians who sit accused of malpractice. During the expert testimony, the judge, already angered by Galvin's poor performance, takes it upon himself to question the witness, a permissible if uncommon practice. During this exchange, the camera films the two men – the expert witness and the judge – in contrast. From the judge's bench, the camera teeters over the edge, looking down in a canted shot of the doctor, reinforcing his incredible testimony. From the witness stand, the camera looks up at the judge who peers over the side of his bench and who fills the screen as he fires harsh criticism down toward the witness and at his weak testimony. The close-up shots and the relational editing in this exchange neatly demonize both characters who both turn out to equally damage Galvin's sympathetic, however losing case. The viewer-subject is made uncomfortable in the position of witness and judge, unable to empathize with either character in this scene; in this alienating exchange, one strongly feels that the role of judge or expert will frustrate the legal system's hortatory goal.

In contrast, during the testimony of plaintiff's surprise rebuttal witness, Kaitlin Costello Price, the camera does not film her testimony from the judge's bench as if to criticize, but from the plaintiff's desk and the jury box as if in compassion and support. When Ms. Price gives her startling testimony – direct evidence of the obstetricians' malpractice – she is filmed close-up and straight on. The camera does not belittle her by filming her from above, nor does it aggrandize her from below. And despite the fact that the defence attorney, in all attempts to discredit her testimony, looms above

108

her as she sits in the witness stand, the camera sides with Ms. Price, sitting on her shoulder as if in support and comfort. It is during this testimony when Galvin finally stands out in court. He does not look confident, however, but slumps behind plaintiff's desk biting his nails. Nevertheless, he figures centrally in this cross-examination of his own witness. The film sutures his expressions in between shots of Ms. Price as she testifies, of the judge as he sits back surprised at the serendipitous turn of events, and of the defence attorney Concannon as he fumbles about trying to positively spin her testimony in favour of his clients. The camera's movement between Galvin and Concannon, the judge and Ms. Price situates the dramatic tension in the credibility and control of Ms. Price's damning testimony. How will the jury judge this testimony?

The answer seems foregone after the judge instructs the jury to disregard Ms. Price's entire testimony for various dubious technical evidentiary reasons. During the judge's instruction, the camera films him centred and from below as he addresses the jury. The camera puts the viewer-subject in that jury box to absorb the admonition of the judge as he admits to his own mistake in allowing such testimony to go on. Despite the centrality of the judge in the shot, however, he looks puny behind the bench, as its heavy wooden moulding forms a cage around him and the bench's corner seems to cut sharply into his body. In contrast, the jury, in whose position the viewer-subject is put, has ample space in front of the bench, comparatively free to decide for themselves how Kaitlin Price's testimony will bear on the verdict, the decision being ultimately in their hands. In this exchange of shots, the judge has lost the prestige and authority that came from his raised position, and the jury has filled out the space that Galvin finally managed to provide for them as the remaining arbiters of justice.

During Galvin's summation, the film rehearses his initial sense of loss and ambivalence with regard to the legal system and its dominating presence. His speech later transforms, however, into a representation of a transferral of power, enacted in the previous scene between Kaitlin, the judge, and the jury, between the institutional rules and the individual people in whose name those rules are supposed to function.

When the judge calls Galvin for his summation, Galvin does not stir. It is easy to miss Galvin in the static camera shot, a shot which looks like a painting because it lasts so long with virtually no movement. Then, however, Galvin rises, as if from a crowd of people; he was there all along only unresponsive, invisible. Called to a final battle, at first he only stands, looking straight ahead. He is not looking at the camera, and the camera keeps an awkward distance from him – filming from the jury box in a far left corner – paralleling Galvin's losing battle in the loss of perspective the camera's distance creates. His words mirror the experience of his image on screen. 'So much of the time we're just lost', he says as he stares straight ahead:

We say, Please God, tell us what is right, what is true. When there is no justice, the rich win and the poor are powerless. We become tired of hearing people lie. We think of ourselves as victims. We become victims, we become weak, we doubt ourselves, we doubt our beliefs, we doubt our institutions. We doubt the law.

This slow and soft diatribe rehearses the story of Galvin's descent from his own glory as a young, successful attorney to the despair of disbarment at the hands of unethical colleagues. It also puts the power of a resurrection from those depths into the hands of the jury. He is sympathizing with them, declaring his similarity to them. He is saying that we have all felt the anger and insecurity that arises from the misdeeds of those whose duty it is to protect us – doctors, attorneys, judges, police.

The camera remains unresponsive to Galvin's plea until the last phrase, 'We doubt the law'. On its repetition, 'We doubt the law', the camera moves slowly and steadily toward Galvin as he turns to face the jury. The camera draws closer to him, drawing a straight line between him and the jury box, appealing to the comparison between this plaintiff's attorney, his case of malpractice and the jury's identity as ordinary citizens before the law. 'We doubt the law', he says to them again 'but today you are the law. You are the law.' Galvin reaches the jury box, laying his hands on their bench, the camera allowing his approach, itself drawing nearer, nearly over the shoulder of the jurors, down their necks. He continues:

[Today the law is] not some book, not a lawyer, not a marble statue or the trappings of the court. Those are just symbols of our desire to be just. They are in fact a prayer, a fervent and frightened prayer.

The camera draws so close to Galvin that for the first time in the trial we see into his eyes, we see the wrinkles beside his mouth and along his cheeks. Galvin fills the screen on that last word 'prayer' and looks at the jury, the camera sitting close to the railing of the jury box. He has just described the experience of the film – full of monuments to justice and God, atriums, marble corridors and columns and yet devoid of even a glimmer of hope for those who pray for guidance and shelter, like the plaintiffs in this case at bar. When Galvin finishes, saying, 'In my religion, they say "Act as if ye have faith, and faith will be given to you". If we are to have faith in justice, we need only to believe in ourselves and act as if there is justice', the camera rests on his face and then follows him back, as he drags himself to his chair, exhausted.

In his final speech, Galvin exposes his vulnerability and his ideals, giving all he can to this case which, despite the merits, was doomed by a corrupt defence attorney, a manipulative judge and a washed-up plaintiff's lawyer. Yet the camera does not minimize Galvin's presence behind the chair as it had done previously. Nor does it leave the position of the jury from atop the railing on the jury box. Galvin's message – of jury nullification, recovered strength, and the power of the common person – continues to resonate with

110

the final decision-makers in the trial as the camera holds back, standing beside the jury instead of following Galvin as he returns to his place at the plaintiff's bench. It continues to resonate as the scene fades out, superimposing onto the images of Galvin and his co-counsel a line of jurors entering the courtroom directly towards the camera and a waiting audience in what seems like an instantaneous verdict in favour of the plaintiff for unprecedented amounts of money. As the foreman reads the verdict, the camera hangs from the ceiling, reminiscent of Galvin's alienation and powerlessness. Upon hearing the verdict in favour of his clients, however, Galvin looks upward, at the camera, which instantly zooms down to reach him, filling the screen with his image, blessing his argument with its heightened and triumphant posture.

After Galvin's speech to the jury, the case could only end with a satisfied faith in the legal system's promise of individual and equal justice. To end with a verdict in favour of the defence would have depleted the signs, relationships, and perspectives that were cultivated throughout the film (and especially in the ending trial scene) that together suggested the possibility of a resurrected faith in individual strength and the law's promise of justice.

3. Step three: interpretive gridlock, the truth be told

Despite the portrait, until now, of the trial film's aim in meting out justice through the viewer-subject's balancing of monumental structure and minute detail, diverse perspectives and acute focus, the trial film's finale is often an unsophisticated revelation of some hidden essential truth – be it the facts of the case or the law's inability to assess those facts fairly. Poised to negotiate the contradictions in law's goal of individual and equal justice with its institutional organization of constant, consistent rules and hoops, the viewer-subject instead is made to experience the conclusion of the courtroom drama as a triumph of neatly-tied loose ends. Rarely is the issue at trial in these films about the perplexing (and sometimes unanswerable) questions of law, such as the ambiguity of legislative interpretation, the constitutionality of a state law, or the problematic dichotomous categories of guilt or innocence. Instead, the framing patterns and courtroom shots that are consistent in so many of these films serve not to make complex the relationship between the legal subject and his desire for justice through the process of law, but to simplify that relationship as an individual's decision between right or wrong, truth or falsehood.

In the genre of the trial film, there are two common conclusions toward which the above mapped framing patterns and courtroom scenes eventually lead:

(i)   trial law helps to uncover a long-kept secret and to fit it, like a puzzle piece, into its proper place, thus perpetuating law's reputation as a means toward the whole truth and its resultant justice; or

111

(ii) trial law is a process through which law extends its authority and power, despite what the viewer knows to be the facts of the case, perpetuating law's reputation as an ever-present social organizer – not because the law is always right, but because it is always the law, the last sanctioned force, the foundation upon which everyone has dared to stand.

In both scenarios, the truth is made known to the viewer-subject eventually, either at the end of the trial as law fulfils its promise, or before the trial, in which case the issue is not who did it and why, but whether the law will be able to account for the truth the viewer understands to be facts of the matter. Likewise, in both scenarios, the law is constituted as an internally consistent and endlessly recursive and discursive practice. As the law inevitably remains standing and in place at the film's end – whether or not it achieved justice through its courtroom procedure – the trial film concludes by propagating a notion of the world already made, only waiting to be found, always occupied by a legal system, and only waiting to be organized by it. This is not a representation of law and its force as tyrannical, but a representation of society which cannot imagine sustainable human civilization without law. It is a very rare film about the legal system (and certainly not a mainstream feature film) whose message is truth at all costs, even anarchy.[12]

Amidst these neat endings, the viewer-subject is left to make sense of the rushed, nearly predictable conclusions to these films in the face of what has otherwise been an internally complicated experience of law. Framed from the beginning in terms of its grandiose structure and its diminutive (though no less powerful) inhabitants, and developing towards a participatory perspective about the adversarial process and its ability to reconstruct a story from diverse angles, the law engages the viewer-subject as an inclusive system, its goal being individual and equal justice that the viewer-subject is made to both desire and effect. But the viewer-subject's engagement with the law is more accurately on a take-it or leave-it basis when the climax of the film is either simply the discovery of previously missing evidence, the revelation of which speeds the trial to a just conclusion, or a disruption of law's orderly process, which exposes its internal corruption and sets the record straight despite its limitations. There no longer remains a relationship with the law to be nurtured through the story's unfolding around the viewer-subject's interpellated identity. Instead, in the end, the law is constructed by the film to stand there, reified, before its subjects as the classificatory social practice that sometimes hits its mark and sometimes does not. When it does, the viewer-subject experiences a sense of triumph and gratitude, somewhat proud of the system that designates him a subject within it; when it does not,

---

12 But see *Sacco and Vanzetti* (Guiliano Montaldo, 1971), the film about the trial and execution of the two Italian immigrant anarchists.

the viewer-subject is rarely surprised, having been warned throughout the film of the law's potential failings and insurmountable burdens, and thus his suspicion is vindicated, his pride remains attached only to those individuals who resisted law's overreaching pull.

The ideology of the trial film genre is most strong here, at the film's overstated and often predictable climax. Made to recognize and expect the ever-present force of law in its fulfilment and its flaws through the patterns previously outlined, the viewer-subject can make claims (indeed the film's story is motivated by such claims) to know how the law's force works to perpetuate its authority and classificatory practice, and particularly how it keeps its promise of justice as truth alive. As the film interpellates its subject both as critical of the film's fiction due to its generic expectations and as desiring of the film's triumphant climax, however generic, the film genre continues the work of establishing a relationship between a viewing audience and a legal system, a relationship that has as its object the constitution and critique of law and its subjects. The viewer-subject as liberal-legal subject – who is both outside (as in a spectator of) the law as represented in the film and part of (as in discursively designated within) the legal representation that constitutes the film experience – figures himself as distrustful of law's totalizing presence as well as integral to the law's promise of individual and equal justice.

For example, in *A Few Good Men*,[13] about the investigation of a murder in a marine corps unit in Guantanamo Bay, Cuba, Tom Cruise plays Dan Caffy, a smart and cocky Harvard Law graduate serving in the Army's Legal Services in order to pay off his law school loans. Caffy has a reputation for plea-bargaining every case, some say because he is committed to expediency, others suggest it is because he fears the commitment a courtroom trial entails. What is clear is that to him law is a game less important and less complicated than his weekly softball games; it is not something to think much about, but to manipulate, fit, and apply. He says as much when asked by his client, 'Do you think we were right?' and Caffy answers, 'It doesn't matter what is right, you'll lose in a court of law.' That right and wrong have nothing to do with winning his cases does not seem to bother Caffy; in fact, Caffy is drawn to the surety, consistency, and predictability of law. He shouts with frustration, and indeed some pride, when he says, 'Don't tell me what is right and wrong, I know the law!', insinuating that he knows what will win the case despite the fact that there are murky moral issues at stake. Here, Caffy represents the legal professional who imagines law as a system that is not about interpretation or context, not about details of individual cases as they relate to larger social and ethical questions, but instead about a maintenance mechanism, a system that keeps order, drawing lines between legal and illegal based on arbitrary social norms.

13 *A Few Good Men* (Robert Reiner, 1992).

Caffy's perspective changes, however, when he realizes that he has been assigned to defend two marines accused of murder so that he will do his usual dance and settle out of court; his weakness – a reluctance to litigate – is being exploited by the system so that this case will be washed away with so many others, its details hidden by the opportunism the legal process can inspire. Out of pride, it seems, he struggles to discover why his superiors are suspiciously eager to have Caffy's clients plead guilty to a lesser offence. Caffy, thus, refuses settlement and pursues the investigation with unrivalled zealousness.

During his preparation for trial, Caffy is bothered by his clients' blind faith in the Marine credo 'Unit, Core, God, Country', a faith that he thinks led them to commit the murder for which they now stand trial. Caffy is appalled that his clients refused to think for themselves and instead obeyed an illegal Code Red order from a superior officer that demanded they 'haze' a fellow marine, an order that resulted in the marine's death. Eventually, however, Caffy finds inner enlightenment; he realises that following orders in the Marines is like blindly applying the law to cases, a tactic he has mastered and exploited to his benefit. Caffy's awakening leads to a new-found sympathy for his clients.

Following a hunch based on very little evidence (and, as such, that could cost him his legal career), Caffy insinuates in open court that Colonel Nathan Jessup, his clients' commanding officer, lied under oath when he denied his involvement in the death of the marine. Caffy effectively accuses Colonel Jessup of violating both military and federal law by ordering the Code Red that eventually cost the life of a marine under his command. In his cross-examination of Jessup, Caffy pressures the Colonel to defend his severe disciplinary tactics, to which Jessup responds: 'We follow orders or people die.' The irony in this response spills from the screen; a person died, in this case, because of an order.

To win his case, however, Caffy knows that irony is not enough; if Caffy's clients are to be acquitted on the first-degree murder charges, Jessup must admit to ordering the Code Red. So Caffy pushes Jessup. 'I want the truth!' Caffy demands of the Colonel. At first amused by the young lawyer's audacity, Jessup now turns angry. At Caffy's suggestion that Jessup is lying under oath and that the marines under Jessup's command fail to follow his orders, the Colonel puffs that they never question him and that they do exactly as they are told. 'We follow orders or people die. You want answers? ... You want the truth? You can't handle the truth!' In this suspenseful and intensely emotional cross-examination, both Caffy and Jessup, representing two competing systems of power and order, confront their breaking point. For Jessup, it is the fact that in a court of law, he is responsible to the rules of law and its representatives despite his towering rank in the Armed Forces. For Caffy, it is the revelation of something as conclusive and unambiguous as the truth of a situation that drives his argument and wins over the jury. Jessup's retort suggests that the truth is not something Caffy, as a lawyer, has

114

had to face, not something he has ever needed to think about, and frankly, something he is incapable of handling. In the end, however, Caffy learns that the truth is the simple admission that Jessup did order the Code Red causing the death of the marine, and that this truth can set his clients free. Upon admitting that he ordered the Code Red, Jessup is dragged from the courtroom in shackles, charged with breaking the Marine Corps code and with the murder of one of the marines under his command. Upon hearing the Colonel's admission, the jury finds the two marines not guilty of murder, not guilty of intent to kill, but guilty of conduct unbecoming a marine. In the end, then, the law as represented by the jury verdict not only reaffirms that the law is a truth-telling process, but also converts Caffy into a believer in trial law as that which binds truth with justice.

A Few Good Men could have been a complicated and interesting commentary on the rule of law – suggesting that the military and its mission may be parallel to, or even a rival of criminal law. Instead, the film ends with a more simplistic message about the relationship between truth, justice, and individual stamina, providing oversimplified guidance for distinguishing between right and wrong, just and unjust orders in the face of rigid rules. Upon being convicted only of 'conduct unbecoming a marine,' young Private Downey asks his more savvy co-defendant Corporal Harold Dawson, 'What did we do wrong? We didn't do anything wrong', implying they just followed orders and that is what marines are taught to do. Dawson replies bitterly, his life as a marine and his blind faith in service to his nation now torn apart by the law's guilty judgment of his own faith in his superiors, 'Yeah we did. We were supposed to fight for people who can't fight for themselves.' As it turns out, for these marines, and for Caffy, the best course of action within the institutions that shaped them was to reject the institution's rigid structure and disobey orders. Dawson and Downey should have ignored Colonel Jessup's order to haze their fellow marine, despite the strength unquestioned allegiance to authority brings to the military; and Caffy was right to have challenged Jessup on the stand, despite the professional and ethical risks he ran had it proven a mistake. Both were potentially illegitimate moves within the institutions that judge them, but both, according to the legal verdict, fit neatly within the trial film's theory equating truth with justice.

At the end of his journey in *A Few Good Men*, the viewer-subject encounters a truth that is not only about an event in history or an individual's culpability, but also about the law's (and the trial film's) constitutive power. This is the truth of the force of the metaphor of the journey toward justice through law: the viewer-subject's struggle to recover diverse perspectives through the organizing principles of the courtroom. In other words, the discursive practice of the trial film (of film form and legal practice) effects a viewer-subject who both sanctions the trial film's and the law's final word (the narrative finale and the legal judgment) and helps perpetuate the notion of legality that promises justice to those who participate in its process. This

115

metaphor for law's process in courtroom drama, and its sojourner, the viewer-subject, is the motor for liberal legalism.

Such a close look at the trial film genre, something understood as a signifying practice with effects beyond its formal existence, demonstrates how trial films are meaningful and affective as instruments of American legal ideology. As productive and transformational interactions that braid a real relation between the film, the viewer, and the communities in which they are situated, trial films perpetuate the authority of law by constituting their viewer-subjects as the liberal legal subject – as desirous of and believing in the power of each individual and the promise of equal justice.

All of these filmic patterns – iconic, relational, and thematic – help constitute the life of law in trial films. The trial, in particular, stands as a metaphor for each individual's journey toward justice, a sense of individual worth as seen through the perspectives of many and as validated by the institution whose rules strive to give meaning to justice in the first place. As patterned, this journey is recognizable, cultivating expectations in its subjects that perpetuate the law's promise whether or not it is fulfilled at the film's conclusion. As a fulfilment or disappointment of these expectations, the trial film enables the relationship between film and viewer-subject as one that both critiques the discursive practices of law and of film as disciplining forces on their subjects and relies on those practices as they designate their subjects as integral to their meaning-making.

In his journey from the steps of the courthouse to the final verdict, the viewer-subject of these trial films experiences more than the triumph of justice achieved or the exasperation of justice soiled; he grows strong with the knowledge of the just result and of the importance of law's struggle to achieve it. By positioning the viewer-subject within the courtroom drama to participate in and witness justice done, the trial film heeds the warning of the by now familiar adage, 'for justice to be done, it must be seen to be done'. In this way, the trial film – an instrument and conduit of popular legal consciousness – cultivates a desire for and perpetuates the strength of law's authoritative endeavour by locating the promise of law in the tenacity and proclaimed self-possession of each individual.

116

JOURNAL OF LAW AND SOCIETY
VOLUME 28, NUMBER 1, MARCH 2001
ISSN: 0263-323X, pp. 117–32

Law in Film: Globalizing the Hollywood Courtroom Drama

STEFAN MACHURA* AND STEFAN ULBRICH*
(English-language version by Francis M. Nevins and Nils Behling)

The courtroom drama is a prominent film genre. Most of the movies in this category are Hollywood productions, dealing with the legal system in the United States of America. What they have in common is that essential parts of their stories take place in court. These movies have a tremendous influence on the public's concept of justice even though very few of them accurately reflect legal reality. Anyone with legal training who watches films of this sort will notice in them all sorts of absurdities[1] which are not thoroughly investigated in this paper. Our concern here is to inquire why even movies that take place in continental Europe follow patterns of the American system and also why certain elements from American movies are repeated over and over again.

I. THE REMARKABLE INFLUENCE OF HOLLYWOOD COURTROOM FILMS

Experience transmitted by media is sometimes a functional equivalent for experience gained in the real world. American movies have influenced the image of legal procedure a great deal – and not just in the United States of America. An English legal expert told us about seeing a young barrister try to proceed before an English court in a manner that is possible only in the United States. A Spanish anthropologist who had filmed legal procedures in California carried her camera into a Spanish courtroom and was shocked to discover that everything was done differently from how it was done in the United States. German defendants and lay assessors have indicated in interviews that they were surprised to learn that procedure in German courts was so different from what watching television had led them to expect. It has

---

* Law Faculty, Ruhr-Universitat Bochum, Gebäude GC 8/135, D-44780 Bochum, Germany

1 F.M. Nevins, Review of P. Bergman and M. Asimow, *Reel Justice: The Courtroom Goes to The Movies* (1996) 20 *Legal Studies Forum* 145; M. Kuzina, *Der amerikanische Gerichtsfilm* (2000).

also been said by German lawyers that some of the changes in German procedure over the last few years have been in the direction of letting the attorneys put on a little more of a show, a performance to impress their clients.

The effect of movies on the appearance of children as witnesses in German courts is particularly noticeable. Children, juveniles, and adults were asked by Petra Wolf what they knew about courts.[2] The source of information they most often mentioned was movies, especially American crime movies and courtroom dramas. A group of psychologists from Kiel who published a book for the preparation of children as witnesses found out that, even after seeing pictures of a German courtroom, children still believed that the judge would have a gavel or at least wear a wig.[3] In the new edition, the authors explain to children that there will be no gavel or wig, both of which are crossed out in red.[4] This picture is repeated at the end of the book, where the children are asked to guess in which country judges have neither gavels nor wigs.

It is beyond dispute that the cinematic portrayal of the American legal system and its personnel is far removed from legal reality. Very few defence attorneys in the real world resemble Atticus Finch as Gregory Peck portrayed him in Robert Mulligan's *To Kill A Mockingbird* (1962), and very few prosecutors are so blind and biased as their movie counterparts.[5] Movies dealing with criminal law and procedure are far more common than films that explore the civil side even though there is far more civil than criminal litigation in the real world.[6] From movies that portray a jury deliberating on a particular case, one gets the impression that most cases in the real world are decided by juries, although in fact they hear only a small percentage of all cases[7] and the rest are either tried before a court sitting without a jury or, thanks to plea bargaining in criminal cases or a settlement in civil matters, never heard by either judge or jury. In the real world, trial by jury is a last resort. In the world of film it is the preferred choice.

Academics in both Britain and the United States have written on law-related films, to the point that one observer has called this subject the 'law

2 P. Wolf, *Was wissen Kinder und Jugendliche über Gerichtsverhandlungen?* (1997).
3 P. Hille, '*Verbesserung der Situation kindlicher Zeugen vor Gericht – Entwicklung und Evaluation von Informationsmaterial für Kinder*' (disseration submitted for diploma, Institut für Psychologie, Christian-Albrechts-Universität, Kiel) (1997) app. F, fig. 4.
4 P. Hille et al., *Klara und der kleine Zwerg* (1996).
5 S. Greenfield and G. Osborn, 'Where Cultures Collide: The Characterisation of Law and Lawyers in Film' (1995) 23 *International J. of the Sociology of Law* 107, at 118; M. Pfau et. al., 'Television Viewing and Public Perceptions of Attorneys' (1995) 21 *Human Communications Research* 307.
6 P. Robson, 'Law and Lawyers in Film – Globalising Atticus Finch' (paper presented to the Joint Meeting of the Law and Society Association and the Research Committee on Sociology of Law, Glasgow, 10–13 July 1996) 2–3.
7 V.P. Hans and N. Vidmar, *Judging the Jury* (1986) 19; P. Duff and M. Findlay 'Jury Reform: of Myths and Moral Panics' (1997) 25 *International J. of the Sociology of Law* 363, at 363.

and cinema movement'.[8] To an increasing extent, law schools are offering courses and seminars on law, lawyers and justice in popular fiction and film.[9] And of course new movies in this category continue to be made, not only in the United States but in Germany where some directors (Norbert Kückelmann, Fred Breinersdörfer, and last but not least, Hark Bohm) are lawyers themselves. TV series dealing with judges, prosecutors and defence attorneys seem to be permanently popular.

II. LAW-RELATED PROGRAMMES ON GERMAN TELEVISION

To what extent does Germany's television schedule offer law-related subjects? Using the German TV guide *Hörzu*, we analysed what was broadcast on forty-four stations over two weeks (from 12 to 25 February 2000) in order to discover the relative frequency of six programme categories, namely:

(i)   Courtroom movies, that is, films like Billy Wilder's *Witness For The Prosecution* (1957) in which scenes esential to the story take place in court;

(ii)   Law-related movies, that is, films like Michael Crichton's *Physical Evidence* (1988) that have lawyer protagonists and deal with law and justice but do not have courtroom scenes;

(iii)   Law-related television series like *Perry Mason*, each of whose episodes tells a fictional story about law, lawyers, and justice;

(iv)   Law-related TV series like *Richterin Barbara Salesch* (something like a German counterpart of *Judge Judy*) in which authentic legal conflicts are presented as entertainment;

(v)   Programmes like *Ratgeber Recht* in which real-world lawyers provide information on various legal problems; and

(vi)   Documentary films, including those that exclusively use authentic material and the so-called docudramas like Claus Strobel's *Sechs Schüsse auf einen Minister* (1998) in which dramatized scenes are added.

8 N. Rosenberg, 'Young Mr Lincoln: The Lawyer as Super-Hero' (1991) 15 *Legal Studies Forum* 215, at 215.
9 P.N. Meyer 'Visual Literacy and the Legal Culture: Reading Film as Text in the Law School Setting' (1993) 17 *Legal Studies Forum* 73; S.N. Gatson '"It's About Law" Accessible Teaching Sources for Law and Society' (paper presented to the Annual Meeting of the Law and Society Association, Toronto, 1–4 June 1995); S. Greenfield and G. Osborn, 'The Living Law: Popular Film as Legal Text' (1996) *The Law Teacher* 33; F.M. Nevins, 'Using Fiction and Film as Law School Tools' in *Legal Education in the 21st Century*, ed. D.B. King (1999) ch. 13; on two examples in Germany: S. Machura 'Rechtssoziologie in der Juristenausbildung' (1997) 37 *Juristische Schulung* 953, at 956.

Figure 1 shows that German television is dominated by our third category, fictional series like *Perry Mason* (54 per cent of the total time our stations devote to law-related shows). Next in frequency comes our fourth category, series along the lines of *The People's Court* and *Judge Judy* (22 per cent). Law-related movies without courtroom action (10 per cent), legal advice shows (6 per cent), courtroom films (6 per cent) and documentaries (3 per cent) are broadcast far less often.[10] Note that our percentages reflect only the programmes broadcast and not their relative popularity. Most of Germany's broadcast stations are on the air twenty-four hours a day and often run repeats of series like Perry Mason late at night when only a few people are watching.

How long is the average law-related programme? Figure 2 shows that the vast majority run for between fifty and sixty-five minutes (sixty-two minutes arithmetical mean, fifty-five minutes median). During the two weeks covered by our analysis, a staggering 8,904 minutes (148.4 hours) of broadcast time were devoted to law-related programmes. (Commercial time has not been subtracted from these figures.) With the help of a VCR and gallons of black coffee one could watch such programmes without interruption twenty-four hours a day for 6.18 days (using the videos of that 14 day period).

As Figure 3 shows, law-related programmes on German television seem to follow a standard pattern, being largely clustered in midweek and falling off on weekends, when movies with courtroom sequences are more likely to be shown.

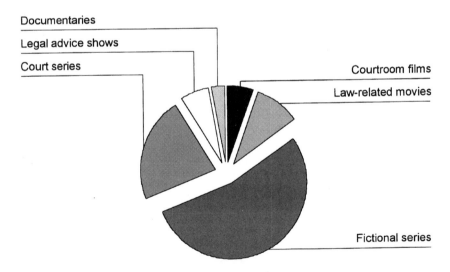

Figure 1: Distribution of film categories

10 These percentages add up to 101 per cent due to rounding.

120

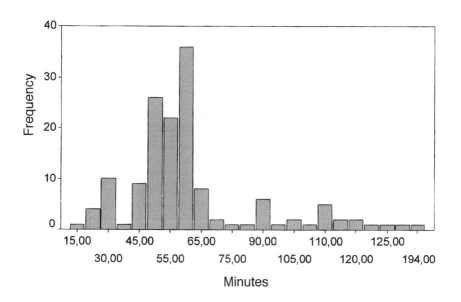

Figure 2: Duration in minutes

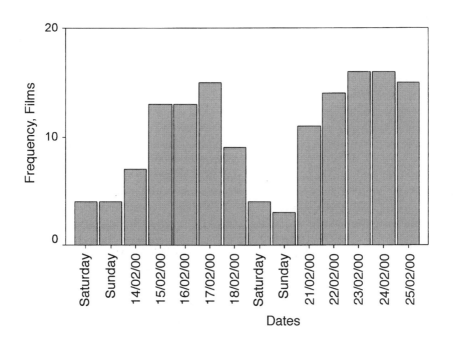

Figure 3: Date of broadcasting

121

III. VIEW OF THE GENRE

Sometimes it seems that all courtroom films are constructed out of the same building blocks. Certain scenes recur in those movies over and over: not only cross-examinations[11] but also motions to exclude evidence and other elements. In *To Kill A Mockingbird* the white girl who claims to have been sexually attacked by the Negro Tom Robinson (Brock Peters) has a bruise on the left side of her face. Cross-examining the girl's father, Atticus Finch asks him to write something and we see the man use his left hand. Later Atticus tosses a glass to Robinson, who catches it with his right hand because his left is crippled. In Peter Yates's *Suspect* (1987), defence attorney Kathleen Riley (Cher) asks the jury to listen carefully to the evidence that indicates the murder victim was stabbed by a right-handed assailant. Sure enough, later in the film she throws an object to the defendant (Liam Neeson) which he catches with his left hand, showing us he is not guilty. In Billy Wilder's *Witness for the Prosecution* (1957) we first see the dome of the courthouse and then a cut into the courtroom. In Jonathan Demme's *Philadelphia* (1993) this sequence is repeated. Both Wilder and Demme use these shots not only to introduce us to the arena of action but to create a visual metaphor for the high ideal of justice. In Wilder's movie the courthouse dome is crowned by a sculptured figure of Justice, on which the ironic director then shows us a labourer working to make it look prettier – or perhaps justice needs to be fixed.

A recurring theme in courtroom films is the rhetorical duel. In the early 1930s, when silent films were superseded by talkies, Hollywood took advantage of the new sound-on-film technology to make dozens of movies with courtroom scenes,[12] not just pictures set in the present but even Westerns about legal disputes between ranchers and cattle barons over water rights. A lengthy courtroom scene became almost a guarantee of a movie's success. After 1933, when the Hollywood studios adopted a production code that strongly discouraged negative portrayals of 'establishments' such as law and religion, American movies did not generally question the judicial system, although they frequently attacked individual lawyers or bureaucrats. From the mid-1950s to the present a number of courtroom films explicitly offer a social message and agitate for social change. Sidney Lumet's *Twelve Angry Men* (1957) argues for community participation in legal decisions; Robert Wise's *I Want To Live!* (1958) opposes trials in the media and capital punishment; *To Kill A Mockingbird* indicts racism; and *Philadelphia* protests discrimination against people with AIDS.

The classic courtroom films from the years that roughly coincide with the peak years of the Supreme Court under Chief Justice Earl Warren tend to portray lawyers as heroes and the legal enterprise as a noble one, but more

---

11 Criticized by Greenfield and Osborn, op. cit., n. 5, p. 117–8.
12 F.M. Nevins, 'Through the Great Depression on Horseback' in *Legal Reelism*, ed. J. Denvir (1996) 44–69 at 45.

recent releases usually present a negative view,[13] with lawyer protagonists portrayed as broken, disillusioned or corrupt, and storylines reflecting the insecurity of American society on issues of crime control. The first half of Peter Hyams's *The Star Chamber* (1983) shows an idealistic young judge (Michael Douglas) who revolts in horror against having to release sadistic psychopaths because of absurd legal technicalities and joins a conspiracy of judges who have engaged an assassin to kill criminals who have wriggled through loopholes in the system. The second half of the film follows Douglas as he frantically tries to stop the hit-man from killing two criminals who he discovers did not in fact commit the child-murder for which they were acquitted. In the final scene, Douglas informs on his judicial colleagues who have gone outside the law to achieve what they consider to be justice.

IV. WHY AMERICAN LEGAL PROCEDURE DOMINATES MOVIES

Prior to our research we operated on the assumption that courtroom films reflected the legal system more or less correctly[14] but we soon found this not to be so. What came to amaze us was the striking uniformity of the legal procedures that are portrayed in movies: predominantly criminal procedures. We discovered that American procedure has provided the foundation for almost all cinematic legal procedures, even in films set in a country like Germany that has a different system.[15]

There are a number of reasons for the dominance of American legal procedure in movies: not only do American films enjoy international box-office success, but American legal procedure is structurally more suitable for a film than is the so-called inquisitorial procedure found in civil law systems, such as we find on the Continent. American courtroom films have created a manner of portraying legal procedure which has been followed in courtroom films set in other countries and other legal systems. We shall analyse this phenomenon in terms of 'self-referential' communication.

Mass communication scholars have often discussed the question what makes something that happened in the real world a news event. According to proponents of what is known as the news value theory, whether something that happened does or does not become news depends on so-called news factors which, if present, make the event interesting to the mass media. This approach can be traced back to Walter Lippmann, who in his classic *Public Opinion*[16]

13 R. Berets 'Changing Images of Justice in American Films' (1996) 20 *Legal Studies Forum* 473.
14 According to the 'reflection theory', 'culture is the mirror of social reality' (C.L. McNeely, 'Perceptions of the Criminal Justice System: Television Imaginary and Public Knowledge in the United States' in *Interrogating Popular Culture*, eds. S.E. Anderson and G.J. Howard (1998), 55–68, at 57).
15 Robson, op. cit., n. 6, p. 3.
16 W. Lippman, *Public Opinion* (1922) 338–57.

set forth the fundamental assumption that news did not represent reality but was the result of decisions made by journalists. Using concrete examples, Lippmann developed what he called stereotypes, that is, criteria which turn an event into news. It was in this context that the concept of news value was born.

News factors of course are variable and various studies have tested them empirically.[17] James Buckalew identified six such factors: significance, unusualness, prominence, proximity, timeliness, and (for televison news only) visuality.[18] The emotional dimensions and 'human interest' aspects of what happened also turned out to be important factors in determining what events are treated as news.

Niklas Luhmann explicitly refers to this tradition of research into news factors in his book *The Reality Of The Mass Media*.[19] Among the news factors he stresses the aspects of conflict and unusualness:

> Conflicts have this advantage as subjects, that they have uncertainty built into them. The information about who wins and who loses is not revealed until later. This creates suspense, and in order to understand the communication one must use guesswork.[20]

News factors like unusualness and prominence are of great significance to our understanding of how legal institutions and procedures are represented on television news programmes. Slotnick and Segal analysed the portrayal of the US Supreme Court on such programmes and showed how the Court's media image has changed in recent decades.[21]

For television news programmes, the information function of the media is central but for law-related movies the entertainment function is more important. We believe that to understand such films it is necessary to develop an entertainment value theory, analogous to the news value theory *vis-à-vis* print and electronic journalism. Such an approach emphasizes film-makers' selective perception of law, without undue emphasis on whether they represent law correctly but focusing on what factors make law interesting to them. We have found in law-related movies the following entertainment value factors.

1. *Dramaturgy*

American legal procedure seems more suitable for movies because it is more hospitable to scenes of intense drama, featuring classical confrontations

---

17 J.F. Staab, *Nachrichtenwerttheorie. Formale Struktur und empirischer Gehalt* (1990) 40–92.
18 J.K. Buckalew, 'A Q-Analysis of Television News Editor's Decisions' (1969) 46 *Journalism Q.* 135; J.K. Buckalew, 'News Elements and Selection by Television News Editors' (1969/1970) 14 *J. of Broadcasting* 47.
19 N. Luhmann, *Die Realität der Massenmedien* (1996, 2nd edn.) 56–81.
20 id., p. 59.
21 E. Slotnick and J.E. Segal, *Television News and the Supreme Court. All the News That's Fit to Air?* (1998).

between two antagonists and conflicts between good and evil which have to be resolved. Such conflicts can be made a great deal more powerful in an adversary procedure than in German criminal procedure, in which the principle of official investigation (*Amtsermittlungsgrundsatz*) requires the public prosecutor to investigate all aspects of the case including those that favour the defendant. In American procedure the parties wrestle to establish their individual version of the facts of the case as well as their legal views. Where the courtroom is seen as a battleground, fierce conflict becomes the norm.

American adversary procedure is in some ways reminiscent of ancient drama. Even the outward appearance of the courtroom is similar to the architecture of the classical Athenian theater. The 'scene,' where the action in Greek tragedy takes place, is similar to the space in front of the bench where opposing counsel act, plead, and question witnesses. The 'orchestra', where the chorus sings and dances, has its functional equivalent in the jury box. The 'theatron', where the audience sits, is also present in the courtroom. The dialectic structure of adversary procedure – thesis of the prosecution, antithesis of the defence and synthesis of the verdict – also uses classical structure elements such as one finds in Sophocles's *Antigone*, which is about the conflict between two opposing positions, each partially right. This structure is also found in courtroom films like *Philadelphia* which portray an ambivalent conflict unfolding before the judge.

The attorneys for the parties present two different versions of what happened. This main feature becomes evident during the opening arguments in *Philadelphia*. The attorneys themselves stress that the jury will hear two different versions of the case and will have to decide which one is more convincing. On the other hand, German procedure as governed by the *Amtsermittlungsgrundsatz* is more abstract and seeks the higher value of objective truth. Here the stress is more clearly on the outcome and the participants invest less effort on the procedure. To a German lawyer, the procedure is nothing more but an almost negligible means to the end of an appropriate verdict. The German type of procedure is much less dramatic. The judge who sits on a case follows his hypothesis based on what he knows from the files. This pattern becomes clear during the scene in Gianni Amelio's *Porte Aperte* (1989) where the judge interrogates the bookkeeper and pushes him into confirming financial manipulation.

A growing body of research has recognized the narrative function of trial lawyers:

> In short, stories are powerful means of transmitting precise interpretations of distant and complex events to people who either did not witness those events or who did not grasp them from the storyteller's perspective.[22]

---

22 W.L. Bennett, 'Storytelling in Criminal Trials: A Model of Social Judgment' (1978) 64 *Q.J. of Speech* 1, at 4.

The lawyer's task in the courtroom is to present a sound story, in which all aspects form a convincing whole. Stories are most successful if they conform to patterns widely shared in the culture.

Besides the 'story in the trial' there is also the 'story of the trial'.[23] The trial itself is the material of this story. Such trial stories again follow typical cultural patterns. The outcome of the trial depends on the acceptance of the story of the trial by the judges. The cultural patterns provide decision-makers and observers with criteria for judging the trial's qualities. Prosecution and defence can work on different types of stories. The defence for instance may present its own performance in court as a heroic struggle against an abusive state,[24] which is represented by the prosecution and its ruthless behaviour at court. As the judges deliberate, they remember the 'stories of the trial' and the 'stories in the trial' and finally correlate them into a single version of events.

When watching courtroom movies we are in a similar situation. We are confronted with stories presented during a trial and we have an impression of the trial itself. Often on fragmentary information, we construct our version of the whole story. Bennett cited as evidence of the power of stories the fact that we who listen add missing links and repair stories that have been poorly told.[25]

2. A question of life and death

In American movies the tension is often built up by putting the defendant's life at stake. Many states impose the death penalty for murder, so that the battle of prosecution and defence is about the irreversible death of a human being. 'The dramatic effect is to raise the stakes not just for the accused but also for the ... lawyer ...'.[26]

3. The jury as representative of the public

The jury is another element that contributes to the usefulness of American adversary procedure for movies. Here too there is a link with ancient Greek drama if one looks at the jury as a replacement for the chorus. In ancient drama, the chorus was responsible for watching and commenting on events on stage in which it is also somehow involved.[27] The parties in court must call not only on the minds but also on the emotions of the jury. The jury is supposed to represent the public and therefore provides a good identification

23 B.S. Jackson, '"Anchored Narratives" and the Interface of Law, Psychology and Semiotics' (1996) 1 *Legal and Criminological Psychology* 17, at 27.

24 R.K. Sherwin, *When Law Goes Pop* (2000) 54–5.

25 Bennett, op. cit., n. 22, p. 4; see, also, Meyer in this special issue.

26 Greenfield and Osborn, op. cit., n. 5, p. 111.

27 B. Seidensticker, 'Chor' in *Theaterlexikon*, eds. M. Brauneck and G. Schneilin (1996) 214–16, at 214.

point for the viewer. When a director chooses to shoot a scene from the viewpoint of the jury box, we understand that the jury members in the movie are standing in for us.

It is supposed to be the function of lay judges and jurors to add legal understanding of the public and to ensure the democratic control of justice.[28] Democracy versus bureaucracy is a central topic in American movies, with the jury serving as a corrective element with which we are invited to identify, although uncritical prejudices and sympathies of the public often sit in the jury box too.[29] Sympathy and animosity are reflected in the faces and body language of movie jurors. Even a juror who remains motionless and with a poker face provokes the viewer to take one side or the other. The facial expressions and gestures of the jurors serve to comment on events in the courtroom and therefore create a meta-level parallel to the actual level of what is going on. If the jurors are dissatisfied, we know that it is up to one party in the case to dispel these doubts. Like the chorus in ancient drama, the jury has the function of commenting and moving the plot along.

4. *The weak judge*

Another factor contributing to the greater intensity of the confrontations in American movies is that the role of the judge in American legal procedure is a great deal weaker than in Germany and other countries. Basically the judge in the American legal system has the job of controlling procedure. This weak role strengthens the positions of the prosecution and the defence, and thereby facilitates greater emphasis on conflict.

The fact that American justice is much more political than justice in Germany also contributes to the dramatic effect of American films. In many states judges and prosecutors are elected by the people, so that their actions are often suspected to be for political reasons.[30] Politically motivated litigation plays a huge role in American courtroom films.[31] In a perfect world the judge is supposed to be a functionary, totally impartial and free from personal motivations. Only the rule of law is accepted, not the rule of men.[32] The mean or corrupt judges often found in American courtroom films add yet another element to their dramatic conflicts.

The judge in American courtroom movies is often not shown as the wise expert alone on the side of objective truth, even though directors also work with this cliché. The American judge's function is to ensure a fair trial. His

28 J.P. Dawson, *A History of Law Judges* (1960) 287.
29 Hans and Vidmar, op. cit., n. 7, p. 131.
30 S.C. Thaman, '*Das Rechtssystem*' in *Länderbericht USA. Vol. 1*, eds. W. Adams et al. (1992, 2nd edn.) 519–45, at 522.
31 Robson, op. cit., n. 6, p. 3.
32 J.M. Landis and L. Goodstein, 'When is Justice Fair? An Integrated Approach to the Outcome Versus Procedure Debate' (1986) 4 *Am. Bar Foundation Research J.* 675, at 675.

role supports the focus on procedure rather than result, and on the crucial nature of what is said in the courtroom.

5. *The strong attorney*

The role of the defence in the American legal system also lends itself to effective use in films,[33] which often portray the defence attorney as a charismatic figure who saves the innocent from unjust conviction. A typical example is John Ford's *Young Mr. Lincoln* (1939), a movie that has drawn the attention of movie analysts worldwide.[34] But for every heroic attorney in movies there is at least one and perhaps several who are corrupt. Often the attorney lives in a privileged social world. But the role of defence lawyers is often very ambivalent. These attorneys are often portrayed as having attended top law schools, and their upper-class clothes and mannerisms may be used by a director either to celebrate this lifestyle with all its status symbols or to strongly criticize it. Fighting for a client can mean fighting for the good and true elements of life or the sophistic art of getting an obviously guilty individual acquitted.[35] This internal ambivalence of the attorney's role is very suitable for telling a story of a lawyer character's evolution, for example, from an ambitious materialist to a fighting idealist (as in *Philadelphia* or *The Verdict*). The extremes of good and evil are options between which the film's lawyer protagonist must choose, for example, *The Firm* (Sydney Pollack, 1993). This conflict often takes on a quasi-religous dimension (as in *The Verdict*).

Furthermore, attorneys traditionally enjoy a strong position in American society which adds to their usefulness as protagonists. They almost always stand for liberalism. In the political life of the United States, mistrust towards government organizations and the fight for civil rights have traditionally had important roles. The lawyer sometimes appears as defender of individual rights against the state, which is often regarded ambivalently.[36] This theme can also be found in German films,[37] but in the German system it is the co-operation of judge, prosecutor, and defence attorney that works to help the innocent and betrayed.

---

33 Greenfield and Osborn, op. cit., n. 5, p. 112–3.
34 Rosenberg, op. cit., n. 8; S. Greenfield and G. Osborn, op. cit., n. 9; N. Rafter, *Shots in the Mirror* (2000) 100; Kuzina, op. cit., n. 1, pp. 38 and 164; see, also, Böhnke's contribution to this special issue.
35 Nevins, op. cit., n. 12, p. 52.
36 S. Greenfield and G. Osborn, 'Justice and Civilisation in Mega City: At the Beginning and Ends of Cinematic Law?' (paper presented the Joint Meeting of the Law and Society Association and the Research Committee on Sociology of Law, Glasgow, 10–13 July 1996) 5.
37 G. Oesterreich, *Im Dschungel der Paragraphen* (1984) 150, 213, fn. 110.

6. *Case law and discovery*

The American legal system is rooted in case law, as opposed to the legal systems in Europe, which operate with written law codes mainly. The decisions of higher courts in an American jurisdiction are binding on that jurisdiction's lower courts, and the job of the opposing counsel is to find cases that can be used as analogies. Arguments over which precedent is controlling offer film-makers another dramatic possibility which is not available to them in a codified legal system. American courtroom justice is the object of a quest, as depicted in *Anatomy of a Murder* (Otto Preminger, 1959), and in American courtroom films there is often a last-minute surprise development that makes for compelling drama (for example, in *Young Mr. Lincoln*). Such dramatic tension is impossible in continental legal systems, where the law is treated as already given in the shape of various codes and the only possible disputes are over matters of interpretation.

Another element that creates dramatic tension is discovery, which is the term for the American procedure whereby defence and prosecution collect evidence before the trial, with the prosecution focusing on material proving the defendant's guilt and the defence of course stressing the opposite. This is why in American films, and in the real world of American law as well, it is often necessary for the defence to employ private investigators (for example, *Suspect*, Peter Yates, 1987). In German criminal law it is the job of the prosecution as 'lord of the investigative procedure' to find evidence both for and against the defendant, and the use of a private detective is therefore hardly necessary and highly unusual. But in the most popular German series *Ein Fall Für Zwei* (*A Case for Two*) a private eye conducted the investigation, a fact which again shows the global influence of American courtroom films.

V. THE SELF-REFERENTIALTY OF FILMS: A SYSTEM-ORIENTED EXPLANATION

These observations suggest the hypothesis that the cinematic portrayal of legal procedures reflects not so much the real world of law but rather their depiction in previous movies. But the fact that adversary procedure is more suitable for movies explains only why American courtroom films have been so successful. It leaves open the question why the American pattern is employed in films from other cultures around the globe.

At this point the systems theory that Niklas Luhmann outlined in *Social Systems*[38] and *The Art Of Society*[39] may be useful. Luhmann tells us that films, as mass-media artistic products, communicate and connect by means

38 N. Luhmann, *Soziale Systeme* (1984).
39 N. Luhmann, *Die Kunst der Gesellschaft* (1997).

129

of references to one another rather than to the outside world. The system of art to which the movies belong and the system of law do not communicate with each other but each creates the other's environment. In Luhmann's view, which has long since gone beyond the borders of sociology to be employed in other disciplines such as theory of literature and art, what differentiates systems are the operations each one uses to become a self-standing entity. This position stems from the theoretical viewpoint known as constructivism: for social operations, communication forms the elementary and ultimate unity that permits social sub-systems like law, science, and art to differ from each other in their typical forms of communication. Thus the communications of the legal system are organized according to the binary opposition lawful/unlawful. In this context, however, 'communication' cannot be understood as a transfer of information from one individual to another but, rather, as a concept that consists of three components – notification, information, and understanding – which refer strictly to the unity of communication and are not meant hermeneutically. Thus, by 'understanding', Luhmann means simply usefulness in the course of further communication, that is, what he calls connectibility.

Imagine a farm that some animal lovers are operating as a home for homeless cats, dogs, and horses. The mewing of the cats, the barking of the dogs, the whinnying of the horses: each of these is in Luhmann's terms a self-referential system of communication, and so also, of course, is the talk among the humans who are caring for their four-footed friends. Our thesis is that the relation between courtroom films and the real world of law is analogous to the relation between any two of the four self-referential systems of communication on the animal farm.

For obvious reasons, systems theory can provide only brief flashes that help illuminate our observations. In this context the predominance of adversary procedure in movies can be understood as a part of a self-referential communication system which operates separate and apart from the legal system. Certainly the legal system provides plot material for movies but beyond that there is no communication between the two systems, especially not in representational form such as exists, say, between Leonardo's Mona Lisa painting and the woman who posed for him. The advantage of this theory lies in its sharp contrast between the systems. It leads, however, to an interesting question: how, if not with the concept of 'communication', can one explain the fact that each of the species on our imaginary animal farm both reacts to and is reacted upon by the others, or the analogous fact that movies both influence and are influenced by the legal system?

Luhmann's *The Art of Society*[40] offers several hints as to why self-reference in courtroom movies operates in this way. So far, we have concentrated on explaining why in connection with these movies one can

40 id.

130

speak of self-referentiality in a system of art, and have pointed to differences between the real-world legal system and the way it is presented in courtroom films, such as the echoes of the American legal system even in movies set in the legal world of continental Europe. Now, taking as given the self-referential nature of films and the proposition that courtroom movies belong to a system of art, we shall use systems theory as a contribution to explaining the manner in which films refer to the legal system. Translated into Luhmann's terms, our discussion revolves around the themes of self-referentiality and external referentiality.

According to Luhmann, within the system of art, external referentiality 'is used only as a screen ... in order to show other possibilities of order.'[41] Courtroom films survive only because they can depart from everyday legal reality. They do not portray the normal treatment of cases but the exceptional cases, and in these portrayals the law is often insufficiently (if not distortedly) described and the situation is resolved thanks only to an unusual person employing extra-legal methods. The abandonment of the normal can even lead into the realms of the fantastic and mythical. For example, in William Dieterle's *The Devil And Daniel Webster* (1941) the devil empanels a jury of the damned and in Akira Kurosawa's *Rashomon* (1950) a medium summons the murder victim's ghost in order to resolve a situation. But provided that viewers find something they can connect with, that is, that their expectations of recognizing *something* that they see are not completely disappointed, incredible and surprising variations guarantee entertainment value. Luhmann stresses that the free choice of external references is what makes possible the autonomous life of art.[42] However, he goes on to say, 'the media substratum still carries the external references against which the self-referentiality of a work of art has to test itself'. It thereby becomes possible for the viewer to make sense of what he sees. Since movies are supposed to be profitable, large segments of the audience have to be able to relate to something in them. Applying to cinema a remark of Luhmann about literature, it is the film-maker's job

> to organize the work so that those who encounter it are able to draw conclusions applicable to their own lives and experiences, whether in the private or the public realm. The individual becomes both the subject and the creator of his own story, with which he identifies.[43]

We have shown with the example of the jury how courtroom films place the viewer in certain perspectives. Luhmann stresses that works of art open some possibilities of observation and at the same time shut off others. Drama plays with what its characters know or do not know,[44] which is why characters like a weak prosecuting attorney or a stupid judge are sometimes

41 id., p. 238.
42 id., p. 252.
43 id., p. 441.
44 id., p. 334.

131

necessary. The film medium can also use sound, light, perspective, and editing to present seemingly straightforward scenes in such a way as to mislead or deceive the viewer. For example, in *Young Mr. Lincoln* John Ford has the murder scene take place in shadows so that what actually happened is not clear to us until Henry Fonda as Lincoln makes the key witness confess during cross-examination. Each viewer must form an opinion of what the picture is about. Tension is created. Thus a good movie is a mixture of known quantities, alienation through surprise, and resolution. If a residue of uneasiness still remains, the film can convey a critical message.

With viewers reconstructing a film's story for themselves individually, it becomes difficult to determine the effect of any movie. This can be seen in Orson Welles' adaptation of Kafka's *The Trial* (1962), where the leading character, who has done nothing and does not know how to help himself, gets caught in a legal spider-web. One viewer might take a nihilistic message from this, while another might feel moved to fight for civil rights. Even though movies usually suggest particular interpretations, two different viewers will still not perceive the same film identically. This is why the interaction of law and film is such a fascinating subject of research.

(An earlier version of this article appeared under the title '*Recht im Film: Abbild juristischer Wirklichkeit oder filmische Selbstreferenz?*' in (1999) 20 *Zeitschrift für Rechtssoziologie* 168. Reprint permission by Lucius & Lucius Verlagsgesellschaft, Stuttgart.)

JOURNAL OF LAW AND SOCIETY
VOLUME 28, NUMBER 1, MARCH 2001
ISSN: 0263-323X, pp. 133–46

Why a Jury Trial is More Like a Movie Than a Novel

PHIL MEYER*

This essay is concerned to note the way in which successful trial advocacy seems to stem from the ability to convert legal discourse into a story form. These stories need to be ones with which a jury is familiar. These increasingly come from visual media, particularly film. It looks in detail at one trial where this process of relating a defence to the jury employed the structure of a Mafia film. The essay concludes by examining the reasons why the nature of the novel differs significantly from that of the film and how in the novel-to-film adaptation process a certain simplification is bound to occur.

> Fiction goes everywhere, inside, outside, it stops, it goes, its action can be mental. Nor is it time-driven. Film is time-driven, it never ruminates, it shows the outside of life, it shows behavior. It tends to the simplest moral reasoning. Films out of Hollywood are linear. The narrative simplification of complex morally consequential reality is always the drift of a film inspired by a book. Novels can do anything in the dark horrors of consciousness. Films do close ups, car drive-ups, places, chases and explosions.
>
> E.L. Doctorow[1]

In a previous essay, I examined the filmic influences upon an attorney's closing argument to a jury in a criminal case.[2] After studying closing arguments and trials, it became apparent to me that trial advocacy, especially argument to a jury in a criminal case, is deeply imbedded in narrative practices, certainly as deeply as in the analytical practices and paradigmatic structures of rule based reasoning traditionally taught in law schools. The essence of successful trial advocacy to a jury is the ability to combine legal analytics with the storytelling ability of the artist within the 'aesthetic' constraints of form demanded by trial practice. This is not a 'novel'

---

* Vermont Law School, Chelsea Street, PO Box 96, South Royalton, VT 05068, United States of America

1 E.L. Doctorow, *City of God* (2000) – quoted in *New York Times* Book Review, 5 March 2000, 7.
2 See P. Meyer, 'Desperate for Love: Cinematic Influences Upon A Defendant's Closing Argument to a Jury (1994) 18 *Vermont Law Rev.* 721.

perception.[3] Many, myself included, have perceived that trial practice requires the ability to marry the analytical work of law school, and convert legal rules into the infrastructure for effective narrative-based storytelling.[4] But my perception, after attending criminal trials, and recalling my own work as a trial practitioner and clinician many years ago, was somewhat different and simultaneously more specific than this.

First, the narratives constructed at trial exist among a wide range of other popular cultural narrative practices. Advertising, the popular song, television programming, 'realist' literature, theatre, all are, of course, guided and informed by particular aesthetics and structures. These practices influence other narrative practices, including the trial of a case to a jury. It is my contention that the narrative practices that are probably most influential upon trial practitioners are not those of 'literary' storytellers or literature so often discussed (often quite romantically and nostalgically) in law and literature scholarship as analogues for and informing the study and interpretation of legal texts. Instead, the dominant influence upon oral and visual narrative practices in court, at least in my observation, are popular 'oral' and 'visual' storytelling practices. The most important of these is the influence of the cinema, particularly the linear, protagonist-centred, theme-based, hard reductionist narratives of 'conventional' genre-based Hollywood entertainment films. These stories and the underlying storytelling practices and conventions are closely related to and, I believe, deeply influence and inform aspects of courtroom storytelling including the substance, style, structure, and content of trial work. In many ways, the narrative practices of the trial practitioner exist in a curious relationship with popular cinematic storytelling (drawing upon the forms and stories from the cinema, just as the popular entertainment cinema draws upon law and the trial as the subject of so many current films).

There are surely many reasons for why this is so. For example, we exist in a post-literate storytelling culture and the dominant and most influential form of storytelling is, I believe, that of the popular cinema. Jurors, and attorneys, are products of this culture and their ways of understanding and meaning making are deeply rooted in the folk psychology and schematic patterns of the popular cinema, as well as in the specifics and cultural vocabulary created by the cinematic stories themselves. The work of the trial practitioner is, specifically, akin to that of the director in many ways. Effective trial attorneys, like Hollywood screenwriters and directors, storyboard evidence into clear structural patterns that are often converted

---

3 For example, the trial is analysed as narrative in W.L. Bennett and M.S. Feldman, *Reconstructing Reality in the Courtroom: Justice and Judgment in American Culture* (1981).

4 P.N. Meyer, 'Desperate for Love III: Rethinking Closing Arguments as Stories' (1999) 50 *South Carolina Law Rev.* 715. Many perceptions in this section of the essay are more fully developed in analysing the inferential structure of the argument in that article and are based upon that analysis.

134

in closing arguments into explicit narratives, and, more importantly, by jurors in deliberations, into the narratives that frame juror understandings of evidence and provide the basis for juror verdicts. Jurors watch the drama of the trial unfolding passively, in the theatrical space of the courtroom, their attention spans, expectations, and story consciousness often shaped and prefigured by the Hollywood cine-myths.

My perceptions about why Hollywood films are important to understanding narrative practice in trials to a jury are not, however, the central concern of this brief speculative essay. Rather, my concern is to simply identify some of the ways that trial practitioners convert evidence and inference to construct effective narratives at trial that are often mimetic of popular cinematic stories. I comment upon why the aesthetics of storytelling in the courtroom are more akin to popular entertainment films than the aesthetics and structures that may predominate in 'serious' literary fiction these days, and why, on the continuum of narrative practices, the work of the trial attorney is farther away from the work of the novelist. This distinction becomes clearer, I think, when I review several recent adaptations of novels into Hollywood films, and try to show why one trial story in a criminal case is more akin to the movie rather than the original novel.

CONVERTING EVIDENCE AND ARGUMENT INTO STORY

In trials to a jury, effective advocates often convert the more fragmented structures of rule-based analytical arguments into unitary and focused narratives.[5] The analytical arguments are structured through logic and inference.[6] Clinical paradigms for teachers of trial advocacy accurately articulate the sequence of steps that the trial attorney employs to create the anaytical structure of a trial argument.[7] First, the advocate converts the more abstract terminology and categories[8] of legal elements into factual propositions. Some of these factual propositions are crucial and highly problematic and contested. Others are not. The advocate in structuring argumentation and proof at trial must establish the linkage between evidence

5 Jerome Bruner has observed, 'There are two modes of cognitive functioning, two modes of thought, each providing distinctive ways of ordering experience, of constructing reality. The two [the analytical and the narrative] (though complementary) are irreducible to one another.' J. Bruner, *Actual Minds, Possible Worlds* (1986) 11.
6 A recent book by Moore, Bergman, and Binder provides a structural model for attorneys and law students constructing trial arguments. This model serves as the basis of my analysis. See A.J. Moore et al., *Trial Advocacy: Inferences, Arguments and Techniques* (1996).
7 id.
8 The nature and importance of legal categories in structuring analysis and argumentation is explored in depth in 'On Categories' in *Minding the Law*, eds. A. Amsterdam and J. Bruner (2000).

135

introduced at trial and the crucial and relevant underlying factual propositions by identifying generalizations that connect the evidence to the factual propositions.[9]

For example, I analysed the trial of a federal criminal case[10] (brought under the federal RICO conspiracy statute[11]) charging a defendant with conspiracy in the attempted murder of another person. The problematic element of the charge was whether the defendant, a reputed mobster and member of a crime family, intended to murder that person. That is, the crucial legal issue was the question of defendant's 'intent,' the *mens rea* component of the crime. The most probative evidence of defendant's intent was his promise to the head of the crime family that he would kill the third person. The 'logical' or 'inferential' legal argument presented by the prosecution may be diagrammed in accordance with the clinical model presented for analysing inferential arguments by Moore, Bergman, and Binder[12] as follows:

Evidence: Defendant promised the mob boss that he would kill the third person.[13]

Generalization:[14] When a defendant promises another person that he will kill a third person, the defendant usually intends to kill the third person. *Especially when:*[15]

1. The defendant is a member of a 'crime family'.
2. The defendant is 'deathly afraid' of the person to whom he has made the promise.
3. The defendant knows that the person to whom he has made the promise has a compelling motive for wanting the third person dead.

---

9 Moore et al., op. cit., n. 6.
10 *United States* v. *Bianco* (1990) no. H-90-18 (AHN) (D. Conn. Dec. 7, 1990), *aff'd*, 998 F.2d 1112 (1993).
11 18 U.S.C. sec. 1961–1968 (1988 and Supp. IV 1992).
12 Moore et al., op. cit., n. 6, at pp. 9–22.
13 The first step in Moore, Bergman, and Binder's clinical model is to convert the abstract terminology of the legal elements (categories) onto 'factual propositions' and then, 'with a crucial proposition and evidence list in hand, select an item or two that you consider to be the most highly probative of the proposition. That is choose the one or two items that you think a factfinder will see as most clearly establishing the proposition.' id, at p. 20.
14 The next step is to establish the linkage between the evidence and the crucial factual proposition. That is, the 'basis for connecting the evidence to the proposition' must be established by 'identifying the generalizations connecting the evidence to the factual proposition.' Then, the advocate should, 'identify additional evidence suggesting that the generalization is especially likely to be true given the unique circumstances of the particular case.' id., at p. 25.
15 'Especially whens' are items of evidence and reasons indicating why a generalization is especially likely to be accurate in the case at hand. Thus, to strengthen an argument add 'especially when' to a generalization and examine a file to identify additional evidence suggesting that your generalization is especially likely to be accurate in the case at hand.' id.

136

4. The defendant conspires with other members of the 'crime family' about how to accomplish the killing.

The defendant responds with counter-propositions ('except whens') that make the prosecution's argument less likely to be true. These counter-propositions must also be supported by evidence submitted at trial. Thus the logic of defendant's counter-argument may be set forth as follows:

Defendant's 'Except Whens':[16]
1. Defendant is not receiving much benefit from being a member of the crime family and does not participate in the family's day-to-day activities.
2. Defendant has a close personal relationship with the third person.
3. Defendant does not really mean what he says and is lying about his true intentions to buy time for the third person.
4. Defendant is prone to hyperbole and exaggeration about his criminal intentions.
5. Defendant has failed to carry out the execution even when he has been alone with the third person and has had the opportunity to do so.

The attorney, hypothetically, could have presented evidence at trial, and structured his argument in just this way, as a series of logical counter propositions. Like many, perhaps most, effective attorneys these days, however, he did not choose to do so. Instead, he converted the 'except whens,' and the evidence supporting these propositions, into an aesthetically compelling narrative similar in tone, structure and content to many hard, linear, protagonist-driven Hollywood cine-myths. The evidence introduced at trial had been presented as if 'story-boarded' and was then recapitulated in closing argument in the form of a three-part structure of a popular, compelling, and entertaining 'Mafia movie'. Theme, character, conflict, narrative structure were intentionally proximate to filmic counterparts about the mob, and the story of the tender-hearted mobster had numerous historical cinematic antecedents. Furthermore, the attorney nested his storytelling in these cinematic models. The story had many of the characteristics of a popular Hollywood mob fable filled with irony and humour, and attempted to fulfill the audience's expectations and understandings about American crime families derived from popular film.

Evidence is converted into story on the spine of a hard narrative structure that is 'thematic.' The theme is like the 'stock' themes and repetitive stories of Hollywood entertainment fables. Here the theme is that of the a redemption plot, where the protagonist moves from selfishness towards selflessness

---

16 Responding to the prosecutor's argument, the defendant's attorney identifies 'except whens' to refute the generalization underlying the argument. These 'except whens' are additional propositions that make the generalization relied upon by the prosecution less likely to be true. Like the 'especially whens' these propositions must be supported by evidence admitted at trial. id., at pp. 40–1.

and ultimately sacrifices himself to a larger cause. The classic Hollywood version of redemption story is, perhaps, *Casablanca* where the protagonist, Rick, a strong but selfish man, moves from cynicism to romantic love and then, at the moment of crisis, sacrifices himself in service of a larger cause.

I have called the 'title' of the defendant's version of the thematic trial story 'Desperate For Love', and explained the plot as the story of a weak but kind man torn between the love of his Mafia family on the one hand and the love of his 'real' family on the other.[17] His dilemma and his internal psychological conflict and the outer plot conflict is resolved at the denouement. Like Rick, the protagonist in *Casablanca* who moves from great selfishness towards love of another and then towards self-sacrifice within the confines of three hard narrative acts, the protagonist, defendant Louie Failla, moves through a similar psychological arc, along the well-trodden character through-line and narrative progression of the contemporary almost-hero.

The perspective of the storyteller, the defendant's attorney, like the director's perspective in *Casablanca*, is focused upon Louie's psychological transformation that is intimated through his responses to the pressures of external events. Like the audience in *Casablanca*, the jurors respond to Louie's psychological transformation. Also, in the end, like Rick in *Casablanca*, Louie, the protagonist/defendant, a weak but kind man, gains strength and sacrifices himself, stringing along his adopted mob family and pretending to participate in the murder conspiracy while, in fact, protecting his son-in-law from the mob.

The 'themes' of certain 'stock' stories or archetypal stories tend to organize the storytelling at trial. This is the type of familiar genre storytelling that, I believe, is much more likely to be found in a popular film (as an entertainment) than in many literary novels. That is, the story that connects evidence into trial narrative enforces rather than defies the conventional shared understandings and the morality of the audience. The story is organized by themes that engage the jurors but do not defy or offend audience expectations; they are often themes rooted in the folk psychology characteristic of the storytelling and aesthetic sensibility of Hollywood cinema.

Likewise, the depiction of character, particularly the depiction of a sympathetic or empathetic protagonist, is more akin to Hollywood genre conventions than the psychological depth that is often characteristic of the novel. There are reasons for this. First, the story in a trial looks 'out' at external events presented through testimony on an 'objective' experiential landscape. The form of questioning of witnesses does not allow for deep introspection, and time is compressed to focus on narrow concepts of relevancy that do not allow for deep exploration of peripheral matters.

For example, in the trial of Louie Failla, although the crucial issue was 'what did Louie intend?', that is, whether he intended to murder another

17 Meyer, op. cit., n. 2.

138

person, Louie never testified. There is no first-person storytelling, no direct exploration of Louie's motivation and character. The trial was thirteen weeks long, and endless government surveillance tapes were introduced. The only exploration of Louie's past, however, his psychobiography, his personal life and motivations, was coincidental, involving some shared nostalgic stories about Louie's sexual exploits. None of these events were legally relevant to the narrower issue of Louie's intent. Louie's deep character, that might have been the material for a marvellous novelistic exploration, was not a relevant issue at trial especially since Louie, like many criminal defendants, did not testify at trial. The dynamics of Louie's character were reduced to the simple story told by his attorney in the closing argument where Louie's character was compressed into the limited dimensionality of a single internal conflict. This was the inner contradiction of the small-time mobster torn between two competing plots and personal goals – securing the respect of his mob family, and obtaining some financial success and security while maintaining his honour on the one hand, and, simultaneously, preserving the love of his 'real' family on the other by defying the order of the *capo* of his crime family. This external conflict caused the central crisis of character that is characteristic of the redemption film genre and fits well with the legal issue (the ambivalence of Louie's intent).

It is my belief that trial storytelling genre conventions – the rules of evidence, the time constraints of the trial itself, the focus on arranging testimony and events into clear narrative progressions that complement juror expectations, and the focus upon events taking place on a shared and external narrative landscape – all shape the defendant's character in the trial story to take the imaginative form of the protagonist in a Hollywood genre film.

Finally, the progression of the character, the through-line, and the overall arc of the plot tends to form itself at trial along the well-defined structural masterplots provided by Hollywood templates. That is, stories that transform arguments at trial tend to be developed in three parts or acts characteristic of the three-act narrative structure dominant in many Hollywood films. There is a linearity to the progression of events that may be characterized in terms of shots, scenes, and sequences. In 'Desperate for Love', for example, the first act is the hook and set-up, where the attorney for the defendant redefines the plot along the theme suggested by his 'except whens' (the counter-propositions to the prosecutions argument). In the second act the dramatic tension is increased as the defences to the lesser charges in the RICO indictment are established. That is, Louie Failla is a small-time mobster engaging in illegal activities but these activities are outside the scope of RICO because 'they put money into Louie's pocket but not into the pocket of the Patriarca crime family'. During this act, the tension between the protagonist and the antagonist is intensified and culminates in a third-act climax and resolution where Louie, the exaggerator, chooses to defy the Patriarca crime family by pretending to go along with the plot to murder Tito Morales while stalling to buy Tito sufficient time and protecting him from

139

the crime family. The story is consistent with the evidence introduced at trial. This hard plot-driven form of narrative while characteristic of many Hollywood films is not characteristic of the structure of contemporary fiction.

These observations may become clearer when I compare the filmic adaptations of two authors in relationship to the Failla trial.

ADAPTATION IN THE COURTROOM AND ON THE SCREEN

As I have argued in the previous section, the popular film maker and the trial attorney employing narrative often convert more complex material into simpler structures of visual and oral narratives that can capture the imagination and understanding of a passive audience sitting to absorb the presentation of the story. Although the conversion process and the conventions of the forms are somewhat different, there are remarkable similarities between the two processes. The attorney at trial to a jury must introduce testimony and evidence and respond to evidence introduced by the other side and reshape this evidence into an effective story that is, primarily, made explicit only when speaking directly to the jury in opening statement and closing argument. The story is usually organized and presented along a spine of a narrative 'theory,' a theme, so that, in jury deliberations, the jury can readily reconfigure the evidence into a unitary, linear, focused 'narrative' that provides a form to process and convert the evidence introduced at trial.

The popular film-maker often makes similar narrative moves. These moves are especially apparent when adapting material from other narrative mediums, particularly from literature. For example, in adapting material from potentially more complex literary novels into film, the popular film-maker, like the defence attorney in *Failla*, often compresses complex and ambiguous characters into sympathetic archetypes, strengthens a unitary and linear plot line around a single and readily identifiable thematic core, and focuses the lens of a story upon the perspective of a sympathetic or empathetic protagonist as both subject and providing point of view. In the process, the adaptation often reduces the potential complexity of literary themes, and sacrifices the perceptions and vision of deeply interior literary voices that might slow the plot and interfere with the audience's enjoyment of recognizable entertainments that fulfill clearly held narrative expectations.

Let me illustrate briefly by identifying Hollywood cinematic adaptations of ambitious literary fictions, and how these works were adjusted to fit the confines of a different genre of oral and visual storytelling. This is somewhat akin to the storytelling practices of trial attorneys converting potentially complex evidentiary materials to fit the genre conventions of effective storytelling at trial.

Numerous 'realist' novels have been converted recently into popular films. Let me here, however, briefly identify two to illustrate somewhat

140

conventional narrative 'moves' in the conversion of a literary work into popular film, and then analogize them to the work of defendant's attorney in *United States* v. *Failla*. The moves pertain to: (i) the use of theme as a linear spine in popular cinema (to convert and provide the plot-based focus for the unifying 'vision' in fiction often accomplished by the power of 'voice'; (ii) the clear redefinition of character as sympathetic or, at least, an empathetic character that the audience can readily identify with; and (iii) the use of a 'hard' three-act narrative structure based upon linear time that cuts away and reconfigures material that does not readily figure into the plot-line.

The filmic adaptation of the works of James Ellroy provide an illustration about how a more complex and searching and extremely dark moral vision and, simultaneously, the perspective conveyed by 'voice' is transformed into a readily defined and acceptable cinematic theme that serves as the spine for construction of a hard, visual, plot-based narrative. James Ellroy's novels, including such books as *L.A. Confidential*[18] and *White Jazz*,[19] and Ellroy's darkly powerful recent memoir, *My Dark Places*,[20] provide recurring visitations to a societal nightmare. The nightmare ultimately has to do, I believe, with corruption so deep that it pervades not only the institutions of the society but infects the souls of the characters, including the voice of the storyteller. The 'plots' of the books are inevitably descending spirals into ever darkening shadows. The clear resolutions of cause and effect, of mysteries solved by hero detectives redeemed through their searches and discoveries are often denied to the reader. The power of the books is in the prose style – the 'voice' of the author – that raises Ellroy above other 'genre' authors: the language stylistically serves like a machine gun fusillade of bullets of language shot against darkening imagery, as if the author, like the protagonist detectives, is attempting to somehow awaken from the dream that envelops him. All of the books, including Ellroy's memoir, are about tracing unsolved murders back to their source and have to do thematically with the consuming nature of the power of evil, that infects all of the characters, including the protagonists. The darkness is so deep and all-pervasive that it is impossible to locate the source of the corruption. The power is in the prose, the style, that compels the reader's attention.

For those unfamiliar with Ellroy, here is an illustrative excerpt taken from the opening of *My Dark Places*, the plot of which is about Ellroy's ultimately failed attempt to find his mother's murderer. Ellroy's circumstances are akin to those of Bud White, one of the protagonist detectives in *L.A. Confidential*, who, unlike Ellroy, has actually witnessed his mother's murder. White's anger is transformed into brutality expressed through vengeance against those who abuse women; Ellroy's rage is expressed through language. *My Dark Places* opens:

18 J. Ellroy, *L.A. Confidential* (1990).
19 J. Ellroy, *White Jazz* (1992).
20 J. Ellroy, *My Dark Places* (1996).

THE REDHEAD

A cheap Saturday night took you down. You died stupidly and harshly and without the means to hold your own life dear.

Your run to safety was a brief reprieve. You brought me into hiding as your good-luck charm. I failed you as a talisman – so now I stand as your witness.

Your death defines my life. I want to find the love we never had and explicate it in your name.

I want to take your secrets public. I want to burn down the distance between us.

I want to give you breath.[21]

*

Some kids found her.

They were Babe Ruth League players, out to hit a few shag balls. The three adult coaches were walking behind them. The boys saw a shape in the ivy strip just off the curb. The men saw loose pearls on the pavement. A little telepathic jolt went around . . .

Deputy Vic Cavallero huddled up the coaches and the kids. Officer Dave Wire checked out the body.

It was a female Caucasian. She was fair-skinned and red-headed. She was approximately 40 years of age. She was lying flat on her back – in an ivy patch a few inches from the King's Row curb line.

Her right arm was bent upward. Her right hand was resting a few inches above her head. Her left hand was clenched. Her legs were outstretched. She was wearing a scoop-front, sleeveless, light and dark blue dress. A dark blue overcoat with a matching lining was spread over her lower body. Her feet and ankles were visible. Her right foot was bare. A nylon stocking was bunched up around her left ankle.

Her dress was disheveled. Insect bites covered her arms. Her face was bruised and her tongue protruding. Her brassiere was unfastened and hiked above her breasts. A nylon stocking and a cotton chord were lashed around her neck. Both ligatures were tightly wound.[22]

The book ultimately concludes with the dramatic juxtaposition back to the intimate first-person voice with Ellroy speaking directly to his mother 'the red-head' once again:

> *I'm with you now. You ran and hid and I found you. Your secrets were not safe with me. You earned my devotion. You paid for it in public disclosure. I robbed your grave. I revealed you. I showed you in shameful moments. I learned things about you. Everything I learned made me love you more dearly.*
>
> *I'll learn more. I'll follow your tracks and invade your hidden time. I'll uncover your lies. I'll rewrite your history and revise my judgment as your old secrets explode. I will justify it all in the name of the obsessive life you gave me.*
>
> *I can't hear your voice. I can smell you and taste your breath. I can feel you. You're brushing against me. You're gone and I want more of you.*[23]

21 id., p. 2.
22 id., pp. 3–4.
23 id., p. 429.

142

In the cinematic version of one of Ellroy's novels, *L.A. Confidential*, Ellroy's vision is recast into the more familiar territory and the dramatic form of Hollywood cinema, a conventional plot structure with a strong thematic spine. The language and 'voice' of the storyteller are no longer crucial. The adaptation by Curtis Hanson casts the theme into the more familiar form of an updated *film noir*, akin to Roman Polanski's *Chinatown*, where the clarity of the familiar story about the corruption of powerful institutional forces is commercially more viable and immediately recognizable to the audience. The criminal enterprise, initially investigated by the protagonist-detective, becomes a clue, and eventually a masterplot of corrupt institutional force, personified by powerful and evil antagonists, unravels. The protagonists here are not beyond redemption, and the story theme obtains clarity at the film's narrative climax, an 'up' ending where the protagonist, Bud White, is redeemed and saved and escapes transformed. The source of the external powerful evil is identified, the plot has a sense of resolution, and the evil does not swallow up all of those within it.

Similarly, in *Failla*, the defendant's story has intentionally chosen a narrative theme that echoes with familiarity of clear Hollywood cinematic precursors. The material was rich and dark and complex and could have provided a fascinating exploration of defendant Failla's complex motivation. The thirteen weeks of testimony and evidence had introduced a huge amount of material. Failla, however, had not testified and no direct testimony had been introduced to clarify Failla's 'intent'. The attorney made important and creative choices and then shaped the plot along the simpler narrative core provided by a familiar theme formulating a readily recognizable and updated version of the Hollywood redemption story, providing a reconfiguration of the evidence.

The trial story, intentionally, had a certain Hollywood familiarity to it: the 'theme' of the story was about a man with a deep inner need to be loved and respected. A theme about a man torn between his real family, on the one hand, and his adopted mob family on the other. A man who exaggerates and tells stories out of a need to be loved, and a desire to be respected and valued. In the end, this character must choose between his two families, and, in doing so, redeems himself through his storytelling and exaggeration. It is an updated version of a long line of redemption stories.

A second familiar move of cinematic adaptation is to reformulate the character of the protagonist into an empathetic or sympathetic character (a flawed everyman) that the audience can identify with. Then, thirdly, to formulate a linear narrative plot from the perspective of the transformation of this protagonist/narrator. The adaptation of Russell Banks's complex multi-perspective novel, *The Sweet Hereafter*,[24] into the excellent and carefully constructed cinematic version, provides an artistic illustration of this principle of adaptation. In Banks's novel about the aftermath of a school bus crash in northern New York, Mitchell Stephens, Esq., one of four first-person

24 R. Banks, *The Sweet Hereafter* (1991).

narrative voices telling the story, is an attorney who travels to the town to sign up the families of the children who died in the crash and those who did not in a lawsuit against as yet unidentified defendants (defendants with financial resources) who could be culpable for the tragedy. He is a dark character, largely unsympathetic, motivated by his rage. Like Ellroy's voice, Stephens transforms fury into language, introspection and self-hatred, simultaneously, into purposeful conduct as he enlists his clients. An initial excerpt introducing Stephens provides an illustration of Williams' 'character' in the novel:

> Angry? Yes I'm angry; I'd be a lousy lawyer if I weren't. I suppose it's as if I've got this permanent boil on my butt and can't quite sit down. Which is not the same, you understand, as being dubbed hounded by greed; although I can see, of course, that it probably sometimes looked like greed to certain individuals who were not lawyers, when they saw a person like me driving all the way up there to the Canadian border, practically, saw me camping out in the middle of winter in a windy dingy little motel room for weeks at a time, bugging the hell out of decent people who were in the depths of despair and just wanted to be left alone. I can understand that.
>
> But it wasn't greed that put me there; it's never been greed that sends me whirling out of orbit like that. It's anger. What the hell, I'm not ashamed of it. It's who I am. I'm not proud of it, either, but it makes me useful, at least. Which is more than I can say for greed.
>
> That's what people don't get about negligence lawyers – good negligence lawyers, I mean ... No, what it is, we're permanently pissed off, the winners, and practicing law is a way to become socially useful at the same time, that's all. It's like a discipline; it organizes and controls us; probably keeps us from being homicidal.[25]

In the cinematic adaptation, however, shot from the perspective of Mitchell Stephens as protagonist, the character is artfully transformed into a somewhat ambivalent and largely empathetic (although not sympathetic) character[26] whose present-tense story of enlisting the victims in a lawsuit is

---

25 id., pp. 89–90.
26 Robert McKee, the highly regarded screenwriting teacher and guru, stresses: 'The PROTAGONIST must be empathetic; he may or may not be sympathetic.' And then explains:

> Sympathetic means likable. Tom Hanks and Meg Ryan, for example, or Spencer Tracy and Katharine Hepburn in their typical roles: The moment they step onscreen, we like them. We'd want them as friends, family members, or lovers. They have an innate likability and evoke sympathy. Empathy, however, is a more profound response.
>
> Empathetic means 'like me.' Deep within the protagonist the audience recognizes a certain shared humaity. Character and audience are not alike in every fashion, of course; they may share only a single quality. But there's something about the character that strikes a chord. In that moment of recognition, the audience suddenly and instinctively wants the protagonist to achieve whatever it is that he desires ... An audience may, if so moved, empathize with every character in your film, but it must empathize with your protagonist. If not, the audience/story bond is broken. (R. McKee, *Story* (1997) 141.)

144

balanced against the past-tense back-story of the transformation and loss of his daughter and family. In Atom Egoyan's cinematic adaptation, Stephens is not possessed by the perpetual linguistic fury that blinds him in the novel, and makes him a manipulator of the broken spirits, his clients, the victims of the accident and their families. The novel's character of Stephens, angry and unredeemed, would be repellant to the audience. In the film, Stephens's character has different and more ambivalent relationships with and feelings for his clients, particularly the paralysed girl Nichole Burnell, who has been sexually abused by her own father. She herself seeks and achieves her delicate revenge against Stephens and her father by undermining the lawsuit in her deposition at the denouement of the film.

Mitchell Stephens is transformed in the film from a dark force, one of four voices and the least empathetic voice of all, into a Hollywood protagonist who, unlike Mitchell Stephens in the book, goes through a process of transformation of character that becomes the subtle climax of the film as his anger is transformed into acceptance, of the loss of his daughter as well as the case. The film, consequently, required the reimagining and creation of new scenes not in the novel to reshape this climax and resolution along the new through-line and character arc for Mitchell Stephens's character, now the focus of the film. The film thus becomes a story about the psychological redemption of the protagonist.

Likewise, at trial and, particularly, in his closing argument, attorney Jeremiah Donovan literally assumes the voice of his client Louie Failla and reformulates a protagonist-centred story. The focalization is the psychological perspective of Louie Failla, and Donovan revisits portions of damaging surveillance tapes and evidence in which defendant Failla plots the murder of Tito Morales. Like Mitchell Stephens as depicted in the film, akin to Rick in *Casablanca*, Failla undergoes a psychological transformation in three carefully structured acts that can be readily identified by the audience of the jury. This conforms both to the reconfigured evidence and the jurors' notions about empathetic characterization derived from folk wisdom, and the complex stock stories drawn from a cinematic repertoire. Akin to the transformation of Stephens' character as he moves from the novel to cinema, Failla becomes a true cinematic protagonist; a deeply empathetic, if not entirely sympathetic, character. In the prosecution's version of events, and in the surveillance tapes played at trial, Louie Failla was but one of eight defendants in a dark conspiracy, an evil agent, unredeemed and unrepentant, his psychology unexplained and unexplored. In the defendant's version of the same events, however, and in the exploration of the same surveillance tapes and evidence introduced at trial, Louie's character is redefined along the familiar path of the psychological transformation of the protagonist in the Hollywood redemption plot. The story is now Louie's story, shot from Louie's perspective exclusively, just as the story belongs to Mitchell Stephens in the cinematic adaptation of Banks's *The Sweet Hereafter*, or to Rick in *Casablanca*. That is, the focus is upon the

145

psychological transformation of the protagonist. Simultaneously, the jury is compelled to reinterpret evidence through the lens of Louie's perspective as protagonist and, in doing so, Louie's static character is transformed. At the end Donovan's version of the plot becomes a genre Hollywood redemption story. Louie becomes a self-aware protagonist who cleverly uses his storytelling abilities to stall off the mobsters by pretending to go along with the plot to murder Tito Morales while securing for him additional time so that he can find safety.

Finally, narrative structure often changes in cinematic adaptation. Fragments become pasted onto a single narrative spine that is often broken into three discrete narrative acts, and a univocal story takes shape centering the story and providing a protagonist-driven perspective for storytelling. For example, in Banks's *The Sweet Hereafter*, there are multiple first-person voices telling the story from different perspectives. Consequently, time is complex, fractioned into elliptical slices into the stories of each of the voices. Time moves backwards and forwards as each of the voices revisits the accident and the events that occur after the accident has occurred. In Egoyan's cinematic adaptation of Banks' novel, however, those multiple voices are transformed into a single focus, the lens of the story is upon the perspective of the protagonist. The story becomes linear, but not purely chronological, rather a series of psychological chronologies with flashbacks interspersed from the perspective of the narrator and the stories of those characters who are interviewed by the narrator, intertwined with the narrator's interior story. Likewise, attorney Jeremiah Donovan, reshaped the multiple narratives of the witnesses at trial and the multiple perspectives of the surveillance tapes played at trial into a single univocal narrative shaped around Failla's perspective, an interior story based exclusively on the reconfiguration of the evidence introduced at trial.

CONCLUSION

In this speculative essay I have summarized my observations based on a close analysis of arguments in a criminal case and, I hope, have conveyed some sense of my belief that the popular cinema provides a model for some aspects of storytelling at trial. Using the jury trial in the criminal case of *U.S. v. Failla* as an illustration in comparison to two cinematic adaptations of recent novels, I have attempted to show why storytelling at trial is more informed substantively and stylistically by the filmic counterparts rather than more literary models such as those provided by 'realist' fiction, especially the often more complex voices and forms of the contemporary novel.

JOURNAL OF LAW AND SOCIETY
VOLUME 28, NUMBER 1, MARCH 2001
ISSN: 0263-323X, pp. 147–63

Adapting the Modern Law Novel: Filming John Grisham

PETER ROBSON*

The essay looks at the process of adaptation of fiction to film. It seeks to build on earlier work which suggested that this process required to be examined in the political and social context within which the adaptation occurred. It focuses on the work of John Grisham and notes how the fiction of Grisham can be divided into thrillers and social issues novels. These in their turn have been turned into films in which, in the process of adaptation, their themes have become both sharper and more focused. They have also in this process become less critical of the social and political structures within which Grisham's fictional protagonists operate. The essay seeks to provide an explanation for this paradox which relates to the fore-mentioned notion of contextual adaptation.

The people who make these decisions are at the top of their professions . . .
there are, though, times when you wish they could have done it more
faithfully to the novel.
(Colin Dexter on the adaptation of his final Inspector Morse novel *The Remorseful Day* – in which Morse dies – but lives on in the adaptation)[1]

SOCIAL ISSUES IN THE MODERN LAW FILM: ADAPTING JOHN GRISHAM

This essay is principally focused on the work of John Grisham and how
this work has progressed in its transfer from mega-selling fiction to a
number of modestly successful films – judged both financially[2] and

* *The Law School, University of Strathclyde, 173 Cathedral Street, Glasgow G4 0RQ, Scotland*

1 *Guardian*, 16 May 2000, G2, 3. Authors must have more influence than Dexter imagined. When the final Morse was screened on 15 November 2000, Morse did indeed die.
2 *Movie Times*: Box Office: Top 100 grossing movies ever – no appearances; *Entertainment Scene*: $100m+ Grossing Movies – *The Firm* at 49 taking $158m and *The Pelican Brief* at 154 with $100m – March 30 1998; no appearances in the top 100 movies, even adjusted for inflation. Grisham is reported to have received for the film

critically.[3] It draws on observations which suggested that to obtain a better purchase on the process of adaptation it is crucial to examine the social and political context within which the films in question are made rather than simply concentrate on the aesthetic and stylistic distinctions between the written source and film[4] as though these are pure processes to be assessed in some kind of artistic vacuum. Grisham has been uniquely successful in the number of his books which have been filmed. Other authors within the sub-genre of modern legal procedurals have made much fewer translations to the screen.[5]

In an earlier essay[6] I sought to look at adaptation in the context of social issues novels and their transformation in British film. In addition to a general overview I looked in detail at one area of social issues, race. The film version of a non-fiction autobiography retained significant areas of the original storyline of a young black man coming to work in Britain in the 1950s whilst having its context radically amended. A much blander portrayal of race and racism in post-war Britain hence emerged. In the other area, poverty, by contrast, a full-length work of radical fiction in three parts was adapted in a highly modified form which emphasized the positive aspects of the struggles of the working class against capital. In the first instance, in *To Sir With Love*, the background of racism was removed from the film. In the other situation, the ambivalence and failures of the Labour movement were airbrushed out of the action in *The Stars Look Down*. That essay sought to explore some of the reasons why this had occurred. The conclusion was that any grounded explanation had to go beyond the artistic imperative and could best be understood by locating the films firmly within the cultural context, political parameters, and economic production process operative at the time. The observations in this essay suggest that the adaptation process has both sharpened the value conflicts between the principal protagonists as well as softening their structural implications.

---

rights an escalating set of payments – $600,000 for *The Firm*, $2.25m for *The Client*, $3.75m for *The Chamber*, $6m for *A Time to Kill*, and $8m for *The Runaway Jury* (source: *Halliwell* (2000)).

3 The Oscar nominations for Best Supporting Actress and Best Actress have been received for the films – Holly Hunter in *The Firm* and Susan Sarandon in *The Client*.
4 R. Richardson, *Literature and Film* (1969).
5 Scott Turrow has had one of his novels filmed – *Presumed Innocent* (1990). No films have emerged from the novels of Richard North Paterson, Philip Friedman, Steve Martini, Ed McBain (writing his Matthew Hope novels) George V. Higgins (writing his Jerry Kennedy novels), William Bernhardt, Lisa Scottoline or William Coughlin. Barry Reed similarly has produced other novels but only his first one, *The Verdict* (1982), has been filmed.
6 P. Robson, 'Fade to Grey: Transforming Social Issues in Film', paper at Critical Legal Studies Conference, London, September 1999.

A major focus of adaptation studies has been on how 'literature' or major works of fiction have fared when they reached the screen, with particular emphasis on the question of 'fidelity'.[7] This has not been without its critics, of course.[8] Given the major cinematic and televisual coverage of some authors' work, it is not surprising that the treatment of writers like Shakespeare, Dickens, and Thackeray has dominated.[9] They are described by the media, if not the academy, as 'the classics'. The most recent intervention in the field of adaptation discusses the question of what indeed amounts to a 'classic' in the context of the impact of cultural studies and multiculturalism. The various authors proceed on the basis that the canon is culturally constructed. There is no permanence to its constitution but it operates as useful heuristic tool and explanatory device. The essays trace the process of adapting from within such a culturally constructed canon and its impact on the films adapted and of the further impact of earlier adaptations.[10]

Different ways of categorizing adaptations have emerged from the writers in this area drawing on the works examined. Wagner produces a triple category of adaptation covering transposition, commentary, and analogy denoting the distinct ways in which the cinema industry has dealt with literary sources.[11] They have sometimes simply rendered their content in a visual form. *Wuthering Heights* (1939), *Jane Eyre* (1944), *Madame Bovary* (1949), *Lord Jim* (1965) are amongst those which fall into this category of Wagner's. On other occasions, film-makers have altered the original, either deliberately or intentionally. Here the fictional work is a point of departure for the new creation. This may involve re-emphasis or re-structuring. *Catch-22* (1970) and *A Clockwork Orange* (1972) are suggested examples of this relationship between fiction and film. Finally *Cabaret* (1972) and *Death in Venice* (1971) are put forward as representing the method which involves using different techniques to make a very different work of art from the original. This may involve shifts in time, location or characters. Wagner also provides a way of seeing the early James Bond films as fitting into each of these categories. Sinyard, for his part talks of adaptation as criticism. He suggests that the best adaptations of books for film involve the adaptation

7 N. Sinyard, *Filming Literature* (1986); J. Orr and C. Nicholson (eds.), *Cinema and Fiction* (1992); J. Bignell, *Writing and Cinema* (1999) – part 3; D. Cartmell and I. Whelehan (eds.), *Adaptations: from text to screen, screen to text* (1999) – part II; P.J. Santoro, *Novel into Film* (1996); J. Lothe, *Narrative Fiction and Film* (2000).

8 B. McFarlane, *Novel to Film* (1996) at 8–11.

9 R. Giddings, K. Selby, and C. Wensley, *Screening the Novel* (1990); A. Davies and S. Wells (eds.), *Shakespeare and the Moving Image* (1994).

10 D. Cartmell, I.Q. Hunter, H. Kay, and I. Whelehan, *Classics in Film and Fiction* (2000).

11 G. Wagner, *The Novel and the Cinema* (1975) part 3.

being seen not as a pictorialization of the complete novel but rather a critical essay, which stresses what, is perceived as the main theme.[12] Such adaptations, suggests Sinyard, provide 'a critical gloss on the novels and a freshly imagined cinematic experience that enrich the appreciation of anyone sincerely devoted to film literature'.[13]

More recently Brian McFarlane has stressed that this concentration on 'fidelity' undervalues the 'intertextuality' of film.[14] He notes that the non-literary, non-novelistic influences at work on any film are often crucial. Such matters as conditions within the film industry and the prevailing cultural and social climate at the time of the film's making are major determinants in shaping any film. McFarlane notes that such notions are difficult to formalize as opposed to questions of narrative 'faithfulness'. This whole question of intertextuality is also further explored in the 'classic' collection where, among other things, the role of 'stars' and their impact on the adaptation process is discussed in the context of the work of a variety of authors including Franz Kafka, Nathaniel Hawthorne, and Arthur Miller.[15] The absence of intertextuality is, however, unremarkable. In his fascinating essay[16] on *To Kill a Mockingbird*, for instance, Colin Nicholson does not explore the wider background to official courtroom murder prevalent in the Southern United States which put Finch's actions into context, concentrating instead on character analysis.[17]

Contemporary Spanish writers and screenwriters in 2000, for their part, talk about the cultural equivalence between film and fiction. Neither art form is privileged in the eyes of the practitioners as the true art form.[18] Beyond this we can note that their relationship is contingent and depends on economic factors. The films which can be made are significantly less than the books which can be produced. Each year in the English-speaking world, some 20,000 new fiction titles are produced. This contrasts with the 200 films which are made.

A slightly different set of circumstances obtains where the adaptation takes place during the life of the author and where popular fiction is the subject of the adaptation. The Grisham books are actually written with film in mind as opposed to being simply apt for the visualization process.[19]

---

12 Sinyard, op. cit., n. 7, at ch. 8.
13 id., at p. 117.
14 McFarlane, op. cit., n. 8, at p. 21.
15 Cartmell et al., op. cit., n. 10.
16 C. Nicholson, 'Hollywood and race: To Kill a Mockingbird' in *Cinema and Fiction*, eds. J. Orr and C. Nicholson (1992).
17 See, for instance, special 400-page issue of the *Alabama Law Rev.* (1964) devoted exclusively to locating Atticus Finch in his political and historical context.
18 '*Cine y literatura, ¿buenos cómplices? Cine, Libros ... Nuestra fábrica de suenos*' *Telva*, May 2000, at 20 – discussing *El Portero, La soledad era ésto, Manolito Gafotas*, and *Tú, ¿que harías por amor?*
19 S. Eisenstein, 'Dickens, Griffith and Ourselves' in his *Dickens, Griffith and Film Today* (1949).

Grisham has explained whom he saw in the roles of his characters before starting work on them.[20] We can also assume, that, unlike Dexter and Sara Paretsky, Grisham has been satisfied with adaptations of his work by his continuing to allow his work to be filmed. He has retained the same director and writers on occasions, which indicates approval. Since his annual income is estimated by *Forbes Magazine* to be around $30m, he is not driven by the same financial imperatives as other writers like F. Scott Fitzgerald and Oliver Goldsmith.[21] This essay seeks to engage in the process of contextualization of Grisham's filmed novels whilst paying due attention to the textual transformations which have occurred in the adaptation process.

ADAPTING THE LAW NOVEL

This section looks at two distinct types of Grisham film. One type is a thriller style – the other involves social issues films. This distinction is one, which is to some extent a heuristic device to explain how Grisham operates as a best-selling novelist.[22] His works have alternated between thrillers and social issues works. Of his eleven novels six are broadly chase/thriller works[23] whilst the other five are strongly centred on social issues.[24] Not every one of his chase novels is devoid of social issues and there is some action in the social issues novels. These are not, however, their dominant feature. The social problem content is, however, much less significant in the thrillers. Three of his filmed novels come from that classification – *The Firm*, *The Pelican Brief*, and *The Client*. The other three derive from his social issues novels – *A Time to Kill*, *The Chamber*, and *The Rainmaker*. Although not written in this order this was the pattern of release as Grisham films adopted a more cerebral and issues content. Although it had not reached the screen at the time of writing, October 2000, his most recent novel for film treatment, *The Runaway Jury*, is from the issues side of his work. All of the films fall firmly within Wagner's transposition model or are pictoralizations, to use Sinyard's terminology. This partly stems from the way in which the book and film industry interfaced in the 1990s. Grisham had sold the rights to *The Chamber* prior to starting fleshing out the outline. He saw Paul Newman as the main protagonist in *The Chamber* and he wrote *The Pelican Brief* with Julia Roberts in mind. The recurrent theme within Robert Altman's *The Player* appears to be transposed to real life. The difference is that, with the

20 *Guardian*, 30 May 1994.
21 Goldsmith is recorded as having sold the rights to his works to pay off bills.
22 P. Robson, 'Images of Law in the Fiction of John Grisham' in *Tall Stories? Reading Law and Literature*, eds. J. Morison and C. Bell (1996).
23 *The Firm* (1991); *The Pelican Brief* (1992); *The Client* (1993); *The Partner* (1997); *The Testament* (1999); *The Brethren* (2000).
24 *A Time to Kill* (1989); *The Chamber* (1994); *The Rainmaker* (1995); *The Runaway Jury* (1996); *The Street Lawyer* (1998).

151

potential audience enhanced by the bookbuyers, the semi-fantasy powerplays on which Altman has us eavesdrop become real. The writer's power is sufficient that this process results in a series of films cashing in on the literary sales. He is in the top 100 powerful names in Hollywood.[25] Two of the films with which Grisham has been involved are known in the *John Grisham's The Rainmaker* and *The Gingerbread Man – based on a story by John Grisham*. He has serious clout.

This is not entirely a new phenomenon. Successful fiction writers in the past have been recruited by the film industry to lend their cachet to films. One would include in this number Dashiel Hammett, Raymond Chandler, F. Scott Fitzgerald, Somerset Maugham and A.J. Cronin. With John Grisham it is the scale that is different. There are estimated to be 60 million copies of his books in print world-wide according to his publishers, Random House, in twenty-nine languages. This then at least provides a perspective as to why these adaptations are within the transposition or pictorialization model. It fitted in with the artistic conceptions of a powerful author and more importantly, perhaps, within the financial risk assessment of the producers. That leaves, however, the question of the socio-political content and the impact on the adaptation process. Although, as indicated, these films are broadly transpositions/pictorializations, subtle changes have emerged in these specific adaptations whose nature this essay seeks to explore.

1. *The 'thrillers'*

The method of the industry has been to seek to capitalize on his vast book sales by changing as little as possible. Standard adaptation techniques are employed. Plots are simplified a little. Peripheral characters receive minimal attention. The novels, are however, very much recognizable as filmed versions rather than distinctive creations in their own right. The question of fidelity to some essential text does not appear to be a major concern. These books are, however, 'classics' in the sense that they are the 'ideal type' popular unisex airport novels of the 1990s. One commentator suggested that the sub-genre of the lawyer novel had during this decade supplanted spy thrillers for men and sex-and-shopping novels for women.[26] There has been an explosion of titles and authors in this field producing over 300 titles during the 1990s.[27] Prior to this era the activities of lawyers were given little attention on either side of the Atlantic.[28]

The ways in which the books of Grisham have come to screen are particularly interesting. The calibre of actors and directors involved has

---

25 In 1997 he was at 52nd dropping to 60 in 1998 – *Mr Showbiz*.
26 M. Lawson, *The Bestseller Brief*, BBC, 2 February 1994.
27 Robson, op. cit., n. 21.
28 Henry Cecil and John Mortimer in Britain and William Coughlin and Caroline Wheat in the United States enjoyed modest success.

certainly not been second rate. The films themselves have been, nonetheless, largely unmemorable. Discussing the pre-Law-School influx into Hollywood and the films of Raoul Walsh, Roman Polanski, and other Hollywood 'old-timers' John Patterson observes 'I'm not saying that the absence of legal qualifications among the participants is the reason they all made great movies, but I bet it helped.'[29] They are, however, part of a trend which has seen 'one legal thriller ... knocked off its chart-topping perch ... replaced by another legal thriller'. One reason tentatively put forward by one commentator is the influx of Ivy League law-school graduates who flooded into Hollywood from the late 1980s onwards, producing a stream of pictures like *The Client, The Rainmaker, The Firm, The Chamber, A Few Good Men, My Cousin Vinnie, The Devil's Advocate*, and *Erin Brockovich*.[30]

Six Grisham films were made in the 1990s. The directors had impressive track records and all have made critically acclaimed films as well as commercially successful ones. Thus we find Sydney Pollack, Alan J. Pakula, Joel Schumacher, James Foley, and Francis Ford Coppola directing the Grisham films.[31]

(a) *The Firm*

The novel *The Firm* was Grisham's second and it was this which started the best-seller phenomenon which emerged in the 1990s. It was published in 1991 and rapidly sold 1.6 million copies. The film version appeared in 1993. Its all-star cast included Tom Cruise, Gene Hackman, Holly Hunter,[32] and Jeanne Tripplehorn.

Director Sidney Pollack had worked on another thriller, *Three Days of the Condor* as well as social commentaries about the nature of the American Dream like *The Way We Were, The Electric Horseman, They Shoot Horses Don't They?, Tootsie*, and (on one reading) *Absence of Malice*. His adaptations of fiction met with varied critical success ranging from *This Property is Condemned* to *Out of Africa*. The screenplay was written by David Rabe, Robert Towne, and David Rayfield.

A bright young law gradute from a poor background is tempted to work for a firm in unfashionable Memphis in exchange for a superb financial package. In the course of working for the firm he discovers that there is some dark secret. This turns out to be the fact that the firm is a money-laundering operation for the Mob. Our newly qualified lawyer is able to bring the firm to justice and escape the clutches of the Mob through a cunning knowledge of federal law and make off with enough Mob money to retire in an undisclosed Caribbean destination.

29 J. Patterson, 'To live and die in law-school' *Guardian*, 14 April 2000, G2, 23.
30 id.
31 *The Gingerbread Man* is a Grisham film in that it is based on an 'original story by John Grisham' – this does not appear to be a published story – it borrows heavily from the storylines of *Cape Fear* and *Body Heat*.
32 Her performance earned her an Oscar nomination for Best Supporting Actress.

This novel contains a minimal amount of comment on the social and legal implications of law practice. Grisham limits himself to what might be regarded as self-regarding plaints about the career sacrifices which have to be made to get ahead in the fiercely competitive world of the fledgling lawyer. This may be good therapy for the soul of someone like Grisham who has endured the long hours and heavy workload associated with legal practice. In *The Firm,* however, the implications of this for justice, as opposed to a full, rounded social and family life are not explored. It is, however, a theme which drives the actions of characters in his later works and creates the character of the desperate lawyer looking for the 'big score' to free him from the rat race.[33]

The notion of the corruption at the heart of the system has been a trope which has sustained many fictional representations of institutions including the halls of justice. The dire implications for the rule of law that result from a corrupt *judiciary* is found in film in *And Justice for All, Suspect,* and *Presumed Innocent* and in a vigilante form in *The Star Chamber.* The representation of the *jury* as a highly suspect device for assessing evidence is demonstrated in *To Kill a Mockingbird, The Sun Shines Bright* and is strongly implied in *Twelve Angry Men.* The novel twist, which Grisham lends to the trope, is the 'mysterious law firm … secretly owned by the Mafia … [and] … nobody ever leaves the firm'.

Grisham, in *The Firm,* highlights the notion that those with power, whether legitimate or not, derive legitimacy from their paid legal functionaries. This is expressed in popular culture by such varied figures as Woody Guthrie[34] and Raymond Chandler:

> Sure there's such a thing as law. We're up to our necks in it. About all it does is make business for lawyers. How long do you think the big-shot mobsters would last if the lawyers didn't show them how to operate.[35]

The assumption by those with power of a smooth and persuasive façade by way of their professional representatives is a feature which again recurs in Grisham's work. What is different here, which makes the issue of limited interest is the clear illegitimacy of the interests protected by the firm of Bendini, Lambert, and Locke. These men – women feature only as '1950s homemakers' – are involved in protecting the beneficiaries from drug trafficking and prostitution. Where the issue becomes more interesting is in the rather more problematic role and function of those protecting legitimate but questionable practices. This is a theme which features in later novels and films.[36]

---

33 *The Rainmaker,* at 229, said by Deck Shiffle.
34 *Pretty Boy Floyd*: 'As through this world you ramble; As through this world you roam; You'll meet lots of … men; Some rob you with a six gun, some with a fountain pen'.
35 R. Chandler, *The Long Goodbye* (1953) at 267, said by Philip Marlowe.
36 *The Pelican Brief, The Rainmaker,* and *The Runaway Jury.*

(b) *The Pelican Brief*

The second film in the Grisham oeuvre, *The Pelican Brief* (1993) starred, as Grisham hoped, Julia Roberts. She was joined by Sam Shepard (albeit briefly) and Denzel Washington. Director Alan J. Pakula started his career as a producer and amongst his works was *To Kill A Mockingbird*. As director, his films include such thoughtful thrillers as *All the President's Men, Klute*, and *Parallax View* as well as *Sophie's Choice*. His *Consenting Adults* (1992) was seen as the work of a director whose powers had waned. He also wrote the screenplay.

At some date in the recognizable future, two Supreme Court justices are murdered. They hold very different views on social issues and how the courts should respond to litigation. What is the link between their murders? A bright law student solves the problem. She commits this to paper. She omits, of course, to make any copies so that her elimination will protect those behind the murders. They discover she has solved the link and seek to silence her. This is the plot of the book. The film follows it exactly.

Again the essence of this book appears to be the evasion of the forces of evil by Darby Shaw. She turns out to be bright and resourceful – although conveniently not so bright that she remembers that credit card transactions can be traced. There is, however, more to the book than a simple chase. The springboard into the reasons for the chase is the political nature of the Supreme Court and a crude version of jurimetrics. From a knowledge of judges' politics we can infer their decisions. We are introduced to two judges whose past decisions appear to be diametrically opposed. They are both killed – it is assumed – because of the impact of their work rather than any other factor. So if the audience learns one thing about the legal process it is that the principles of law are the product not of some abstract or objective notion of justice but of personal preferences or biases about the public good. Given, though, that Darby Shaw ends the novel on a Caribbean island in an embrace with the journalist who helped her gain access to the secret services and bring to justice the wrongdoers who perpetrated the original murders, readers might be forgiven for overlooking this. In the film the ending is more enigmatic. Whether Denzel Washington has bid his final farewell to her is unclear as the film closes with Julia Roberts watching Washington being interviewed on television about the mysterious person who solved the Supreme Court murders.

Whilst it contains the major political lawyer figures of any of Grisham's works, *The Pelican Brief* does not concentrate on the work of lawyers. The main protagonist, Darby Shaw is a neophyte, as yet only being inculcated into the mysteries of law. She is not, unlike Mitch McDeere, complicit in the necromancy of law whereby power is transformed into right. We get only hints as to her scepticism as to the whole enterprise and there is no suggestion that she will be returning to the world of study which the threat to her life caused her to abandon. Her mentor, law professor Thomas Callahan, retains only a tenuous hold on his liberal ideals but he is a man going nowhere until propelled into the New Orleans sky by a car bomb wired to his Porsche.

155

(c) *The Client*

In the 1994 adaptation of *The Client*, as in the earlier Grisham adaptations, leading players, directors, and screenwriters are employed. Susan Sarandon and Tommy Lee Jones play the two main protagonist roles in the film. This has the effect of centralizing the conflict between the State Prosecutor and the caring lawyer. The genesis of non-ambitious lawyer Reggie Love's character is explored at some length in the book and is briefly mentioned in the film. Reggie was a fifties homemaking mother-of-two who fell to pieces when her husband traded her in for a younger model. The portrayal of this role of the crushed trophy wife who turns to law for personal salvation is effectively enough portrayed by Sarandon for her to have received Oscar and British Film Academy Award nominations for the role.[37]

The director, Joel Schumacher's previous work included popular box-office successes like *Batman and Robin, Batman Forever, Flatliners, St Elmo's Fire* as well as suffering reverses such as *Dying Young* and *The Incredible Shrinking Woman*. He also directed the ambivalent 'message' work *Falling Down*. The screenwriters were Akiva Goldsman and Robert Getchell. Goldsman subsequently worked with director Schumacher on the adaptation of *A Time to Kill*.

A young boy witnesses the suicide of a mob lawyer and has probably been told a crucial secret. His information must be gleaned from him or, from the point of view of the Mob, he must be silenced. Although only ten, he equips himself with a lawyer. An ethical struggle ensues between the authorities and his own lawyer as to how this is best to be achieved. Both have as their aim obtaining information. In the end the vital information is made available to the authorities and the boy and his family enter a witness protection programme. In the inevitable process of simplification a number of elements like the politics of prosecution are, of course, omitted. What is noteworthy is the retention of the basic theme of the hidden witness.

For some reason, however, the Mob in the film, although they have their informers within the legal system, do not exploit their access to the crucial witness. In the book there is some clarity that there are protection measures in place. In the film the Mob's heavies are able to make their threats in person. Quite why the witness is not silenced permanently is not clear.

On first analysis the author typified this novel as a chase novel likening it to *Witness*. There is an extent to which this can be seen as a critique of the treatment of children in the justice system and the significance of lawyer-client privilege. The impression from closely viewing the film is less of a chase novel than a conflict of ethics – between the overriding interests of the public and the inalienable rights of the individual. These are, however, sketched in and determine the plot rather than having their implications fully or even partially argued for. In the same way, the exposure there is to

---

37 Jessica Lange won the Oscar for her work in *Blue Sky* – also co-starring Tommy Lee Jones.

chiselling, low-rent lawyers grubbing around with poor people's accident claims is no more than the merest glimpse.

The recurring theme here is the concept of the wholly corrupt lawyer. The difference between *The Firm* where this was hidden and used for covert money-laundering purposes is the openness of the activities of the suicidal Romey Clifford. He is a hired hand of the Mob who will lie, cheat, and murder on their behalf. In that sense, he is a quite distinct character within the work. In this instance we have a world of gangsters and hit-men co-existing with politically ambitious lawyers, ambulance-chasers, and honest selfless pursuers of justice.

There are many fewer lawyers in the film version of *The Client*. Essentially it boils down to a struggle between recovering alcoholic defender of the weak, Reggie Love and the bible-quoting political candidate, Roy Foltrigg. There are cameo appearances from one of Grisham's constants, the ambulance-chaser. In this instance we see Gill Beal hustling for business at the hospital trying to sign up accident victims and when Mark Sway visits his offices looking for a lawyer, he is repulsed by the formidable receptionist who informs him that the firm only does personal injury claims. There is also a brief sight of the sympathetic judge, Harry Roosevelt. The judge represents a man doing his best in a legal system where the judiciary are the traffic directors rather than play powerful role, as implied in *The Firm*. This tunes in with traditional representations of the judicial role in courtroom dramas.[38]

What alters in the film version is the depiction of Foltrigg. Each time he is mentioned in the book it is to emphasize his insincerity in the quest for justice and the sublimation of any vestige of human concern in exchange for advancement of his own career towards governor. Whilst he is not sleazy or necessarily insincere, he is untrustworthy. His concerns are driven by his political ambitions and nothing is going to get in his way. This changes in the film in both the language and in the relationship he develops with Reggie. This fits in with the predilection in films and adaptations for pairings and romantic resolutions. This we can observe from *Adam's Rib* through *First Day in October* and *Legal Eagles* to *Suspect*.

The limited number of social issues in this work is altered interestingly in the film so that the question of the individual versus the state assumes a greater significance in the film than in the book. There are however fewer indications of the journey of expiation which Reggie Love has undertaken from being an oppressed housewife to a protector of the poor and dispossessed. In addition there is the question of the cavalier treatment of children by the legal system which the film addresses rather more than the book.

38 P. Robson, 'The Judge in the Picture', Law and Society Association, Aspen, May 1998, and P. Robson 'Judges in Film – a Reappraisal', Law and Society Association, Chicago, May 1999.

2. The 'social issues' novels

Although, as indicated, the dichotomy between the thriller and issues novels is only an interpretation it is one which may have interesting implications for the commercial success of the Grisham enterprise. The first two films grossed over $100m whilst the rather more cerebral courtroom dramas have played less successfully.

(a) *A Time to Kill*

Grisham's first novel, *A Time to Kill,* sold well enough on re-issue[39] to merit a film version in 1996. It starred Matthew McConnaghy, Samuel L. Jackson, Sandra Bullock, and Donald Sutherland. Important support was given by Kevin Spacey and Patrick McGoohan. Again the direction was by Joel Schumacher with the screenplay by Akiva Goldsman. John Grisham was one of four producers.

The book's tale of the brutal rape of a ten-year old African-American girl by two racist rednecks and their apprehension by the criminal justice system and their death at the hands of the victim's father, *à la* Jack Ruby, is faithfully reworked on the screen. What ensues is their defence by a young inexperienced small-town lawyer, Jake Brigance. In the book a considerable amount of time is spent dealing with the twists and turns of seeking to secure a change of venue with a smaller proportion of white jurors on the panel. The defence of temporary insanity collapses with the credibility of the defence team's witness's exposure as a felon. In a powerful speech the young lawyer recreates the events and asks the all white jury to assess their reaction had the victim been white. Tears in their eyes they acquit. There is no deviation from the basic plot in the screen version.

The implications are to say the least interesting, not least for Grisham himself. Vigilantism appears in both the book and film versions of *A Time to Kill* to be acceptable as long as the crime is repugnant and the legal process can conveniently be dispensed with. In the context of the responsibility of the artist for copycat actions John Grisham has suggested that '[t]he artist should be required to share responsibility along with the nut who actually pulled the trigger'.[40] He was referring, however, here to Oliver Stone's *Natural Born Killers* (1994).

The venal old boys network (here almost a 'good ol' boys' network) is seen as the key to the operation of law in this portrayal of the phenomenon of law. It determines how the prosecution and judge interact and the potential for justice available in the courtroom of Omar Noose. We are not clear what drives Kevin Spacey's prosecutor – politics, career or perhaps justice. His personal and political ambitions *in the book* are not even hinted at. Like Roy

---

39 The original print-run by Wynwood Press was 5,000. After the success of *The Firm* the book rights were bought by Doubleday.

40 L. Halliwell, *Figures in Film* (ed. J. Walker, 2000).

Foltrigg he becomes an altogether more driven, albeit lawyerly character. He is not above pressing to remind the judge that his running for re-election is only months away. In a system of elected judges this is not an idle threat.

The main protagonist, Brigance, obliquely sees the Carl Lee Hailey murder trial as his springboard away from balancing creditors and the daily grind of law practice in small Southern town. In a slightly belated marital reconciliation, his wife ascribes rather higher motives to Jake's keenness to take the case. She assumes that he felt he had to take the case because the victim could have been his daughter. This seems somewhat as odds with Jake's enthusiasm for the cameras and appearing on television.

The other 'bit' players in the film have qualities that in 130 minutes the film can only hint at. Burned-out radical Lucien Wilbanks (Donald Sutherland) is restricted to uttering law-affirming aphorisms. The rule bending and shifty 'fixing' Harry Rex Vonner is limited to looking sweaty in a crumpled white suit. The NAACP law team, as in the book, come and go with a morally ambivalent agenda hinted at but no more. The implication seems to be that they are driven by the organizational imperative to expand and root out the competition. Given the number of death-row cases and levels of representation throughout the Southern states this does not seem entirely plausible.

(b) *The Chamber*

The dark and action-free film of *The Chamber* in 1996 starred Gene Hackman, Faye Dunaway, and Chris O'Donnell. With the exception of the initial Klan killing of a liberal Jewish lawyer in the opening sequence, this is an exploration of how individuals react to the reality of the death penalty. Director James Foley is well versed in the claustrophobic exploration of feelings and issues. His films include the acclaimed adaptation of David Mamet's play, *Glengarry Glen Ross* (1992) as well as the excellent *After Dark, My Sweet* (1990) and *At Close Range* (1985). Less recognized was his early work, *Who's That Girl* (1987) with Madonna. He has gone on to further success with *Fear* (1996) (Cape Fear for the Teenage Audience) and *The Corruptor* (1999). The screenplay was by noted Hollywood writer William Goldman along with Chris Reese.

Based loosely on the Byron de la Beckwith case and the killing of Civil Rights activist Medgar Evers this traces the retrial of a Klan activist from the 1960s and his treatment by the judicial system. The crucial narrative device is the discovery by a young liberal lawyer that a notorious racist killer on death row is, in fact, his own grandfather. He seeks permission from his rich corporate employers to leave the comfortable world of take-overs and leverage buy-outs to save his grandfather from the death penalty. This is a voyage of self-discovery. It is Grisham's longest book. The surly and cantankerous old man does not wish to be saved. His soul is not available for redemption. There is no dramatic resolution. There is no real sense in which the horror of death row and its interminable waits is communicated. The book has the advantage of repetition to convey the weight of time. This is not available to the modern film-maker. Nothing much happens other than the daughter of the killer relapsing into her old alcoholic ways. Then the old man suffers the death penalty.

Unlike Jake Brigance who was comfortable with the notion of the death penalty, Adam Hall is against the barbarity of judicial murder. There is, however, not a lot more in this film than a parade of the indignity of the process in a country with a complex hierarchy of courts and system of challenges to decisions. We see clearly the arbitrary nature of the concept of clemency depending as it does on short-term political considerations. The trick of Grisham in this instance, which recurs in *Dead Men Walking,* is to avoid appealing to sentiment in the battle over how to deal with those who take the lives of others. The problem is that, along with Gene Hackman's Sam Cayhall, the audience is unlikely to be that bothered about him ending his life a little prematurely.

In *The Chamber* the other lawyers, Chris O'Donnell apart, have little to say or do. The fervent anti-death penalty campaigner from the book, makes a brief appearance, but the rationale for his stance is omitted. The corporate world from which Hall comes is sketched in very lightly.

(c) *The Rainmaker*

Again an all-star cast appeared in this 1997 film including Matt Damon, Danny de Vito, John Voight, and Mickey Rourke. The director was no less prestigious. Director Francis Ford Coppola also wrote the screenplay. It was scripted by Michael Herr.[41]

Young law student, Rudy Baylor, looks for an easy life picking up credits for graduation in a clinical law course. Here learning is experiential and students get to help poor people in a legal clinic. With an eye to the main chance Rudy sweet-talks his way into a legal firm. He thinks he is on his way with two cases from the poor law clinic at an old folks day centre but these claims turn out to be less than unqualified blessings and he is required to engage in ambulance chasing in the company of a streetwise paralegal serial Bar exam failer. In the course of this he meets and befriends a victim of spousal violence. The rich widow from the centre turns out to have spent all the money she inherited. He does, however, raise an action on behalf of a poor family denied hospital benefits under their medical insurance plan. He successfully sues the firm and, against all the odds, secures a multi-million dollar settlement. The firm duly declares itself bankrupt and he is back to square one. He quits the law practice together with the ex-wife of the abuser whom he has beaten to death with an aluminium baseball bat. The future will be less stressful and more fulfilling - teaching history in high school – or, in the film, teaching in Law School!

The moral responsibility of lawyers for their clients dominates this tale of spiritual self-discovery. Rudy Baylor goes from a self-seeking cynic to a

41 N. Bradshaw, *Time Out Film Guide* (8th edn., 2000).

160

principled human being within the book's narrative. In the film he is driven by the inspiration of what the Civil Rights movement showed lawyers could achieve for society. By accident he stumbles into a morally arresting scenario where the limited legal protection available to women from spousal abuse and the full impact of the pursuit of profit remove the scales of scepticism about justice from his eyes.

The lawyer 'Bruiser' Stone operates on a most unusual financial basis. It is a version of 'sharecropping'. Like sharecropping, however, the young lawyer, stands to end up in debt if he cannot generate enough business. He gets to set a proportion of the fees he generates against the money allowed from the firm to him each month/week. The other lawyers have in their various ways 'sold out' to those who pay for their expensive suits and fancy cars. At the end Rudy is aiming somewhere simple to do something he sees as involving no moral compromise – he is planning to become a law professor.

SUMMARY

On the basis of examining the filmic representation of race and poverty fiction in British film, my initial view was that the transformation in the adaptation process could better be understood by looking at the specific pressures and influences operating on film-makers. This material and ideological context seemed to provide a richer picture of the adapted novel than seeing this as merely an abstract artistic process concerned chiefly with fidelity. Further, the relationship between social and economic developments had to be examined to see what kinds of constraints operated on writers and film-makers in their work.

The situation we can see in relation to the work of Grisham is that adopting this contextual perspective seems to provide a fascinating, albeit restricted, window on the American justice system in the 1990s. The films, in their adapted form, provide a sense of how certain social and legal debates were conducted during this period. The domain concerns of different eras, of course, vary. In the context of law in film writing, Richard Sherwin, for instance, makes a telling contrast between the way in which the lawyer and the ethical standards of the legal profession are represented in the two film versions of *Cape Fear*.[42] Some issues which seem to go to the very core of legal debate turn out to be recent controversies. The concern, for instance, with freedom of speech under the First Amendment is something which has only in the post-war years become an issue for liberals.[43]

42 R.K. Sherwin, 'Cape Fear: Law's Inversion and Cathartic Justice' (1996) 30 *University of San Francisco Law Rev.* 1023.
43 S. Walker, *Hate Speech: The History of an American Controversy* (1994).

The concerns which arise in the Grisham films are, of course, specific to Grisham's experiential writing rather than a wide-ranging critique of the operation of the legal system. As we have seen they reflect the themes of the books. These are Grisham's preoccupations and there are a number of recurrent issues. An underlying feature is the availability of representation in the legal system. This is a legal system to which access is systematically denied to the disadvantaged – ethnic minorities (*A Time to Kill*; *The Chamber*), the poor (*The Client*; *The Rainmaker*), and women (*The Client*). A complementary aspect is the perceived impact of the almost uncontrolled market in legal service providers. The need to make money in the fiercely competitive market place drives those outwith the cushioned corporate world into providing a second-rate, shabby service in the desperate hope of landing a big case at some time to free them from the cut-throat world of ambulance chasing either through their percentage cut or through the glare of the ensuing publicity. (*The Client*; *A Time to Kill*; *The Rainmaker*). In addition the elected nature of prosecutors distorts the operation of the whole criminal justice process (*A Time to Kill*; *The Client*; *The Chamber*).

The impact of the law on the disadvantaged is an issue which develops in the books which have not been filmed (*The Runaway Jury*; *The Street Lawyer*; *The Brethren*) but which is prefigured in the early work, particularly *The Client* and *The Rainmaker*. The rather less worrying aspect of these social concerns is the high level of work and commitment required of lawyers to get on in the world of corporate law firms (*The Firm*; *The Pelican Brief*) as well as the practices of these lawyers in overcharging their well-off clients (*The Firm*; *The Pelican Brief*; *The Chamber*; *The Rainmaker*).

There are, additionally a whole range of interesting issues which receive no sustained attention like race and gender and their impact on the lives of minorities. Thus we find the whole issue of the impact of race in the jury selection process which is a major feature of the book does not feature in the film, *A Time To Kill*. The lawyers in the Grisham books are overwhelmingly white. Apart from the fleeting appearance of the NAACP lawyers in *A Time to Kill*, there are two judicial appearances in *The Client* and *The Rainmaker*. Perhaps even more interesting is the low profile of female lawyers in the Grisham canon. We have only one practitioner from *The Client*, Reggie Love, while the only other female lawyers whom we see on screen are the students Darby Shaw (*The Pelican Brief*) and Elaine Roark (*A Time to Kill*). Given the make-up of the legal profession this is worthy of note. Sexual orientation seems to be entirely missing. This comes as little surprise, however, given that sexuality is not a feature of the characters in Grisham's work.[44]

Commercial pressures may help explain the limited adaptations of the other lawyer/writers of the 1990s. Even Scott Turrow and Richard North

---

44 The only characters who do express themselves sexually are made to pay for their weakness – Mitch McDeere and Lamarr Quinn in *The Firm*, and Rich Magruder in *The Gingerbread Man* (1997).

162

Patterson have featured little in this arena. Patterson suggested that the law is the focal point for political debate in the United States. The novel had become the preferred forum for such political issues which might previously been discussed in the realm of representational politics. The next stage is to write about such issues, he suggested. Grisham has been able to go further and produce films on these personal concerns from the happy juncture of having a brand product – a Grisham novel. This implies both excitement and an audience. None of the others writing in the lawyer novel field have quite achieved this. Even Grisham is not immune. Although, as indicated, the dichotomy between the thriller and issues novels is only a heuristic one, it does appear to have had certain implications for the commercial success of the Grisham enterprise. The first two 'thriller' films grossed over $100m whilst the rather more cerebral courtroom/prison dramas with their emphasis on social issues have played less successfully.

CONCLUSION

Adaptation of films dealing with social issues can better be understood by locating such films in their cultural and political context rather than simply focus on the aesthetic and stylistic distinctions between the written source and film.[45] The process of adaptation involved requires to be looked at outwith an artistic vacuum. The same kind of situating or contextualization operates in a slightly different way in relation to recent lawyer novels. The social agenda and concerns of John Grisham are subject to significant alteration.

In some situations, the simplifying process of film makes these broad social concerns even more explicit. On the other hand the conventional domination of consensus in film has altered the portrayal of the legal profession to a more oblique critique as we have noted in relation to the State/individual dichotomy in *The Client*. The continuing and extended critique of the private profit basis for allocating legal services which surfaces in all the Grisham novels evanesces under the time constraints of the film process. The fiction is able to call attention to the stultifying and corrosive effect of profit on the pursuit of truth and justice. The cinematic conventions of conflict and resolution, however both sharpen and simplify this underlying analysis. Rudy Baylor's clients are short-changed. By what is not made clear. We are left with 'radical lite'. Structural analysis is replaced by a simplified personal struggle against evil individuals. Even the debates about capital punishment and vigilantism dissove into questions of empathy rather than principle. The solution is exemplified by Jake Brigance's notion, in *A Time to Kill*, of taking on the world 'one case at a time'. Which case and why is overlaid in the films. There is no worked through overview. Given the much touted 'end of ideology' and the role of Hollywood as emblem of United States economic hegemony, this is perhaps an over-optimistic expectation.

45 Richardson, op. cit., n. 4.

JOURNAL OF LAW AND SOCIETY
VOLUME 28, NUMBER 1, MARCH 2001
ISSN: 0263-323X, pp. 164–75

Borders and Boundaries: Locating the Law in Film

Guy Osborn*

The essay examines the emergence of law and film in the curricula of law schools in the context of Britain. It outlines the development of legal education in England and Wales and the relationship between legal education and training. It notes the broadening out of the syllabus to encompass more politicized courses taught within their socio-economic context like family law and labour law. From this shift of academic focus the politically contextual has extended to the cultural context. The relationship between law and culture both in literature and in other areas has been the end result of this relaxation of focus on professional education. Finally, the precise nature of law and film and its boundaries are discussed.

> Breadth of knowledge, wider culture, adaptability, perseverance if not determination (often fostered by great personal suffering), an ability to look at the law – in Roscoe Pound's words 'from without' as well as 'from within' – all great comparatists had these attributes to a lesser or greater extent. That is true of those who worked in England as well as of those who operated in the United States; and is also true of the autochthonous giants like Harry Lawson and Jack Dawson. But are we likely to find such features in the next generation? Natural optimism apart, I must admit, that prima facie the signs are not propitious'.[1]

It is undoubtedly the case that law and film is something of a rarity on law school curricula,[2] and that research in the field has been somewhat piecemeal in the past. There are a number of reasons for this. In terms of undergraduate law teaching, it is trite to note that the curriculum is to a large degree predicated on the requirements of the Law Society and Bar Council.

* School of Law, University of Westminster, 4 Little Titchfield Street, London W1P 7FW, England

1 B. Markesinis, 'The Comparatist (or a plea for a broader legal education)' in *Pressing Problems in the Law. What are Law Schools For?*, ed. P. Birks (1996).
2 A module, Film and Law, was validated at the University of Westminster as part of the LLB validation in 1993. This module was inspired, to a degree by a short course run out of the Extra-Mural Department of Birkbeck College in the early 1990s, and since the Westminster module there have been developments at UNL and New College Oxford amongst others.

Because of this, the undergraduate programme is heavily prescriptive.[3] With the 'core subjects' under pressure to expand, it is often difficult to find a place in the curriculum for other subjects not considered as 'core' by the professions. Indeed, in the 1990s the traditional core that took up at least half of the undergraduate curriculum was supplemented by a requirement to study EU law, and it seems likely that human rights law will soon be similarly required.[4] In addition to this 'spatial' difficulty, some subjects have been viewed with suspicion, at least initially, in some quarters. In terms of research, law and film is beginning to attract more attention and signs such as this special issue of the *Journal of Law and Society*, previous special issues of American journals,[5] and the emergence of texts in the field[6] lie testament to this.

However, even if it is taken that the area is one worthy of serious study, a related question concerns subject matter; what is to be included within its penumbra? This article seeks to place film and law within the context of the developing law curriculum, and argue that it has a legitimate place in the curriculum by virtue of its contextual potentiality. In addition, having drawn parallels with the law and literature movement and examined how film can be used within law teaching, an attempt is made to sketch out the subject matter of the area.

THE LEGAL CURRICULUM AND THE INCURSION OF POPULAR CULTURE

Whilst there have been shifts in recent years, it is probably still the case that law school curricula are largely dominated by the black-letter tradition. As Sugarman has noted, 'its categories and assumptions are still the standard diet of most first-year law students and (it continues) to organise law textbooks and case books'.[7] The black-letter tradition assumes, of course, that the law is predicated upon a rational and coherent body of rules that, once identified and applied, will provide the answer to the problem.

---

3 This may be exacerbated by the internal requirements or regulations of the Law School or University.

4 The six core subjects were law of tort, contract law, criminal law, equity and trusts, pubic law, and land law. The most recent 'Joint Statement' of the Bar and Law Society requires that half of the three years of study must be spent on the study of seven foundation subjects, and that two-thirds of the three years must be in law subjects.

5 See, for example, (1996) 30(4) *University of San Fransisco Law Rev.*, which included the symposium 'Picturing Justice: Images of Law and Lawyers in the Visual Media'.

6 See, for example, P. Bergman and M. Asimow, *Reel Justice – the Courtroom Goes to the Movies* (1996); J. Denvir (ed.), *Legal Reelism. Movies as Legal Texts* (1996).

7 D. Sugarman, ' "A Hatred of Disorder": Legal Science, Liberalism and Imperialism' in *Dangerous Supplements. Resistance and Renewal in Jurisprudence*, ed. P. Fitzpatrick (1991) 34.

165

However, whilst such an assumption might underpin much teaching, even a cursory incursion into legal study reveals a labrynth of confusion and non-conformity:

> Like any closed model of rationality, the 'black letter' tradition is shot through with contradictions, omissions and absurdities, which generations of judges and jurists have sought to repress. For instance, the notion of law as resting upon an objective body of principle founders when we consider that the quest for underlying principles must involve a selection from the sum of principles and thus has a strong evaluative element.[8]

These contradictions become apparent early in legal undergraduate study, and often create difficulties for students categorized by the notion that law is in some way exact or precise.[9] Seeing the law at work, and seeing that issues such as policy (a value issue) may affect the outcome of cases may lead the student to take a more critical approach towards the law and its application.[10] To a large degree this is where developments in areas such as the sociology of law and the shift towards 'law and ...' approaches comes in. Legal education is however resistant to change. Writing about the new wave of law professors that followed the golden age of legal scholarship in the late nineteenth century, Sugarman noted the following:

> New texts were discouraged. The great intellectual undertakings of the classical period gave way to a narrowing of vision, seeking to learn in greater detail about smaller areas. Of course, this process had its critics and one can certainly detect a number of counter-currents. What is striking, however, is the extent to which these critics and counter-currents were repressed. Why? In addition to those factors enumerated above, it is undoubtedly the case that high staff-student ratios, the elevation of teaching over research, the isolation of legal education and thought within the scholarly community, the hiring of law teachers based on prowess in examinations rather than flair for scholarship, the failure to provide adequate financial support for research, and the legal profession's control over what law schools taught and how they taught and examined it, all inhibited reform from within.[11]

To a degree this repression still takes place, although the forms and objects of repression may have altered. Significant shifts have occurred both within the legal curriculum, and within the wider world of scholarship and education that have necessitated such a shift. Government interventions into legal education have included a Select Committee on Legal Education in 1846[12] that

---

8 id., p. 35.
9 At my own institution, and from my own experience, this is most openly revealed when dealing with precedent in contract and tort.
10 On the role of policy and judicial creativity, see, for example, G. Osborn and T. Sutton, 'Of new orders and new dawns. Freewheeling returns to negligence' (1996) 12 *Professional Negligence* 2.
11 Sugarman, op. cit., n. 7, p. 64.
12 The report of which was produced quickly but with remarkable perception:

recommended, among other things, the revival of the law faculties at the universities which had fallen into abeyance and that a proper system of degrees should be introduced to replace the rather piecemeal situation that existed. As Ormrod wryly notes in the 'Historical Introduction' to his 1971 report:

> (t)he history of legal education in England over the past 120 years is largely an account of the struggle to implement the recommendations of the 1846 Committee and the effects of that struggle.[13]

A number of further studies followed the 1846 Select Committee, including the Haldane Commission report in 1913[14] and the Atkin Committee of 1934[15] before the Second World War. After 1945 the expansion of higher education, coupled with the introduction of grants, led to a new wave of potential lawyers and posed a whole new set of questions for legal education. This culminated in the Ormrod report which produced a series of recommendations including the following objectives for the academic stage:

> In the scheme of training for the practice of the law, the objectives of the academic stage should be to provide the student with:-
>
> (i)   a basic knowledge of the law, which involves covering certain 'core' subjects ...
> (ii)   an understanding of the relationship of law to the social and economic environment in which it operates; and
> (iii) the intellectual training necessary to enable him to handle facts and apply abstract concepts'.[16]

It is interesting to reflect on Ormrod, some thirty years ago, stressing the importance of an appreciation of the social and economic environment in which law operates. The most recent attempt to analyse the shape of legal education is the Lord Chancellor's Advisory Committee on Legal Education and Conduct,[17] established under the *Courts and Legal Services Act 1990* that also reiterated that '... the degree course should stand as an independent

---

Within the amazingly short period of three months, it produced a Report which contains a remarkable and far-sighted study of the whole problem of education for the legal profession. it revealed that there was virtually no institutional law teaching of any kind in England, with the exception of Professor Amos's teaching at University College, London.

Report of the Committee on Legal Education (1971; Cmnd 4595; Chair, The Hon. Mr. Justice Ormrod) 5.

13 id., p. 8. Subsequent pages reveal a fascinating insight into the evolution of law teaching from the mid-nineteenth century.

14 *Final Report of the Royal Commission on University Education in London* (1913; Cd. 6717; Chair, Lord Haldane).

15 *Report of the Legal Education Committee* (1934; Cmd. 4663; Chair, Lord Atkin).

16 Ormrod, op. cit., n. 12, p. 94.

17 Lord Chancellor's Advisory Committee on Legal Education and Conduct, *First Report on Legal Education and Training* (1996).

167

liberal education in the discipline of law, not tied to any specific vocation'.[18] Notwithstanding this, there has been a shift towards vocationalism on many undergraduate degrees, certainly in terms of the integration of legal skills as free-standing subjects or being integrated into other subjects.[19]

New areas of study have emerged, partly as a reaction to what Sugarman identifies as law's isolation within scholarship more generally. Many of these moves have been viewed with suspicion by the academy although, as can be seen above, both Ormrod and the Lord Chancellor's Advisory Committee stress that academic legal training should be seen within a broader socio-economic context and that it should not operate purely as a practitioner conveyer belt. Within the legal curriculum we have seen a number of developments that illustrate the potential for new subjects that do site the law within its broader social, political or economic context. Both family law and labour law are, for example, good examples of this phenomenon; both are responsive to societal and legislative changes. However, a key aspect of such 'new' subjects is not so much the subject matter itself but the approach adopted. For example, labour law could be seen on one level as a particular sub-stratum of contract, tort and EU law, although on another it might be seen as a heavily politicized course and the approach and coverage would reflect this accordingly. Similarly, as recounted below, any new subject can be reactionary and mundane and not necessarily as vibrant and dynamic as the area might suggest; 'new' does not necessarily equate with 'critical' or 'contextual'.

Within this backdrop, the study of law and film, along with other areas of law and popular culture, is of comparatively recent origin. This may be in part due to a reticence on the part of the academy to embrace new areas of research and disciplines that veer outside the traditional framework. However, a shift towards more contextual, or socio-legal, approaches to legal study has allowed some developments to be made.[20] Of particular note within areas of law and popular culture is that there is no obvious body of law; to a large degree, the delineation of subject matter is highly subjective. This echoes the point above concerning approach. It is, in addition, further complicated by the fact that popular culture is itself a loaded term, and within notions of culture generally, 'high' and 'low' culture are perceived differently. It is probably easier to make a claim for interdisciplinary investigation of high culture than it is low – certainly the study of 'law and literature' has a higher profile, and is more easily acceptable, than 'law and

---

18 id., p. 108.
19 Of course, such skills, whilst legal in nature, may fulfil a number of broader objectives and be perceived as applicable in a wider environment (transferability).
20 For example, writing in 1986, Hunt welcomed the arrival of the critical legal studies movement and its potential for shaking up legal scholarship and forcing it to debate the nature of its development. A. Hunt, 'The Theory of Critical Legal Studies' (1986) 6 *Oxford J. of Legal Studies* 1–45.

168

film'. This to a large degree explains why law and popular culture has not had a particularly high profile, and why historically the intersections of law and popular culture have not been heavily examined.

This reticence to analyse the relationship between law and wider issues of mass culture was identified by Chase in 1986,[21] and the *Yale Law Journal* took up the gauntlet some three years later with an issue dedicated in part to the burgeoning effect of *L.A. Law* upon the legal profession. Friedman, writing in that issue, noted the symbiotic relationship between popular culture and the law:

> Popular legal culture and popular culture are related to one another in two important respects. First, popular culture gets its ideas of law, or at least some of them, from popular legal culture.[22] In other words, popular culture *reflects* popular legal culture.

The upshot of this is that much of the appreciation and understanding we glean about the legal profession is obtained via the cultural *representations* of the law.[23] By the same token, there is much to be learned about the law by appreciating the way in which it interacts with other areas and disciplines – much in the same way that Ormrod argued for law's relationship with social and economic forces to be understood, and that the 'living law' should be experienced.

Recent years have seen the emergence of a number of courses that have attempted to map the trajectory of law and popular culture. These have ranged from courses that have merely used an area of popular culture as a vehicle to discuss areas of law, to (perhaps more ambitious) courses that have attempted to excavate what our understanding of popular culture(s) tells us about the law itself.[24] This reinforces the point that there is nothing necessarily radical about new subject matter in itself – it is the *approach* to that subject matter that truly maps the subject.[25] For example, areas such as sport and law, or media law, could be explicitly 'black-letter' in approach, rather than attempting something more contextual or critical.

---

21 A. Chase, 'Lawyers and Popular Culture: A Review of Mass Media Portrayals of American Attorneys' (1986) *Am. Bar Foundation Research J.* 281.
22 L. Friedman, 'Law, lawyers and popular culture' (1989) 98 *Yale Law J.* 1579.
23 There is, of course, a vastly different approach to the study of film and the law which has nothing to do with the visual content but is concerned with the application of legal principles to the film industry. Such a curriculum would cover issues such as copyright, contractual issues, merchandizing, and so on.
24 At my own institution I have been involved in the validation, course development, and teaching of courses in entertainment law, media law, sport and the law, film and the law, among others. All of these have differing aims and objectives and attempt to achieve different things.
25 I am indebted to a valuable exchange of ideas with Steve Greenfield in our Senior Common Room for this point.

> Legal scholarship can and should include studies of works of literature dealing with law. Fiction may not be particularly helpful as a way to learn legal rules or history, but it can tell us much *about* law, defined broadly to mean the legal order ... The assumption of traditional legal education, that law is a technical and insular matter grasped entirely or largely on its own, has been replaced by the belief that it is inextricably bound up with politics, morality, culture and life ... the center of legal scholarship will always be law, but scholars should approach it as part of a broader civilisation.[26]

On one level, an appropriate comparator for film and law would be with the law and literature movement, an area that is now fairly well established. Films may be viewed as the poor relation to literature given the long traditional history of the novel in comparison with the more recent development of film studies as part of the curriculum. The study of literature provides a good example of how difficult it is for a discipline to remain isolated from wider influences. Literary theory has been subject to numerous critical perspectives that have great value:

> ... literary theory is not an arid form of scholasticism, speculating about the number of angels that can exist on the head of a pin. Rather, literary theory raises important issues about texts, readers and audiences of texts, and the relations of works of art and culture and cultural matters to society and politics.[27]

Accordingly, the academic study of literature has become increasingly influenced by other disciplines such as psychology, sociology, and philosophy. By the same token, it is unrealistic to assume that the study of law can demand to remain in arrogant isolation from other perspectives, particularly those that offer some reflection on law.[28] Writing in *Legal Studies* in 1993,[29] Ward excavated developments in the law and literature movement and illustrated how interdisciplinary studies were able to give new possibilities to the teaching of law. In particular, he argued that law and literature had a number of positive attributes, whilst at the same time following Dunlop's warning against the possibility of over-intellectualization:

---

26 C. Dunlop, 'Literature Studies in Law Schools' (1991) 3(1) *Cardozo Studies in Law and Literature* 69, quote reproduced in D. Black, *Law in Film. Resonance and Representation* (1999) 111–12.

27 A. Berger, *Cultural Criticism* (1995) 38.

28 The phrase is Alan Hunt's, and is here appropriated to a different end. Hunt was arguing about the place of legal theory within law degrees, see Hunt, op. cit., n. 20, and also our analysis of this within the context of law and film: S. Greenfield and G. Osborn, 'The Living Law: Popular Film as Legal Text' (1995) 29 *The Law Teacher* 33.

29 I. Ward, 'The educative ambition of Law and Literature' (1993) 13 *Legal Studies* 323–31.

170

The great virtue of Law and Literature is its potential to be user friendly. That quality, above all, must not be lost. Too many long words are a dangerous thing. As Dunlop suggests, law is already beset by far too many words that do not really mean anything, either to lawyers or to anyone else.[30]

Whilst the fact that the subject can be user-friendly, and can provide a useful interface or point of contact between student and tutor, is important, other aspects of the educative functions of law and literature are equally relevant. In particular, following Cook's argument that the art of teaching lies in the use of analogy and metaphor, literature, like other areas of 'law in context', allow scope for explanation via example.[31] In addition, as can be seen below with regard to film, the non-threatening nature of the 'texts' provides a particularly useful point of entry for legal study. Perhaps most interestingly, Ward illustrates that whilst law students may exhibit a tendency to erase, or dismiss, 'non-legal discourse', teaching in this way might encourage a broader understanding and a more rounded appreciation, both of the law and society itself. The prime virtue of law and literature is, he argues, its educative function; 'The process is one of 'learning by osmosis'. Even if the structural distinction between law and literature remains, as Posner suggests that it should, the functional distinction need not. The educative ambition of law and literature, it is submitted, is both a credible and a creditable one. Moreover, it is one which teachers of law should not seek to dispute, if they do indeed cherish the ambition of educating lawyers to be more than just lawyers'.[32]

This is certainly something with which I can empathize having taught film and law since 1993. Even within the confines of this course, there are a number of different, and perhaps competing educative functions, and this may be replicated throughout other courses. Dunlop puts it thus in terms of research: that there is a crucial difference between research *in* law and research *about* law. The latter allows an appreciation of a subject by utilizing the tools and experience of a different discipline, whilst the former:

> consists of doctrinal analysis of texts ... tends not to involve empirical study of the actual workings of the legal order or of its economic or social consequences ... It apparently has a coherence and an autonomy enabling one to call it a discipline.[33]

The difference between the two is that research about law allows the law to be discussed, interrogated, and critiqued. Dunlop has refined this

---

30 id., p. 324.
31 Ward later cites the following example, regarding the historical antecedents of law and literature; 'Two and a half thousand years ago Socrates was using the literary techniques, metaphors and parables, and telling "stories" as a means of educating his students about all things, justice included' (id., p. 327).
32 id., p. 331.
33 Dunlop, op. cit., n. 26.

categorization to explain the difference between the competing, but arguably complementary approaches of 'Law *in* Literature' and 'Law *as* Literature'. Here, the former looks at representations within the field of literature, whilst the latter adopts some of the tools of literary criticism to assist in the analysis of legal texts. My approach has generally been to utilize the first model (law *in* film) in order that it might tell us something *about* the law.[34]

Whilst the use of film opens up many possibilities, not least in terms of providing an accessible and non-threatening entry point to the law, there are of course problems utilizing such a medium.[35] This is partly a question of asking what the objectives, or learning outcomes, of such a project should be. A further concern arises from the nature of the area itself – that is, where is the law and where is the law text? This is a challenge that has been faced by other emerging areas and 'disciplines', but here it is exacerbated by the answer that 'the film is the text', or at least the primary source. One of the great problems this creates, apart from debating whether or not 'law and ...' subjects are in fact law disciplines (and whether we would want them to be) is what is the subject matter of the (non-)discipline. This is the realm of asking – what should be covered by a course on law and film, and the related question – 'what is a law film'?

WHAT IS A LAW FILM? THE BOUNDARIES OF FILM AND LAW

One of the major problems when setting out to analyse legal films is determining the question of what constitutes a legal film. In essence this is where we have to look to film theory to provide some assistance in determining the edges of our inquiry. This raises the issue about how far we rely on film studies to delineate our own boundaries without becoming too involved with questions of interpretation rather than substance. We need to remain legal scholars studying law films rather than film theorists studying law films. Whilst there will undoubtedly be some crossover, our context is quite different; being rooted in the study of the theory and practice of law and lawyers as opposed to other areas of film studies. The most fundamental question is to decide the law film genre, what are its constituents or perhaps more pertinent what is outside it. Genre is an important means of classification:

---

34 See, for example, S. Greenfield and G. Osborn, 'Film, Law and the delivery of justice: the case of Judge Dredd and the disappearing courtroom' (1999) 6(2) *J. of Criminal Justice and Popular Culture* 35; S. Greenfield and G. Osborn, 'Where Cultures Collide. The Characterisation of Law and Lawyers in Film' (1995) 23 *International J. of the Sociology of Law* 107–30.

35 In two articles, (Greenfield and Osborn, op. cit., n. 28, and 'The Empowerment of Students: the Case for Popular Film in Legal Studies' in the American Bar Association's *Focus on Legal Studies* (1995) 6) we have argued the case for the advantages of using film to enhance law teaching.

We talk about genres because of our need to classify things, which we do to get a sense of how texts relate to one another and to gain some perspective on them. There is an interesting philosophical issue related to genres, namely, whether or not 'classes' of things exist and what their ontological status is.[36]

The most obvious classification for legal film is to draw a line around courtroom drama.[37] This is however problematic as few films are set entirely within the courtroom: one of the best known is *Twelve Angry Men*, yet this takes place within the confines of the jury room. The question would be how much in terms of either quantity or quality needs to take place in court for a film to be classified as a courtroom drama? For example, *A Dry White Season* contains a minimal amount of courtroom action, yet the scene with Marlon Brando as the defence lawyer seeking justice is memorable.[38] Some of those films with courtroom scenes might be classified as comedies (*A Fish Called Wanda, Brothers in Law, My Cousin Vinny*) or as a thriller (*Cape Fear*). The argument can be taken further with a consideration of the spatial requirements of the courtroom scene. An argument can be propounded, for example, that even films such as *Judge Dredd* could be considered as a courtroom drama notwithstanding the paucity of traditional courtroom scenes within the film:

> Dredd is as much the master of his 'courtroom' as any previous cinema judge, the change is the arena not the authority, his judicial robes are signposted as clearly as those historically trimmed with ermine. When Dredd indicates his judicial supremacy by declaring 'I am the Law' he is still acknowledging the legal process albeit is one vested within him, only that the parameters of the courtroom are no longer fixed.[39]

In any event, considering law films as only courtroom dramas is a very narrow interpretation of what law is concerned with. The majority of legal practice takes place outside of the courtroom, and to suggest that a film such as *The Firm* (that is essentially concerned with the construction of law practices) is not a legal film is difficult to justify. In essence then, law films are far more than just courtroom drama. The question then is, 'what are the limits to the law film genre'?[40] It might be argued that the key concept is that of 'justice', and hence lay claim to all films with an element of justice

36 Berger, op. cit., n. 27, p. 18.
37 See, here, the discussion of Black, op. cit., n. 26, ch. 3.
38 Brando's performance was described by one critic: 'Brando's star turn as a lawyer jaded by the realisation that justice cannot exist in matters of race, puffing, pausing, snorting, looking like he's wandered in from another movie'. D. Wells, *The Time Out Film Guide* (1993).
39 Greenfield and Osborn, op. cit. (1999), n. 34, pp. 35, 43.
40 Of course, the question could also be one of stratifying 'law films' and creating a series of genres or sub-genres beneath this. This would be an inquiry that I would argue would have little purpose.

173

contained within the film.[41] Other writers have sought to draw lines around films because of certain characteristics such as the main character, the author, and so on. Rafter's work, for example, considers crime films which she considers a category that encompasses a number of genres including courtroom drama.[42] One of the main problems with identifying and developing a genre is that any film within the genre that has a new feature indelibly alters the genre itself. In many ways approaching the question of genre from the outside has given those working with legal films a freedom to classify and refine their approach. The attempt to construct arguments across strict genre does have some support:

> Ultimately we need to be alert to the possibility that in constructing an argument around a particular genre, auteur or star, we may be producing a neatly organised overview – but we may also be constructing a fiction every bit as credible but every bit as contrived as the narratives of the films themselves ... The temptation to force the film into the framework we have constructed, by the most convoluted of means if necessary, is great. Neatness will have been prioritised over genuine complexity and truth.[43]

No doubt some film theorists would find such an approach rather cavalier, but there is a strong argument that law is an important feature of many films and does not fit into any realistic genre classification with ease. Rafter, for example, makes the point that courtroom dramas have changed over time and identifies three phases of development.[44] Genre as a method of classification within film studies has also been criticized because of the problem of 'isolating intentions', and the related issue that any classification is only useful in terms of what it is designed to achieve; namely, that the classification should have some *point*:

> To take a genre such as a 'Western', analyse it, and list its principal characteristics, is to beg the question that we must first isolate the body of films which are 'Westerns'. But they can only be isolated on the basis of the 'principal characteristics' which can only be discovered *from the films themselves* after they have been isolated, for which purposes a criterion is necessary, but the criterion is, in turn, meant to emerge from the empirically established common characteristics of the films.[45]

This dilemma can be solved in one of two ways. First, by classifying on the basis of the critical purpose of the inquiry, genre as a specific term becomes

41 This may, of course, create problems of size.
42 N. Rafter, *Shots in the Mirror* (2000).
43 P. Phillips, 'Genre, Star and Auteur: An approach to Hollywood Cinema' in *An Introduction to Film Studies*, ed. J. Nelmes (1996) p. 125.
44 She identifies the 1930s–1950s, which she categorizes as 'Experimentation and the Law *Noirs*', the mid 1950s–1960s – 'The Heroic Tradition', and 1970s to the present – 'Depletion of the Genre'. Rafter, op. cit., n. 42.
45 A. Tudor, 'Genre and Critical Methodology' in *Movies and Methods, Vol. 1*, ed. B. Nichols (1976).

174

redundant as the classifier can make their own 'genres'. The second way to solve the dilemma is to reach a common consensus as to what a 'Western' or 'Law Film' (or whatever) is, and then establish conventions to go with this. This is clearly an issue that those working in the area will have to explore in greater depth as the subject develops: at present it remains unresolved.[46]

CONCLUSION

As can be seen from the above discussion, the coverage of an area such as 'film and law' is difficult to define and delineate. Often this will be led by the objectives of the actual course. On the film and law course at Westminster there are a number of learning outcomes including 'to critically examine the portrayal of the law and legal personnel in film' and 'to develop a wider critical awareness of the law'.[47] As such, the course is clearly fulfilling a number of functions in that it was both research/teaching *in* law and *about* law,[48] and in order to facilitate this, the selection of films that was selected for appraisal was necessarily wide. Even once the area is delineated, there is still the issue of curriculum pressure to contend with. Current pressure comes not only from the professions via the Joint Statement, but also from the requirements of the Quality Assurance Agency that has produced a number of benchmark standards. Whilst the QAA benchmarks are less prescriptive and deal more with student outcomes, these outcomes are still largely cognitive. The QAA position may at least more easily facilitate the development of 'law and ...' disciplines. Brayne noted as regards the professions:

> As with previous declarations on the content of the academic stage, the professions have confined their prescriptions to matters of subject coverage in law and development of academic legal skills. The real change from 1995 to 1999 is the increase in the amount of time which is to be spent on law, thereby reducing the scope for widening the horizons of law undergraduates by studying other disciplines.[49]

Whilst there is undoubtedly more pressure upon the curriculum, my position would firmly be that there is a place, and that there are a number of educational reasons, for subjects such as film and the law on the law school curriculum. Our perspective should be framed by our answer to the question of what the law school is for, and what are the objectives of legal study.

46 A further attempt to map this terrain will be made by S. Greenfield, G. Osborn, and P. Robson, *Film and the Law* (2001, forthcoming).
47 Another more specific objective was to '... appreciate the psychological effects of dress and court layout upon perceptions of the law'.
48 See, further, Greenfield and Osborn, op. cit., n. 28, p. 33.
49 H. Brayne, 'A case for getting law students engaged in the real thing – the challenge to the sabre-tooth curriculum' (2000) 34 *The Law Teacher* 17, 20.

Whilst the position and wishes of the professions must be taken in to account, at least to a degree, it must be firmly borne in mind that a law degree can, and should '... provide preparation for a whole range of occupations, and insight to numerous aspects of public life'.[50] With that in mind, subjects that view law within its wider social and economic context should be supported and developed, and film and law specifically should be appreciated for the educative potentiality it contains.

---

50 N. Savage and G. Watt, 'A "House of Intellect" for the Profession' in Birks, op. cit., n. 1.